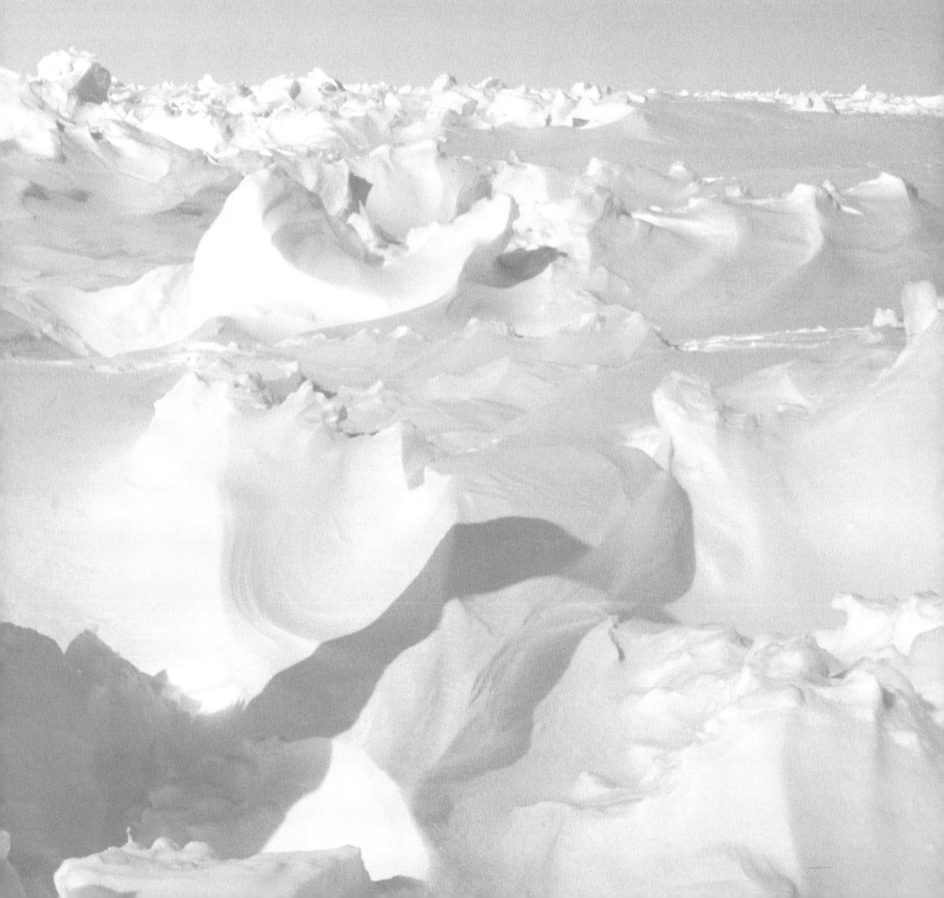

ANTARCTICA

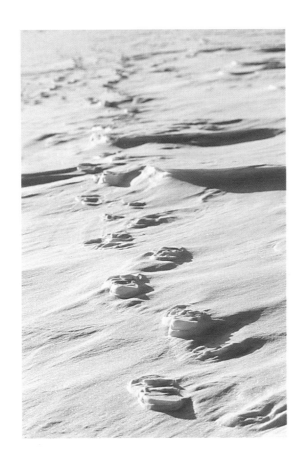

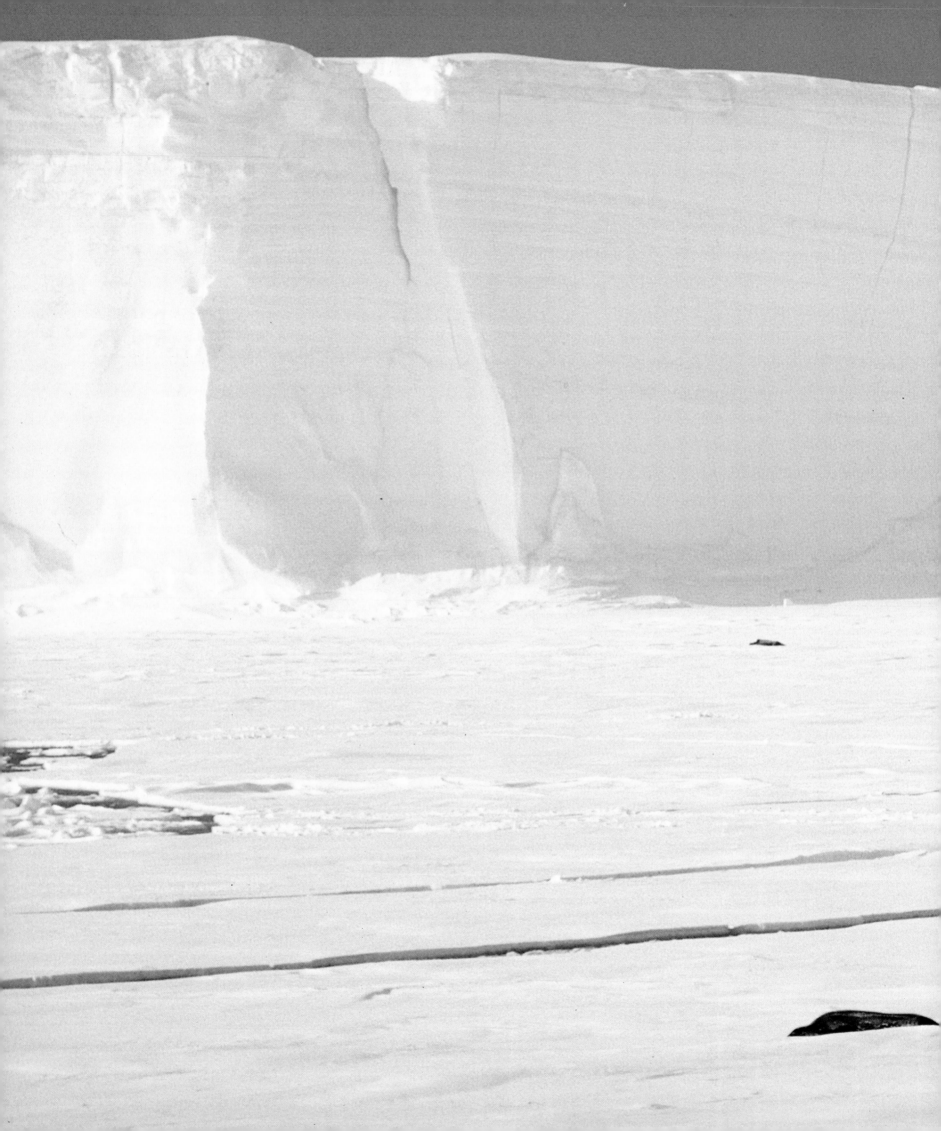

ANTARCTICA

MIKE LUCAS

ABBEVILLE PRESS   PUBLISHERS
NEW YORK • LONDON • PARIS

First published in the United States of America
in 1996 by Abbeville Press
488 Madison Avenue
New York, N.Y. 10022

First published in Great Britain in 1996 by
New Holland (Publishers) Ltd
London • Cape Town • Sydney • Singapore

24 Nutford Place
London W1H 6DQ
United Kingdom

Reproduction by cmyk prepress
Printed and bound in Singapore by
    Tien Wah Press Press Pte Ltd

First edition
10 9 8 7 6 5 4 3 2 1

ISBN 0-7892-0257-3

Senior Designer TRINITY FRY
Editor ANOUSKA GOOD
Publishing Manager MARIËLLE RENSSEN
Illustrator ANNETTE BUSSE

Consultant PROFESSOR PATRICK QUILTY,
Assistant Director Science, Australian Antarctic Division

PICTURE CREDITS

CONTENTS

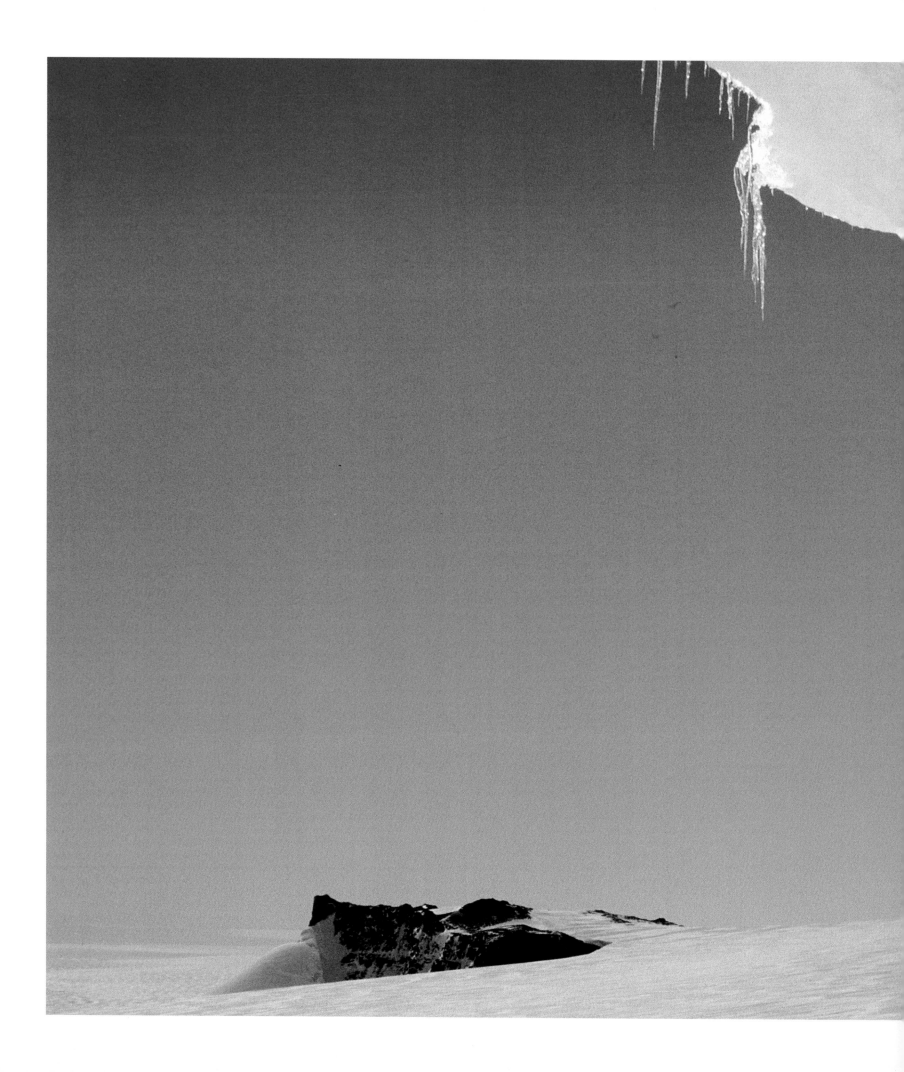

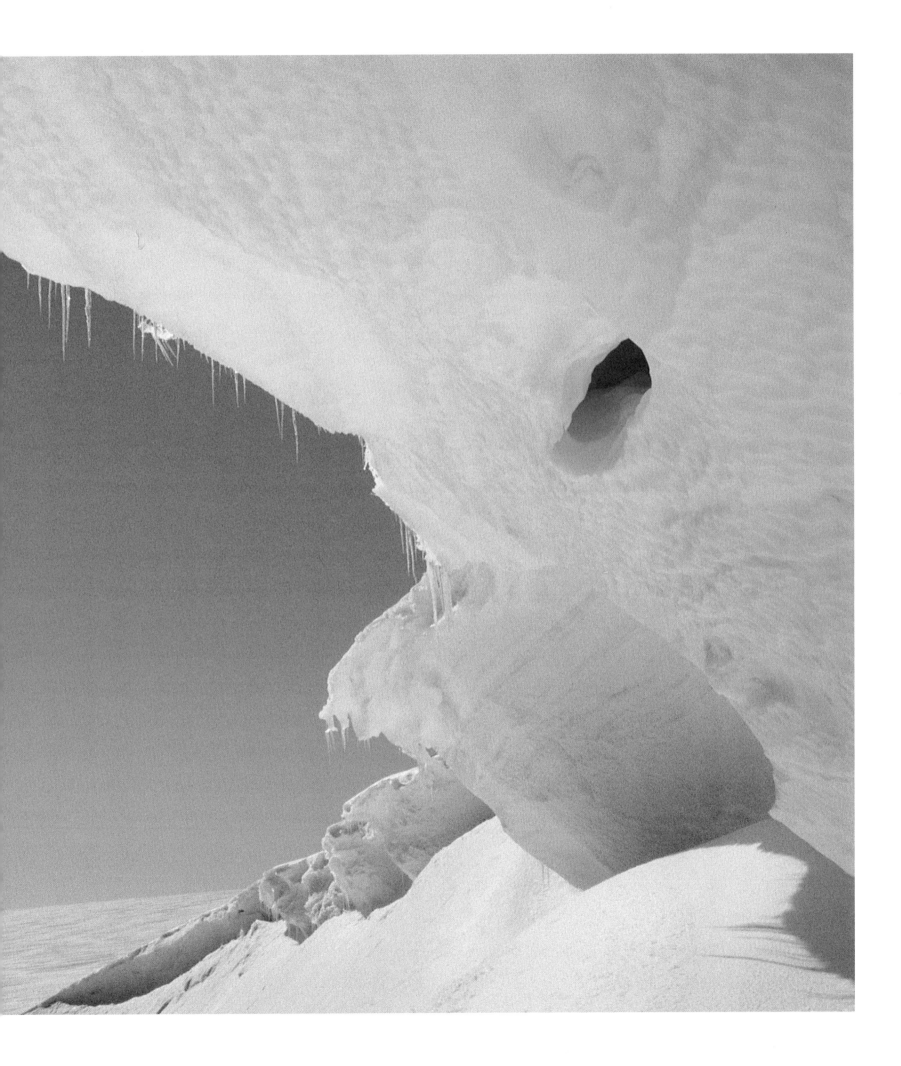

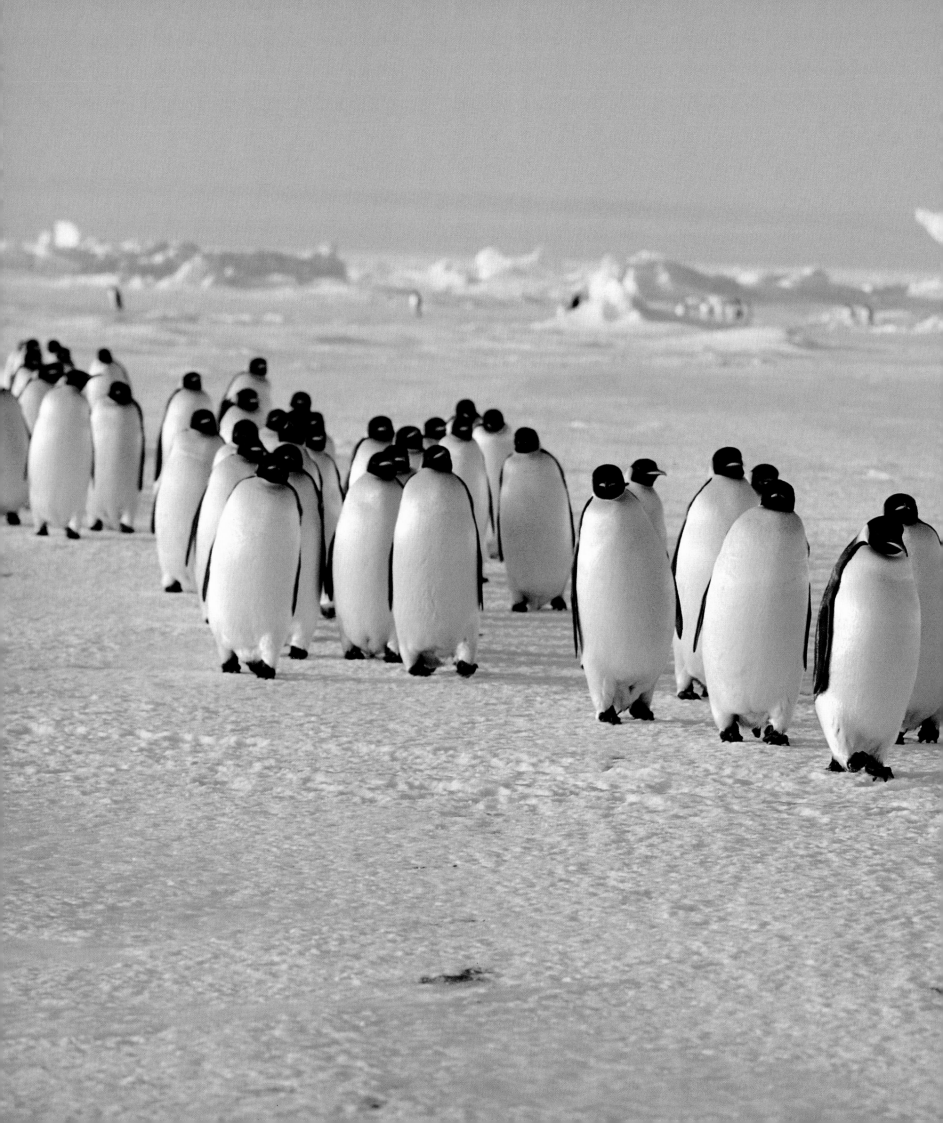

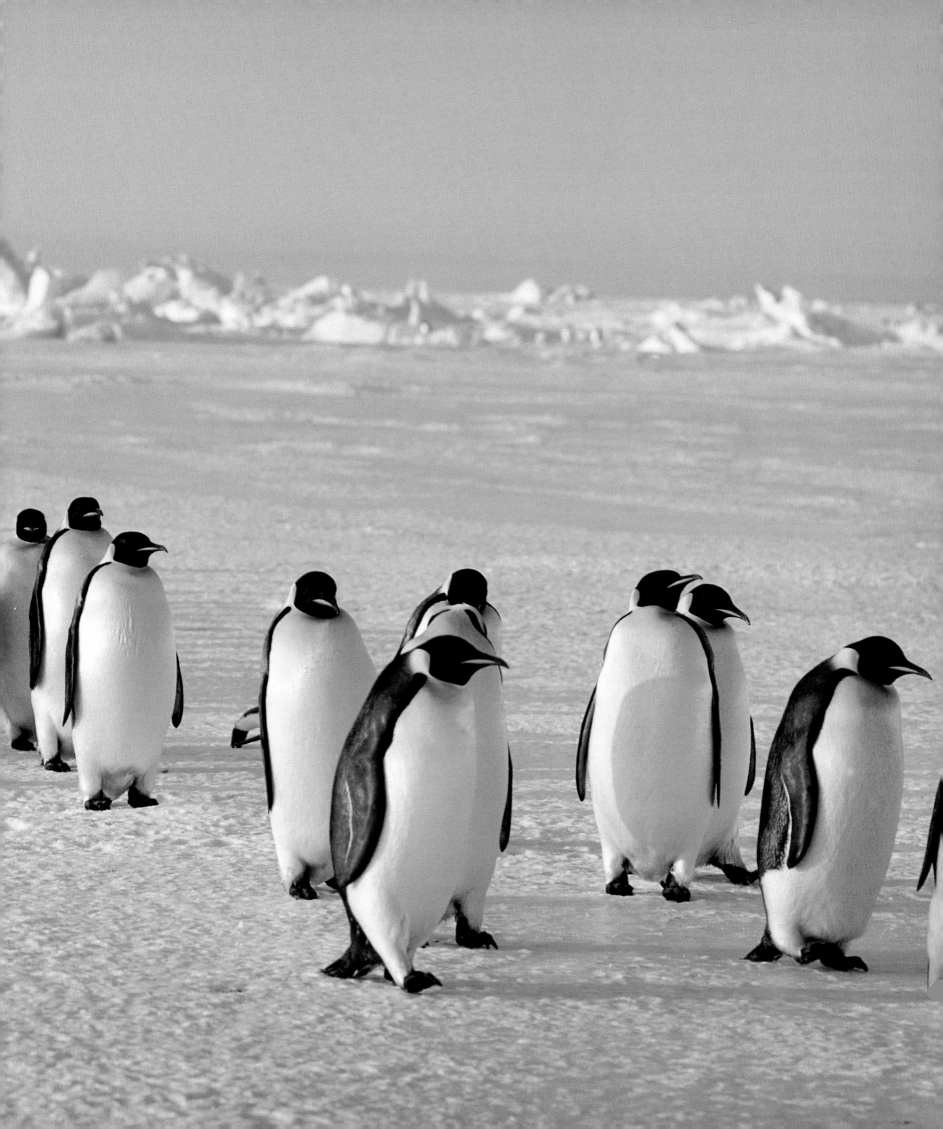

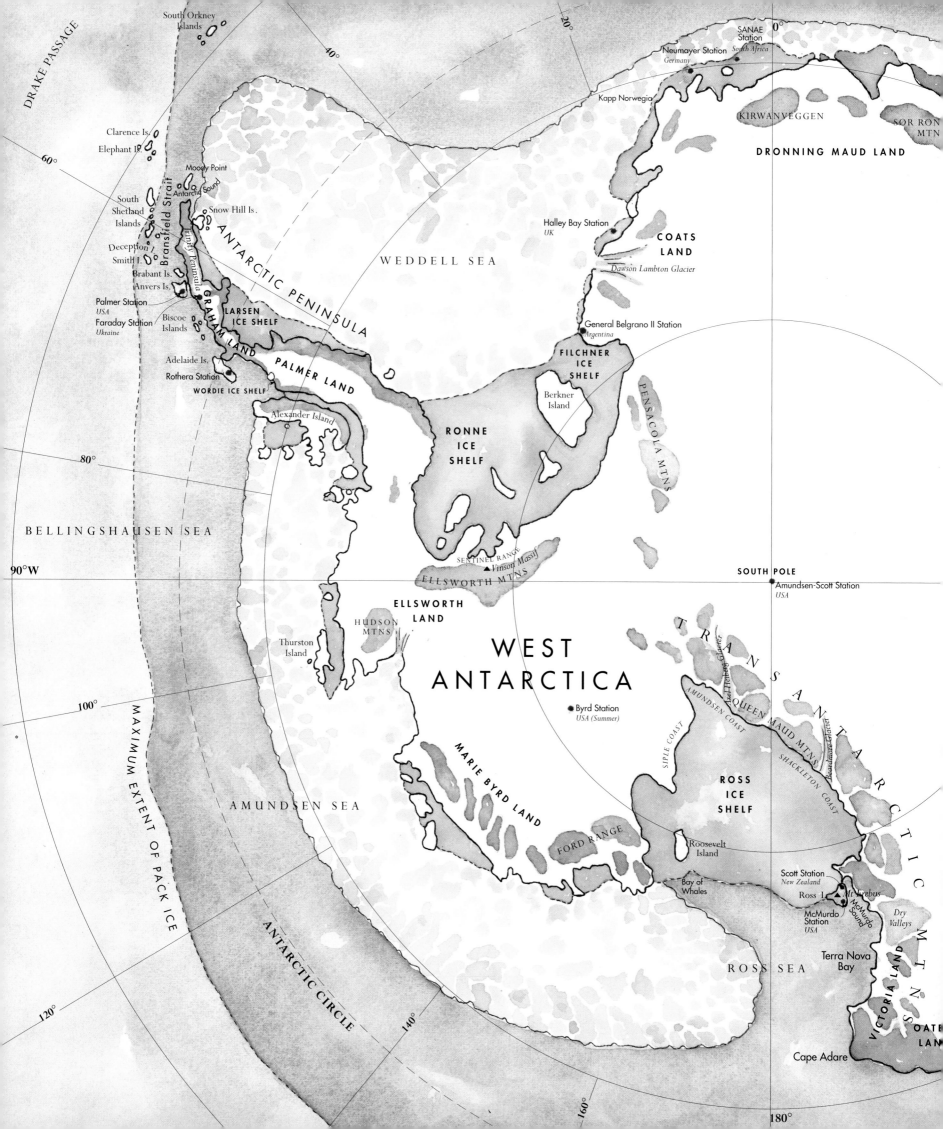

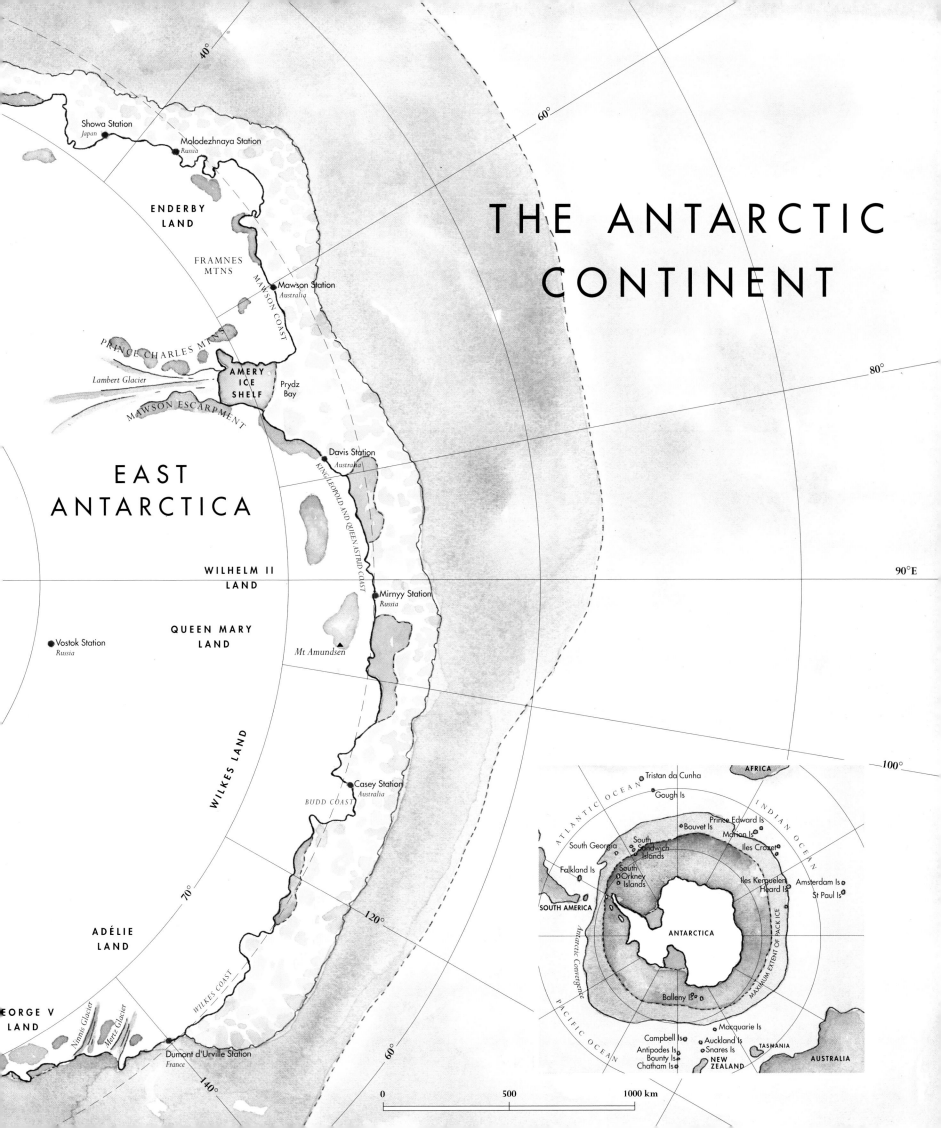

THE ANTARCTIC CONTINENT

ENDERBY LAND

Showa Station
Japan

Molodezhnaya Station
Russia

FRAMNES MTNS

MAWSON COAST

Mawson Station
Australia

PRINCE CHARLES MTNS

Lambert Glacier

AMERY ICE SHELF

Prydz Bay

MAWSON ESCARPMENT

EAST ANTARCTICA

Davis Station
Australia

KINGLEOPOLD AND QUEEN ASTRID COAST

WILHELM II LAND

QUEEN MARY LAND

Vostok Station
Russia

Mirnyy Station
Russia

Mt Amundsen

WILKES LAND

ADÉLIE LAND

Casey Station
Australia

BUDD COAST

WILKES COAST

EORGE V LAND

Ninnis Glacier

Mertz Glacier

Dumont d'Urville Station
France

40°
60°
80°
90°E
100°
70°
120°
60°
140°

Inset map

AFRICA

Tristan da Cunha

Gough Is

ATLANTIC OCEAN

INDIAN OCEAN

Bouvet Is

Prince Edward Is

Marion Is

Iles Crozet

South Georgia

South Sandwich Islands

Falkland Is

South Orkney Islands

Iles Kerguelen
Heard Is

Amsterdam Is

St Paul Is

SOUTH AMERICA

Antarctic Convergence

ANTARCTICA

MAXIMUM EXTENT OF PACK ICE

PACIFIC OCEAN

Balleny Is

Macquarie Is

Campbell Is

Antipodes Is

Bounty Is

Chatham Is

Auckland Is

Snares Is

TASMANIA

AUSTRALIA

NEW ZEALAND

0   500   1000 km

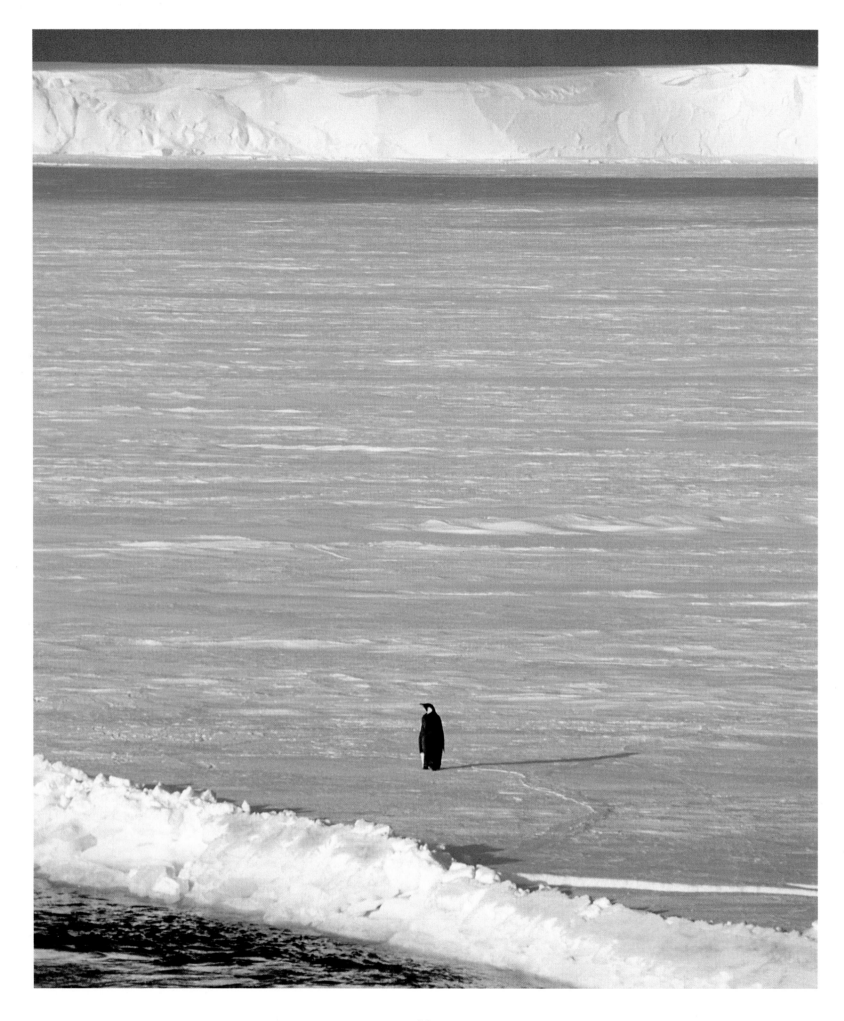

INTRODUCTION

For well over 60 million years Antarctica was indeed a 'lost paradise'. Lost at the end of the earth and witness only to swirling snows that started to accumulate there 15 million years ago, this distant and isolated continent developed alone, while the rest of the world followed another, very different path. Great whales roamed the mysterious depths of the newly emerging Southern Ocean, early primates made their presence felt in the forge of Africa and marsupials followed their own evolutionary track under Australia's burning sun while, far to the south, the ice sheet of Antarctica consolidated and chilled the airs and seas.

This new tempestuous land of snowstorms and icy turbulent oceans underwent its own evolution dominated by flightless penguins and thickly insulated seals able to take advantage of a cold but relatively constant ocean. While fishes proliferated in other, warmer oceans, these ice-bound seas were too harsh for most, and lowly crustaceans such as Antarctic krill exploited a rich untapped niche of phytoplankton. Grasses, flowering plants and mighty trees dominated many corners of the still-developing earth, but the icy cold of Antarctica pushed such luxuriant vegetation northwards to more welcoming climes. Only mosses and lichens hung grimly on, where land escaped the ice cover.

Without much vegetation and subject to extreme cold, Antarctica was too hostile for permanent terrestrial animals save for a few simple forms of invertebrates able to colonize small, more amenable micro-habitats. Antarctica became a unique kingdom of ice and snow and rocks, of savage cold, of raging blizzards and windswept lonely seas, where only a limited number of life forms managed to flourish.

Beyond this flood a frozen continent
Lies dark and wilde, beat with perpetual storms
Of whirlwind and dire hail, which on firm land
Thaws not, but gathers heap, and ruin seems
Of ancient pile; all else deep snow and ice…

Paradise Lost, *John Milton (1608–1674)*

Two-thirds of the earth's landmass is in the northern hemisphere, whereas in the southern hemisphere, 80 per cent is covered by water. To the south of Africa, South America, Australia and New Zealand lie the forbidding Southern Ocean and the frozen continent of Antarctica. Inhospitable and restless, the vast Southern Ocean completely surrounds this continent at the 'bottom of the world' and has isolated Antarctica and the subantarctic islands from over 2000 years of human exploration and discovery. After Greek philosophers, in 500BC, proposed that the world was round and not flat, they argued that the known continental landmasses in the northern hemisphere had to be 'balanced' by some equivalent landmass in the southern hemisphere. By the early 16th century, evidence began to accumulate that such a landmass might indeed exist, but it was not until barely 150 years ago that the 'unknown southern land', *Terra Australis Incognita*, was finally sighted for the first time. Since then, Antarctica has captured the imagination of nations, explorers and scientists, provoking a quest for minerals, seal and whale products, fish and krill, and engendering both the greed and nobility of humankind. More recently, tourism has become a growing industry, particularly in the Antarctic Peninsula region, while global concern over the greenhouse effect and the ozone hole may significantly affect this threatened continent. Fortunately, the Antarctic Treaty system, launched in 1960, monitors such concerns and conflicting interests by a process of rare international consensus and agreement. Antarctica may yet prove to be the jewel in the crown of human conservation efforts, but we should not delude ourselves… it will require commitment and a common vision for the future. Education will be the key.

LEFT *The vastness, emptiness and stark beauty of the Antarctic continent is dramatically captured by the solitude of this majestic emperor penguin, seen here standing at the edge of the fast ice.*

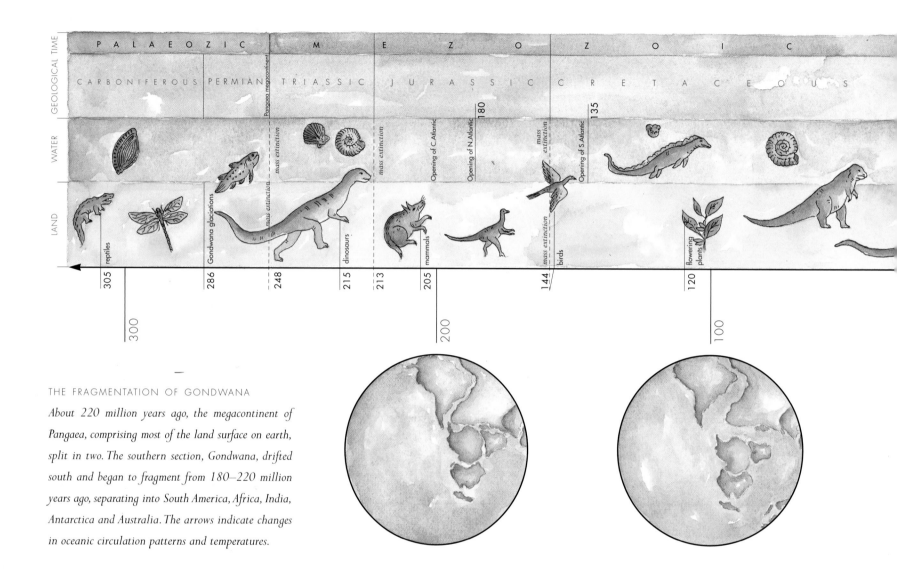

THE FRAGMENTATION OF GONDWANA

About 220 million years ago, the megacontinent of Pangaea, comprising most of the land surface on earth, split in two. The southern section, Gondwana, drifted south and began to fragment from 180–220 million years ago, separating into South America, Africa, India, Antarctica and Australia. The arrows indicate changes in oceanic circulation patterns and temperatures.

BIRTH OF A CONTINENT

Two hundred and fifty million years ago a map of the world would have looked very different from the one with which we are now familiar. Most of the continental landmasses had unrecognizably different shapes and positions on the earth and many continents were still joined together. However, as these continental landmasses broke up and started to drift apart towards their current positions, changes in global climate occurred which have shaped life on earth. In fact, the process of continental movement, known as plate tectonics, continues to this day. Africa is gradually drifting northwards on a collision course with Europe which

will ultimately close the Mediterranean Sea. The eastern part of Africa is splitting from the main African continent all along the Great Rift Valley, while the South Atlantic Ocean grows wider by approximately 3cm (1.2in) each year. Earthquakes and the occasional sudden appearance of new islands engulfed in billowing steam and flowing lava are evidence of the continuing heavings of the earth's crust.

The earth's coal reserves were formed from the great forests that covered much of the planet, including the Antarctic continent, in the Carboniferous era. Evolution of the continents, seas, climate and life has occurred steadily over

the last 250 million years. In the mid-Triassic era the megacontinent Pangaea split in two, forming Gondwana in the southern hemisphere and Laurasia in the northern hemisphere. From the supercontinent of Gondwana, Antarctica was to emerge over the next 200 million years. Fragmentation of Gondwana began in the early Jurassic era, the age of the dinosaurs, and continued throughout the Cretaceous period. This was when Australia separated, only 55 million years ago, while Drake Passage between South America and Antarctica opened up 25 million years ago, finally severing Antarctica from any other landmass on earth.

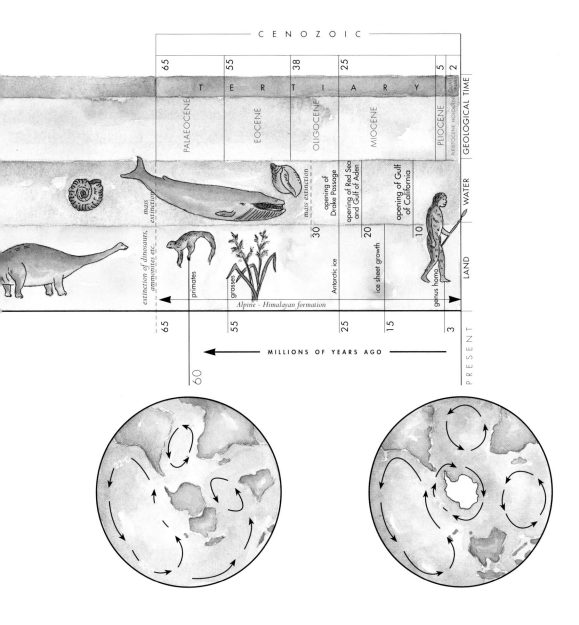

The age of the earth and its moon dates from about 4600 million years ago, while the first recognizable form of life occurred about 3100 million years ago when the first single-celled micro-organism appeared in the young seas — the so-called 'primordial soup'. Life exploded in the shallow seas into a number of different forms 570 million years ago and, when plants appeared on land 400 million years ago, it was possible for animals to emerge onto the land. Over the next 100 million years insects, ammonites, early fish, amphibians and reptiles made their entrance — at the start of the time line, 305 million years ago.

Solid vertical lines mark the first appearance of plants and animals along with milestones of geological interest. Broken vertical lines mark the numerous mass extinctions that have interrupted the evolution of life on earth, often associated with major upheavals in the earth's geology and climate. The process of evolution is therefore marked by periods of great change which create opportunities for new species and new directions in which to adapt and evolve.

Notice that the human race is a very recent arrival, at only seconds before midnight if the evolutionary process were to be compressed into a 24-hour period.

At that time, however, Antarctica was not an ice-covered continent and climates throughout the world were warm. But, as the earth's polar regions slowly cooled and Antarctica settled in its position over the South Pole, the freshwater ice sheet and sea ice began to form about 40 million years ago in the Tertiary period, which extends from 65 to two million years ago.

A major part of the ice sheet formed 15 million years ago with modern ice sheet growth occurring just 2.5 million years ago. Over this period, the circumantarctic Southern Ocean developed as we know it today. Sea water temperatures decreased from about 15°C (59°F) to the present

range of −1.8°C to +2°C (28.76°F to 35.6°F). A relatively warm sea and continent had gradually become extremely cold, forcing animals to adapt, leave or face almost certain extinction.

The appearance of sea ice was an important milestone. As the surface of the sea freezes, it ejects the salt it contains, making the underlying sea water saltier and heavier, thus causing it to sink to the bottom of the ocean.

Antarctic Bottom Water formation, as this process is called, and its spread northwards into all of the world's oceanic depths helps to cool the deep ocean and drive global oceanic circulation patterns. Ocean currents are a powerful

regulator of climate around the world. For example, the city of Tromso on the far northwest coast of Norway lies at latitude 70°N and is kept relatively ice-free under the influence of the warm Gulf Stream originating in the Gulf of Mexico. By contrast, latitude 70°S marks the edge of the Antarctic continent in many places. Trapped in ice for most of the year, it is a world where, in winter, buckled sheets of pack ice can extend more than 1000km (620 miles) from the coast. Indeed, ever since its first appearance, the vast Antarctic ice sheet and pack ice has made a considerable contribution to keeping the world significantly cooler.

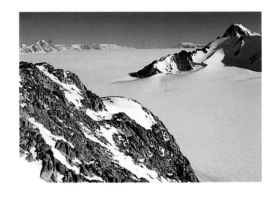
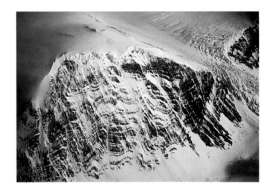
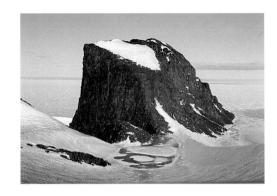

AN OVERVIEW OF ANTARCTICA

With most of the Antarctic continent lying south of latitude 70°S, this icy wilderness is a place of extremes. At such high latitudes, it is light for 24 hours of the day during the summer months, while in winter, there is total darkness for nearly four months of the year.

The polar ice sheet and sea ice reflect most of the incoming heat from the sun back into space, making the Antarctic continent and the over-lying atmosphere the coldest on earth, with an annual average temperature of −40°C (−40°F). Some idea of the scale of this huge global refrigeration unit and its influence on the rest of the earth's climate can be made by comparing Antarctica with more familiar landmarks.

The frozen centre

Antarctica's continental landmass covers an area of 12.4 million km² (4.8 million sq miles), although the permanent ice sheet extends this area to almost 14 million km² (5.4 million sq miles), making it the fifth-largest continent and greater in size than Europe. Only the Antarctic Peninsula, the highest of the Transantarctic Mountains and smaller areas near the coast escape from its cover. The ice sheet is divided into the larger East Antarctic ice sheet, bounded to the west by the Transantarctic Mountains, and the smaller West Antarctic ice sheet. This includes the great floating Filchner-Ronne and Ross ice shelves, the latter being about the size of France. Adjacent to the Ross Sea, in Victoria

Land, lie some of the few places on Antarctica that have escaped the blanket of ice. These are the 'Dry Valleys' of exposed bedrock, which emerged at the end of the last Ice Age when the ice sheet retreated. Here, evaporation by 'freeze-drying' exceeds precipitation, in the form of snow, so that ice does not accumulate.

Rivers of ice

Flowing gently down from the high plateau of the polar ice sheets are major glaciers, frozen rivers of ice, falling from 2000–3000m (6500–9800ft) down to sea level. These glaciers of all shapes and sizes grind inexorably downwards, eventually 'calving', or shedding, great fresh-water icebergs into the coastal seas. This tends

ABOVE *From left to right, ancient peaks of the granitic and folded sedimentary Transantarctic Mountains, the younger Antarctic Peninsula and a nunatak in Dronning Maud Land all unveil the history of the earth itself to geologists.*

BOTTOM LEFT *Rays from the midnight sun sweep across Adelaide Island which, along with several other islands, forms part of the Antarctic Peninsula archipelago.*
BOTTOM RIGHT *Gentoo penguins catch the last few rays of the evening sun.*

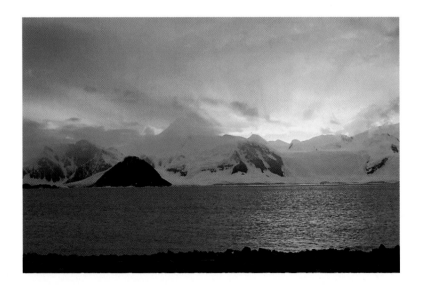
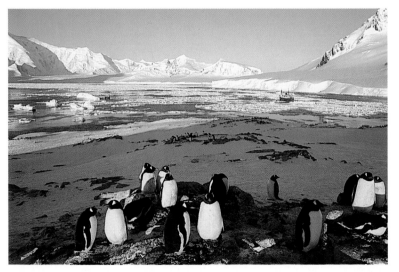

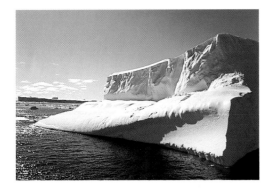

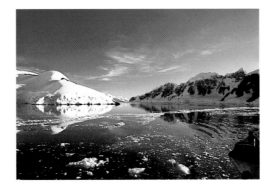

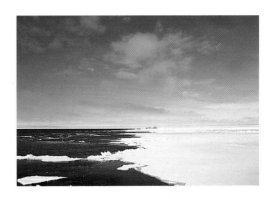

to occur erratically, with periods of ice shelf growth followed by an increase in the frequency of calving. Over time, the shedding of icebergs more or less balances the slow accumulation of ice in the interior, although ice accumulation currently exceeds iceberg shedding.

At the edge of the continent

By the time the glaciers meet the sea and break off as icebergs, these rivers of ice will have flowed far to the north. Here, in the maritime region of Antarctica, climatic conditions are considerably less extreme and are influenced in the summer by the relatively mild temperatures of the Southern Ocean (–1.8°C to +2°C; 28.76°F to 35.66°F). Cooled by the polar ice

sheet, the air above the continent is extremely cold and heavy, so that it accelerates down from the high plateau reaching speeds of over 200kph (125mph) at times. These cold 'katabatic' winds help to freeze the ocean's surface in winter. In summer the sun's warming rays bring milder weather, and the snow and ice fields of some coastal regions retreat to expose bare rock, encouraging an invasion of penguins, seals and petrels. Rocky outcrops in these regions have more abundant, but still simple, examples of year-round resident life. These include mosses and lichens; mites, which are related to ticks; and fleas associated with the summer nesting sites of visiting snow and other petrels located among the rocks and crevices.

Gateway to Antarctica

Because it reaches further north than any other part of the continent, the Antarctic Peninsula, in particular, is seasonally transformed. Its alpine-like mountains and island-dotted coast-line of inlets and fjords come alive in the short summer. Penguins and seals take advantage of the emerging land to find a place to mate and breed. Elsewhere around Antarctica, the ice sheet and 20- to 30m- (65- to 100ft-) high shelf-edge ice cliffs are still impenetrable, but on the remaining pieces of 'land-fast' ice (sea ice permanently attached to the land or ice-shelf edge), Weddell and Ross seals haul out to breed. For a few brief months, the pack ice breaks up and it is possible to navigate right up to the

TOP LEFT *A tabular iceberg may last as long as four years before finally melting.*
TOP CENTRE *Neumeyer Channel, between Anvers Island and the Antarctic Peninsula.*
TOP RIGHT *Over 1000km (620 miles) from the coast, the pack ice begins.*

BELOW LEFT *Buckled and wind-scoured, pack ice stretches across the Weddell Sea.*
BELOW *Heat lost from the sea to the atmosphere in winter, seen here as plumes of 'frost-smoke', maintains large ice-free 'lakes' in the ocean known as 'polynyas'.*

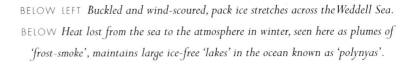

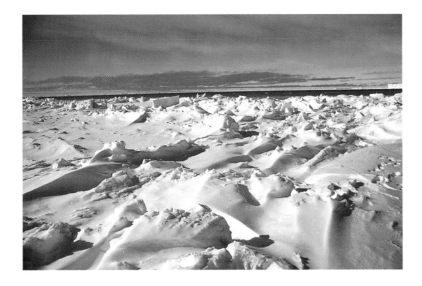

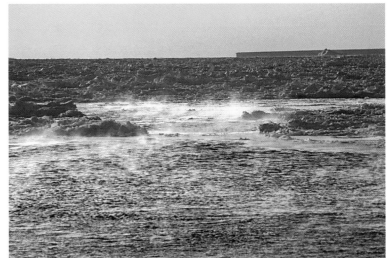

rocky coastline as the early explorers did. Not surprisingly, therefore, most of the early voyages of exploration took advantage of the Antarctic Peninsula, making this the gateway to the interior. Tourists, the new explorers, also make use of the brief period of ice-free coastal waters to follow in the footsteps of Scott and Shackleton. Here, too, scientists have established the greatest density of Antarctic bases.

Fields of ice

The pack ice reaches its maximum (20 million km²; 7.8 million sq miles) in September while the minimum extent (4 million km²; 1.5 million sq miles) occurs in February. Extending as far as 1000km (620 miles) from the ice shelf, the sea ice is about 1 to 2m (3 to 6.5ft) thick on average. It is only partly salty, having ejected most of its salt during the freezing process. As the sea ice expands and is subjected to strong winds and currents, enormous pressures develop, causing ice floes to raft over each other and form 'pressure ridges' several metres thick. Such pressures first crushed the timber planking of some of the early ships of discovery, such as Shackleton's *Endurance*. Even today, ice-breakers can find themselves temporarily captive within the ice, sometimes crippled with damaged steering gear or worse, sunk.

Sea ice remains a harsh environment, but is 'home' to many Antarctic animals. It provides a unique habitat for a number of penguins and seals and also supports a complex microbial and algal community in brown brine channels within the ice. Exposed algal mats on the underside of the ice provide food for krill during winter when concentrations of phytoplankton (microscopic single-celled plants) in the open ocean have disappeared due to insufficient light.

Sea ice is crucial in controlling the earth's heat balance, as it reflects more than 80 per cent of the sun's rays back into the atmosphere. The ice also acts as a barrier between the relatively warm ocean and the cold atmosphere in winter to prevent too much heat being lost from the sea. Should sea-ice extent retreat as a result of global warming, it might shift the current balance between global heating and cooling. Seals, penguins, snow petrels and Antarctic krill would also lose most of their seasonal habitat, with potentially dire consequences for the functioning of this unique ecosystem.

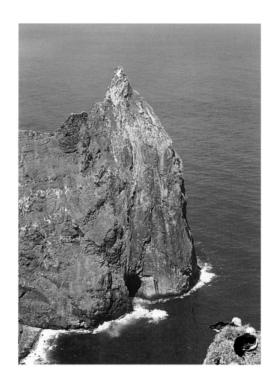

ABOVE *Rugged, volcanic cliffs rise almost sheer from the surrounding subantarctic seas. Vegetation clings tenaciously to the precipitous slopes, while a pair of albatrosses doze peacefully on their lofty perch.*

Stormy seas

The Southern Ocean, averaging nearly 4000m (13,000ft) in depth, is the second largest in the world. It is cold and turbulent, with the area close to the Antarctic continent being seasonally covered by sea ice. Driven by prevailing westerly winds, the Antarctic Circumpolar Current is the ocean's major conveyor belt, marked at its most northern boundary by the Subtropical Convergence at a latitude of about 40°S (see illustration on page 92). This oceanic boundary separates warmer subtropical water to the north from cold subantarctic water to the south. At about latitude 50°S, a second oceanic boundary, the Antarctic Polar Front, or Antarctic Convergence, marks the transition from subantarctic to truly Antarctic waters.

Despite the cold, the Southern Ocean supports a wealth of life, most dependent in one way or another on the small shrimp-like crustacean, Antarctic krill. This small creature is food for many species of birds, seals, fish and baleen whales. Since the early 1800s, humankind has also considered krill to be a potentially lucrative, exploitable resource.

Islands of refuge

South Georgia, Bouvet, Marion, Kergeulen, Crozet, Heard and Macquarie are just some of the windswept, mountainous subantarctic islands which rise from the depths of the Southern Ocean. Marking the ocean's most northerly fringe, they all lie more or less within the latitudes 40 to 55°S in the Roaring Forties and Furious Fifties. Buffeted by huge seas and gales that sweep eastwards unchecked by landmasses, these are among the most remote islands in the world. Without exception they are wet! Storms originating close to the Antarctic continent track east and north across the Southern Ocean, gathering moisture and then releasing it as drenching rain, swirling mists or driving snows over the craggy peaks and sodden marshes of these treeless outposts.

However, in a bleak and lonely world, these islands with their tussocky grasses are sheltering arks, home and refuge to thousands of oceanic birds, penguins and seals which come to breed and escape the worst of the polar winter.

Theirs is a life-long race against the freezing seas and icy winds whose grip is loosened for only a few short summer months each year. Even so, some have had worse to endure, particularly in the early period of Antarctic exploration (1790–1830) when vast numbers of sealers and whalers, intent on financial gain, caused widespread devastation.

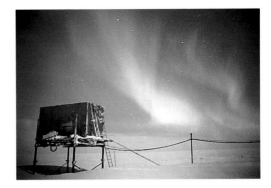

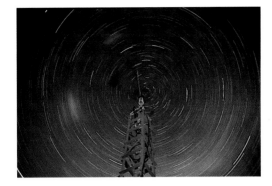

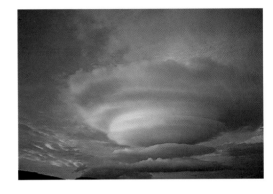

ABOVE LEFT *The* aurora australis *plays eerily across the winter sky above the polar ice sheet.*
ABOVE RIGHT *Time-lapse photography captures the celestial bodies 'spinning' around the earth's south polar axis. It is actually the earth that spins.*

LEFT *Soft, pastel hues on these orographic clouds mark the end of the day over Marion Island.*

HEAVENLY LIGHTS

Not only is Antarctica unique for its ice and wildlife, it is also one of the best places on earth from which to peer out into space. The atmosphere above is free of pollution and here at the geomagnetic pole, the interaction of solar winds and the earth's magnetic field produce the spectacular southern auroral lights, the *aurora australis*. The same event, but this time known as the *aurora borealis*, also occurs at the North Pole.

But what is this amazing phenomenon? When subatomic particles of the solar wind reach earth, they interact and excite subatomic particles in the earth's magnetosphere and atoms in the lower thermosphere. The collision of these particles, which stream down the magnetic axis of the earth (between the North and South Poles), induces electric disturbances which generate the rainbow-coloured lights of the aurora. Depending on the particular atomic composition of the particles, the aurora takes on the different hues of indigo, violet and green that so impressed Scott in 1911, as it does those fortunate enough to witness these heavenly light shows today.

Apart from the aurora, the stars of the Southern Cross are another familiar sight to anyone living in the higher latitudes of the southern hemisphere. On dark moonless nights, the heavens seem to be just an arm's length away. There is nothing quite like watching the stars through the gently swaying rigging of a yacht at sea. It is a double image, with the night sky mirrored in the surface of a calm black ocean. Here too there are other lights – the phosphorescence of a myriad tiny organisms disturbed in a yacht's wake. Scott, Shackleton and others must have seen all of this as they followed the pointers of the Southern Cross towards Antarctica, across the lonely expanse of the Southern Ocean.

BELOW *Layers in the earth's atmosphere as well as ice and clouds play a vitally important role in controlling the earth's temperature, shown here in the illustration by the colour variation, and in regulating the amount and type of solar radiation reaching earth. Charged particles of the solar wind reaching the upper atmosphere cause the auroral lights (see panel). As incoming electromagnetic waves from the sun (heat and light) reach the upper atmosphere, they are heated to over 800°C (1472°F). However, the lower, denser layers of the atmosphere are cooler as most of the heat has been filtered out or is reflected back into space. Ozone in the stratosphere is particularly important in filtering out the harmful ultraviolet (UV) radiation.*

ATMOSPHERIC LAYERS

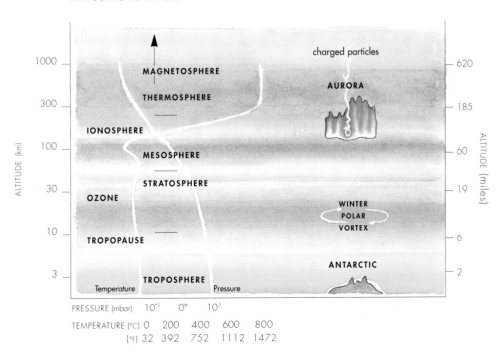

UNVEILING OF A CONTINENT

Curious about the world they lived in, Greek philosophers of 2500 years ago gazed at the stars above the North Pole and pinpointed the constellation *Arktos*, the Bear. Since these stars revolved around a pole, they argued that the world must be round and, in addition, that a southern landmass opposite to ('Ant-') that already known in the north must exist: the continent of *Antarktos*, or 'Antarctica' as it would come to be known.

The early voyages

However, the first known voyages into the Southern Ocean occurred only in the mid-18th century, in small, but sturdy wooden sailing ships. The epic round-the-world voyages of Captain James Cook from 1772–75 added New Zealand to existing maps, but despite crossing 71°S into the pack ice and sailing through Drake Passage, he failed to see Antarctica. The extreme cold and savagery of the oceans and ice fatefully persuaded him to turn north but, by reporting an abundance of seals and whales, he ensured that further discovery, accompanied inevitably by exploitation, would take place. Over the next 50 years, sealers and whalers drove these populations almost to the brink of extinction, while Antarctica, not far to the south, lay undiscovered. By 1830, there were no fur seals left to hunt and with so many sealers then in the Southern Ocean searching for new hunting grounds to plunder and profit from, it is not at all surprising that they figured prominently in the continent's discovery.

A merchant seaman named William Smith may have been the first to sight Antarctica in 1819. Unfavourable winds caught him in Drake Passage, forcing him southeast where he glimpsed land through a break in a snowstorm. However, he did not accurately record his position so his claims were considered dubious by some. Edward Bransfield, a naval officer from Britain, was asked to survey and secure the land Smith had seen a year earlier. In doing so, he claimed Livingston, King George, Deception, Hope, and Elephant and Clarence islands, all between January and February 1820. These were the South Shetlands. News of the discoveries prompted a rush of further exploration with adventurers all trying to push south through the pack ice to reach the continent they thought must exist.

NOTABLE ANTARCTIC ROUTES OF THE 20TH CENTURY

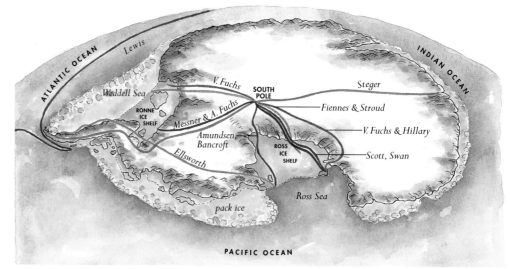

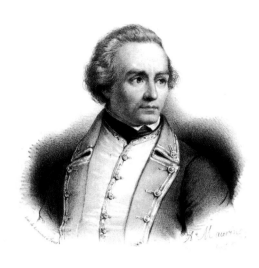

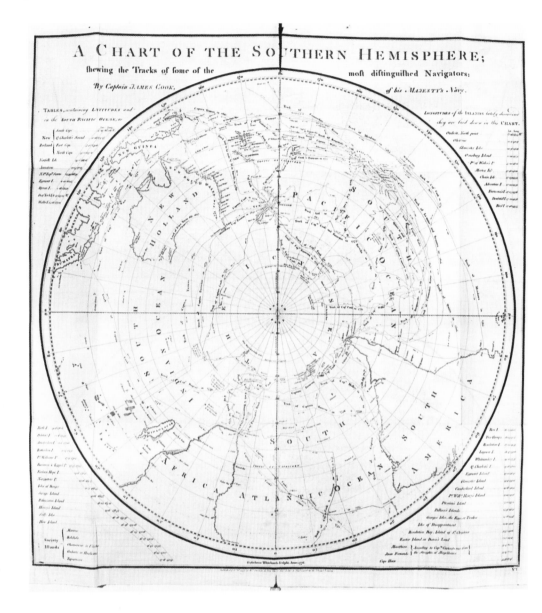

ABOVE *Captain James Cook claimed Australia for Britain and also circumnavigated New Zealand.*
RIGHT *James Cook's map of 1776 charts the sea routes taken by some of his contemporaries in the early years of Antarctic discovery and exploration.*
OPPOSITE TOP *James Weddell, British explorer.*

OPPOSITE BOTTOM *This map charts the routes of some of the modern explorers starting with the first transantarctic flight in 1935 by Ellsworth. The 1956–57 Commonwealth Trans-Antarctic Expedition was led by Sir Vivian Fuchs, who started from the Filchner Ice Shelf and met up with Sir Edmund Hillary at the South Pole on 19 January 1958. Lewis's 1974 solo voyage in Ice Bird was marked by dismastings and near catastrophe. In 1989–90, Will Steger and a team of five made the longest ever crossing — covering 6450km (4008 miles) in 220 days using dog teams. Reinhold Messner and Arved Fuchs man-hauled across Antarctica with air support in 1989–90. In 1992–93, Ann Bancroft led the first all-woman trek to the South Pole, pulling sledges and following Amundsen's 1911–12 route. The first unsupported and man-hauled crossing was achieved in 1992–93 by Sir Ranulph Fiennes and Dr Mike Stroud. Pulling 400kg (880 lb) sledges, they were left physically and emotionally exhausted.*

The great Russian explorer, Thaddeus von Bellingshausen, and Nathaniel Palmer, an American sealing captain, also laid claim to the discovery of Antarctica in 1820. The American, Captain John Davis, is credited with first setting foot on the Antarctic Peninsula in 1821. Two years later, a British sealer, James Weddell, penetrated the Southern Ocean and pack ice to 74°15'S (in the area now known as the Weddell Sea) — a record which was not bettered until the German Wilhelm Filchner reached what is now the Filchner Ice Shelf in 1911.

By the 1820s, the discoveries of land had all been in the vicinity of the South Shetlands, the Antarctic Peninsula and the western Weddell Sea. This would change with the remarkable year-long voyage of a Briton, John Biscoe, who, despite numerous trials, setbacks and near disaster, finally completed the circumnavigation of Antarctica in February 1832.

France was the first nation to lay a territorial claim to a part of Antarctica through the voyages of Jules-Sébastien-César Dumont d'Urville from 1837–40; he called the new territory Adélie Land (Terre Adélie) after his wife. Between 1839 and 1843, Captain James Ross led one of the first fully scientific voyages of discovery, lending his name to the Ross Ice Shelf and the Ross Sea, and associating himself with the first sighting of the Transantarctic Mountains. The only active volcano on Antarctica, Mt. Erebus, is named after one of

Ross's ships. In addition, he contributed greatly to science with discoveries about the earth's magnetic field. In the same period (1838–42), the American naval captain, Charles Wilkes, led an ill-prepared United States Exploring Expedition, charting over 2000km (1200 miles) of the Wilkes Land coastline. Although the voyage ended acrimoniously with his court-martial, his scientific endeavours received subsequent, albeit belated, recognition.

During the 50 or so years between Ross's discoveries and the turn of the century, other pioneers of Antarctic exploration left various milestones of discovery, without quite igniting the imagination of the world at large. However, two expeditions, in 1898 and 1901, captured the imagination of three Antarctic explorers, Roald Amundsen, Robert Falcon Scott and Ernest Shackleton, who would later fulfill their destiny in the age of 'romantic exploration'.

In 1898 a Belgian, Adrien de Gerlache de Gomery, was caught with his ship, the *Belgica*, in the pack ice of the Bellingshausen Sea for 12 months, becoming the first ship to overwinter. During the long cold months, temperatures

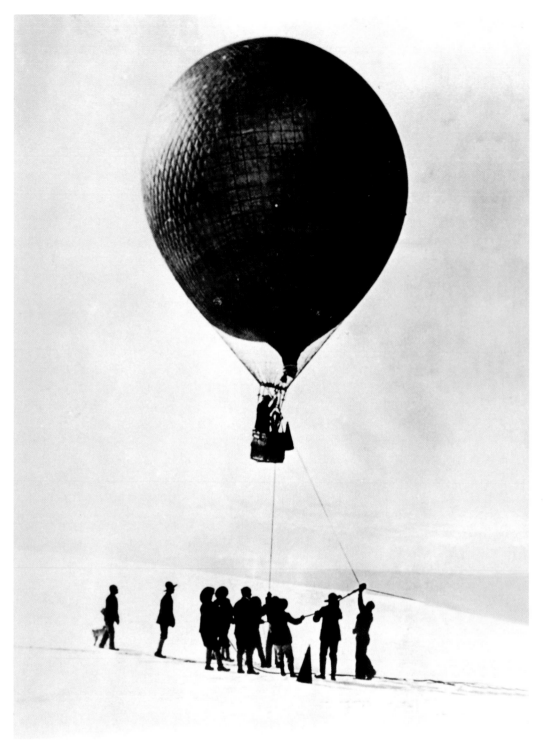

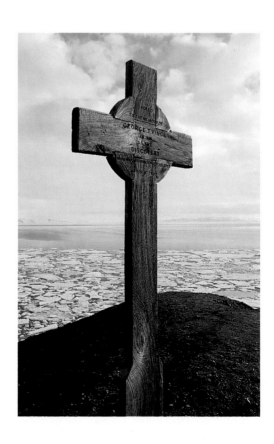

ABOVE *The hot-air balloon, Eva, was supplied by the army in order to assist Scott with his research. Inflated by 19 gas cylinders, the balloon was able to rise to a height of nearly 250m (820ft) and was moored securely to the ground with a wire cable.*

LEFT *The tragic death of George Vince during Scott's 1901–04 expedition emphasizes the hostility of the Antarctic continent. During a violent snowstorm,*

the sailor had fallen to his death over a precipice. The young man's body was never recovered but this cross at Hut Point was erected in his memory.

OPPOSITE *This chrome sphere marks the precise location of the South Pole. Since the ice sheet is continually moving, it is necessary to return the sphere, mounted on a barber's pole, to the exact geographic position at regular intervals.*

plummeted, night was endless and, in their cramped quarters, the men began to quarrel and fights were frequent. Despondency, despair, apathy and insanity overtook many of the crew. However, in de Gomery's crew was a young and very determined man, a Norwegian called Roald Amundsen, who helped his captain and the ship's doctor, Dr Cook, restrain and encourage the crew until the ice released its grip in March 1899.

Amundsen was not alone, however, in his determination to conquer this untamed continent. History and circumstance had thrown together two other, similarly driven men.

From 1901–04, Robert Scott, a British naval officer, led the *Discovery* expeditions of scientific exploration to the Antarctic continent under the patronage of the Royal Geographical Society, the Prince of Wales and Queen Victoria. One of his goals was to make a serious attempt to reach the South Pole using dogs and sledges for transport. Also on board was Sub-Lieutenant Ernest Shackleton, who would later take part in one of the legends of polar survival and become, himself, a household name.

Discovery was specifically built for this venture and sailed from the Isle of Wight on 6 August 1901, arriving in Christchurch, New Zealand, on 30 November. From New Zealand, Scott set sail on 21 December 1901, bound for McMurdo Sound and the Ross Ice Shelf where the expedition hoped to spend the winter, finally arriving in January 1902. Here, Scott and Shackleton became the first men to make an ascent in a hydrogen-filled balloon which was tethered to the ship. From 250m (820ft), they were able to photograph and chart potential routes across the ice.

After overwintering at McMurdo, Scott, Shackleton and Edward Wilson (the medical officer and zoologist who accompanied Scott again in 1912) finally made their bid to reach the South Pole on 2 November 1902. Initial good spirits were quickly tempered by harsh realities. In freezing cold and frequent blizzards, they became frostbitten and developed scurvy. The dogs became weak and started to die one by one. Man-hauling the sledges drained their energy, while hunger gnawed at them, weakening them terribly. Realizing that his team was in grave danger, Scott had no alternative but to turn back after eight weeks of struggling south. They had reached 82°16'S, further south than any other man.

The return trip became a race against time as the men continued to weaken. Finally, on 3 February 1903, after four months on the ice, they reached their ship. It had been desperately close to disaster.

The trial was not yet over, however, as it proved impossible to release *Discovery* from the grip of the pack ice. After sending some of his team back on the relief ship *Morning*, Scott and the remaining crew settled in for another long winter. The following year, in January, *Morning* and another ship, *Terra Nova*, arrived to assist in *Discovery*'s escape from the ice. Finally, on 16 February 1904, they were freed after explosives had been used to break up their icy prison. Undaunted, Scott was to return just seven years later.

Two stories capture the imagination of polar exploration more than any other. The first is the race to the South Pole between Amundsen and Scott in 1911. The second is Shackleton's heroic adventure of survival and rescue from 1915–16 after his ship, *Endurance*, crushed by ice, had sunk in the Weddell Sea.

DOUGLAS MAWSON

Tales of survival and heroic adventure in Antarctica fill the pages of many books. Some explorers have achieved prominence while others, equally brave and resourceful, have been eclipsed by the telling and retelling of Scott's triumph and tragedy. One such explorer is the Australian Douglas Mawson, who from 1911 to 1912 mapped the Antarctic continent to the south of Australia, in the region of King George V Land. After overwintering at his main base camp, inland from Cape Denison, his party split to survey both to the east and west along the ice shelf. Mawson's party, containing two men called Mertz and Ninnis, was exploring the easterly route across what were to become known as the Mertz and Ninnis glaciers, 300km (185 miles) to the east of the main base. After crossing a number of snow-covered crevasses in a particularly treacherous area, Ninnis, along with his sledge and dog team, suddenly disappeared. They had all been claimed by a gigantic crevasse when a snow-bridge collapsed.

Suddenly Mawson and Mertz's survival was placed in terrible jeopardy since Ninnis's sledge had carried most of their provisions. They were in a desperately serious situation and a long way from safety. Worse was to follow. On their slog back to safety, Mertz died 160km (100 miles) from the hut, leaving Mawson alone with no remaining dogs and precious little food. Struggling on, his progress was painfully slow as he quickly weakened, in the same way that Scott, Wilson and Bowers had done. But he was tough and had an astonishing will to live. Despite falling down a crevasse, out of which he eventually managed to pull himself, he finally made it back to his base hut, 10 weeks after Ninnis had died. It had been a truly remarkable escape from Antarctica's treacherous landscape.

First to the Pole

Robert Scott's experiences from his 1901–04 *Discovery* expedition to Antarctica had crucially shaped his planning and thinking about overland sledging. By now he had no faith in dog teams and chose instead to use ponies and ski to the pole while man-hauling sledges. Amundsen, on the other hand, had been convinced of the value of dogs by his experiences in the Arctic; he had no senti-mental objections to using dog teams, which he consid-ered as both transport and food for man and dog alike.

On 4 January 1911, Scott nosed his ship *Terra Nova* towards the shore at Cape Evans on Ross Island. By mid-January the hut had been completed and his party could begin the task of laying out food depots along the route before winter set in. He planned to establish his last and major 'One Ton' food depot at 80°S. On 2 February 1911, a party of 13 men, ponies, dogs and sledges carrying food set out to achieve this. Bad weather, blizzards and soft snow were particularly unsuitable for the ponies, although the dogs were unaffected. Progress was excruciatingly slow, only about 15km (9 miles) a day, and they started to fall behind time. By mid-February Scott was anxious to return to Cape Evans, so he decided to lay his last food depot 48km (30 miles) short of his goal and turn back. Ultimately, this was to be 18km (11 miles) too soon.

By 13 May, when the icy grip of the long polar winter had started to tighten in earnest, Scott and his various exploration parties had retreated to Cape Evans to sit out the winter. They were in sombre mood. Earlier, they had learnt that Roald Amundsen and his team had been put ashore together with over 80 dogs on the Ross Ice Shelf to the east, at the Bay of Whales, where they had established a winter

camp. Well-equipped and organized, Amundsen oversaw preparations for what was developing into a race to the pole the following summer. To the west, at Cape Evans, Scott and his team lived life according to the British colonial ideals of stoic discipline. Nevertheless, the hut was comfortable, if small. Inside, living quarters were divided into space for the officers and scientists and a separate area for the ship's crew. Space was also set aside in the officers' wardroom for meteorological, physical and biological investigations of their white world. For enter-tainment they had a gramophone and there was even a pianola which was no doubt played at the end of the feast to mark Scott's 43rd birthday – his last.

Amundsen's South Pole party of five men, four sledges and 52 dogs set off from the Bay of Whales on 8 September 1911 in fine weather, heading for their food depot at 80°S. In three days they covered 50km (30 miles) as the willing

dogs strained at their harnesses and the sledges hissed across the snow-covered ice of the vast Ross Ice Shelf. Scott started his bid later, on 24 October, but he was held up by the unreliability of the motor sledges with which he had decided to experiment and the unsuitability of his ponies.

By the time they reached the Beardmore Glacier, which links the Ross Ice Shelf with the high polar ice plateau beyond the Transantarctic Mountains, the ponies had been shot.

The Beardmore Glacier falls from 3000m (9800ft) to sea level and, after struggling to the top, the men were already exhausted. Scott's final support party and the dogs turned back, leaving Wilson, Edgar Evans, 'Titus' Oates, 'Birdie' Bowers and Scott himself to face the long trek to the pole. On 9 January they passed Shackleton's furthermost position south at 88°23'S. Amundsen had passed this point exactly a month earlier, on 8 December, and had only 153km (95 miles) left to reach the South

LEFT *The Norwegian explorer, Roald Amundsen.*
BELOW *Scott, at the head of the table, celebrated his 43rd and last birthday in the winter of 1911.*

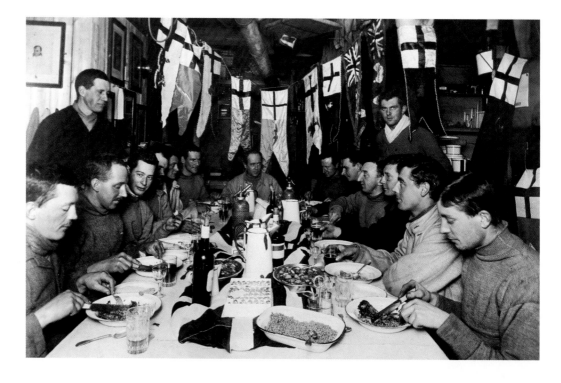

Pole, which he did on 14 December 1911. On the route, Amundsen had shot half of his dogs for food. His men had food, and the remaining dogs to pull the sledges on the return journey.

Scott, Evans, Oates, Wilson and Bowers finally reached the pole on 18 January 1912, only to find the Norwegian flag flying in the breeze, a pitched tent and inside, some letters to Scott. After all their preparations, struggling across deep snow and enduring the physical torture of man-hauling, nothing had prepared them for the bitterness of their failure to be first. Scott wrote in his diary: 'The pole. Yes, but under very different circumstances from those expected – Great God! this is an awful place and terrible enough for us to have laboured to it without the reward of priority.' After building a small cairn, hoisting the Union Jack and taking a photograph of themselves, Scott wrote a prophetic line: 'Now for the run home and a desperate struggle. I wonder if we can do it?'

They had a 1290km (800 mile) march ahead to the safety of the hut at Cape Evans, but they were dispirited, exhausted and now suffering from undernourishment. In 1911, the modern science of dietetics was poorly understood and their provisions simply did not contain enough energy to replace that expended in the arduous business of man-hauling sledges.

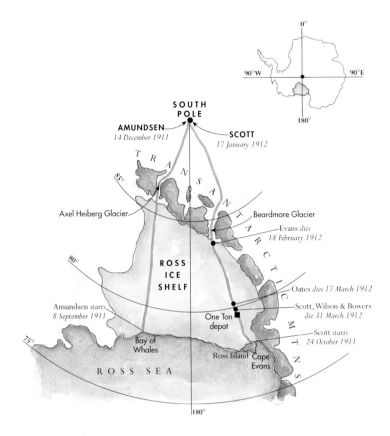

The first man to weaken badly was the normally powerful Evans. Descending the Beardmore Glacier, he finally succumbed to frostbite and starvation on 18 February. Thirty days later, they were only a few kilometres from their 'One Ton' food depot – but it was 18km (11 miles) too far. In a blizzard, the four survivors pitched their tent to sit out the storm: they were all near the end. In stoic British fashion, Oates said to his companions: 'I am just going outside, I may be some time.' He never returned.

From 21 to 29 March the remaining men, Scott, Wilson and Bowers, were tent-bound and too weak to move. Hypothermia-induced sleep was soon to creep up on them. Scott's final diary entry on 29 March was: 'We shall stick it out to the end, but we are getting weaker, of course, and the end cannot be far. It seems a pity, but I do not think I can write more. For God's sake look after our people.' Their frozen bodies were found eight months later.

The British public responded to the news by elevating Scott and his men to heroic status. They had lost – but lost nobly, with heads held high in spirit at least. They had displayed all the characteristics that Britain so admired – courage combined with steadfastness in the face of extreme discomfort, danger and death.

And so, it was thus that the legend of 'Scott of the Antarctic' began, eventually eclipsing the achievements of Amundsen who had been first to the pole, but who had survived.

BELOW *Captain Scott's hut, built on a lava flow on Ross Island, witnessed history in the making from 1910–12. The hollow wooden walls were* lined with dried seaweed for insulation against the bitter winter cold. It was cosy but cramped for the 16 officers and scientists of Scott's expedition. *Tinned food lines the galley shelves, studded leather boots hang from the beam and the dining room table remains just as it was in 1911.*

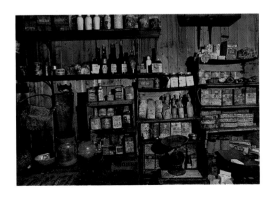

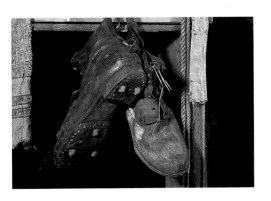

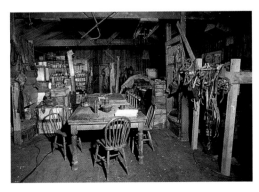

Shackleton's survival against the odds

For different reasons, Shackleton's attempt to cross the Antarctic continent from the Weddell Sea to the Ross Sea via the South Pole was to become another legendary tale. On the eve of World War I, in August 1914, he sailed south from Plymouth to establish a base on the frozen Weddell Sea. By January 1915, *Endurance* was in the unrelenting grip of the pack ice on the eastern side of the Weddell Sea, and the struggle for survival quickly overtook Shackleton's plans of an Antarctic crossing. Caught in the moving ice, his ship was taken first south, then west. Winter's frozen sea had by now extended more than 1000km (620 miles) to the north of their position and the grip of the pack ice was tightening relentlessly. As the grinding ice and currents toyed with the ship, it began to break up and, on 21 November, *Endurance* finally sank. Shackleton and his men were left stranded on the ice nearly 600km (370 miles) from the

nearest land (Paulet Island). With the advance of summer, the ice would soon break up: they had no choice but to get to land. Fortunately, Shackleton and his men had retrieved the lifeboats from *Endurance* before she was overwhelmed by the ice. Now, in a race against time, the crew struggled to reach land with the boats before the ice completely disintegrated. Shackleton and his flotilla of three boats carrying 28 men made landfall on Elephant Island, 16 months after sailing from Plymouth. Twenty-two of them were not to be rescued for another five months, by which time they would have survived the long winter sheltering beneath two upturned boats, eating penguins and seals.

Knowing that no-one would think to look for them on Elephant Island, Shackleton realized that he would have to seek help. The nearest inhabited place offering them a chance of salvation was the whaling station at Grytviken on South Georgia, 1300km (800 miles) to the northeast, across some of the worst seas in the world. The vessel that Shackleton chose was a 6m (20ft) open lifeboat, the *James Caird*, to which was added a crude deck, two small masts and sails. With only six men able to accompany him, Shackleton's epic voyage to South Georgia remains one of the most incredible feats of seamanship, due in no small measure to the brilliance of Frank

Worsley, the navigator. They finally sighted South Georgia on 8 May, 16 days after leaving Elephant Island. Landing was no easy task, however, since South Georgia is an extremely mountainous island surrounded for the most part by cliffs and pounded by furious seas. After waiting off the coast for two nights, Shackleton took his chance with a break in the weather and finally made landfall at King Haakon Bay, on the southwest of the island.

However, between them and the whaling station in Stromness Bay lay 30km (19 miles) of snow-covered mountains and glaciers, dominated by the 3000m (9800ft) Mt. Paget. Leaving the weakest men behind, Shackleton started his attempt on 15 May with two men, Thomas Crean and Worsley. Nearly 24 hours later they finally staggered into the whaling station. The climb had been an amazing feat of willpower and endurance that has defeated many mountaineers with modern equipment and clothing. It had been the first crossing of South Georgia.

After picking up his men from King Haakon Bay, Shackleton was loaned a Norwegian whaler, *Southern Sky*, to make the return voyage to Elephant Island, but heavy pack ice forced the crew to return to the Falkland Islands. Two other rescue attempts ended the same way. Finally, the Chilean government lent Shackleton the ship *Yelcho* under the command of Captain Pardo, who finally succeeded in reaching the stranded men. All were alive: not a single man of Shackleton's expedition had been lost.

SHACKLETON'S JOURNEY

1 Sailed **5.12.1914**
2 Beset in pack ice **18.1.1915**
3 *Endurance* crushed in ice **27.10.1915**
4 *Endurance* sank **21.11.1915**
5 Took to life boats **9.4.1916**
6 Shackleton sails from Elephant Is. **24.4.1916**
7 Lands on South Georgia **10.5.1916**
8 Crosses mountains to Stromness Bay in 24 hours
  Finally rescues his crew from Elephant Island **30.8.1916**

ABOVE *Shackleton's ship,* Endurance, *caught fast in the winter pack ice of the eastern Weddell Sea in 1915 shortly before sinking, is dramatically captured by the expedition photographer, Frank Hurley.*

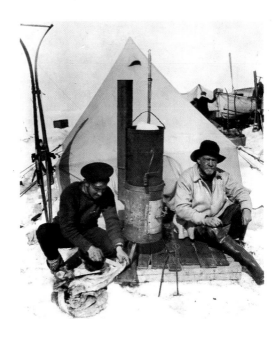

ABOVE *Adrift on the pack ice, Shackleton perhaps contemplates a bleak future while Hurley skins a seal in order to provide blubber for the stove.*

Shackleton's insatiable yearning to return to Antarctica drew him back there in 1921, at the age of 47. He never arrived. On the way, in a creaky old Norwegian sealer named the *Quest*, he died of a heart attack. His grave can be seen at the foot of the hills close to the whaling station at Grytviken. A simple white cross bears the inscription: 'Sir Ernest Shackleton, explorer. Died here 5 January 1922. Erected by his comrades.' In early morning sun, the peak of Mt. Paget glows orange and gold high above his grave, and across the bay stands another white cross, a memorial to this remarkable man.

After that, many more expeditions of discovery and exploration were initiated by a host of nations scrambling to get a foot in the door and the last frontiers of Antarctica tumbled quickly away. With the ratification of the Antarctic Treaty in 1961, scientific concerns began to assume greater importance. Research bases were established, while in the years following the 'heroic' explorers, a pioneering breed of men and women sought to undertake privately funded expeditions of exploration.

Modern exploration

In 1935, after several false starts, the American millionaire, Lincoln Ellsworth, became the first person to fly across Antarctica, while in 1958, Sir Vivian Fuchs succeeded in crossing the continent by land via the South Pole. Nearly 20 years later in 1972–74, David Lewis sailed single-handedly to Antarctica on his tiny yacht *Ice Bird*. However, perhaps the best known modern explorer is Sir Ranulph Fiennes. Not only did he become, in 1980, one of the first men ever to complete a pole-to-pole circumnavigation of the earth, he also, together with Dr Mike Stroud, succeeded in making a totally self-contained and unsupported crossing of Antarctica on foot, in 1993.

Recently, during the 1995–96 season, in a rivalry reminiscent of the race to the Pole between Amundsen and Scott in 1911–12, Roger Mear, a Briton and Børge Ousland, a Norwegian, each attempted to become the first man in history to cross Antarctica solo and unsupported. Sadly, both expeditions failed.

Also during this period, David Hempleman-Adams succeeded in becoming the first Briton to walk solo and unsupported to the South Pole, reaching his goal on 5 January 1996.

In 1996–97, Robert Swan, a renowned polar veteran, plans to lead a transantarctic expedition. Billed as the *One Step Beyond* challenge, it will involve an eight-person international expedition of both young men and women, pulling sledges, on a 1300km (800 mile) trek across Antarctica. Swan estimates that the journey will take approximately 80 days, during which time progress will be televised and beamed live via satellite to over a hundred countries. This will surely focus attention on Antarctica as the world's last true wilderness.

One concern being expressed in some circles, however, is that these expeditions are taking on something of a circus quality. It would be a pity if this great continent were to be reduced to some kind of global playground. If the public starts to view these expeditions as being driven by commercial interests, it would be to the detriment of genuine conservation efforts. It seems likely that the Antarctic Treaty may yet have to adopt the role of policeman.

BELOW *Ernest Shackleton, standing by a broken sledge which was replaced at Grish Depot.*

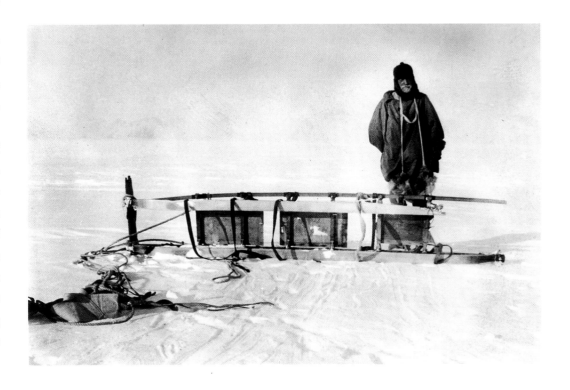

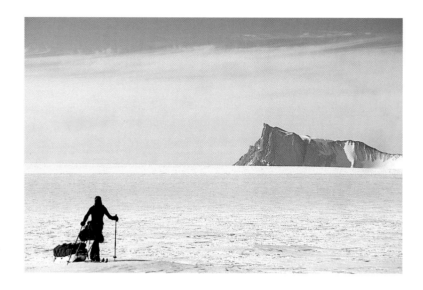

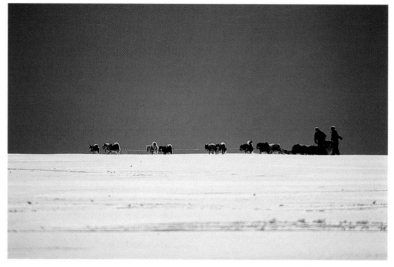

HUMAN INVOLVEMENT IN ANTARCTICA

In the years of discovery, nearly all of the islands were witness to the plundering of sealers and later, the whalers, until finally there was little left to kill for profit. Humankind has irrevocably changed the natural landscape of many of these islands, not only through hunting, but also through the introduction of alien plants and animals. In many instances, these have upset the delicate balance of their ecosystems and most of the islands are now far from pristine.

As human activities, interests and pressures in Antarctica and the Southern Ocean have grown, conflicting interests have developed among nations as well as scientists. Exploitation of seals, whales and the potential harvesting of Antarctic krill have become contentious issues which impact also on Antarctic food webs as a whole. Myths of mineral and oil wealth in Antarctica and on the Southern Ocean sea bed have raised the spectre of commercial mining operations and led to conflict with conservationists, although the prohibitive economics of deep-ocean drilling offer their own protection. Clashes of sovereignty for overlapping territorial claims, and differing interpretations of the Law of the Sea have implications for potential exploitation of living and nonliving resources. Other concerns are environmental threats from pollution on a global or regional scale as well as at Antarctic bases.

In response to these various threats, scientists proposed that Antarctica and its resources should be protected for peaceful and scientific purposes without political interference. Their efforts became the basis of the Antarctic Treaty System which exercises jurisdiction over the area south of 60°S, although some of the conventions to the Treaty, such as the 1980 Convention for the Conservation of Antarctic Marine Living Resources (CCAMLR), include the subantarctic islands north of 60°S.

During the International Geophysical Year (IGY), 1957–58, scientists from 12 nations undertook collectively to improve their understanding of the earth and its environment.

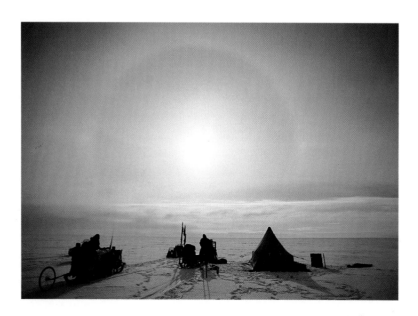

TOP LEFT *Taken during the 'Footsteps of Scott' expedition led by polar explorer Robert Swan in 1985–86, Gareth Wood man-hauls his sledge across the Beardmore Glacier. Mt. Kyffin rises in the background.*

TOP RIGHT *Husky teams and sledges like this took Amundsen to the South Pole in 1911. Used until very recently for polar travel, they have been outlawed on Antarctica since the 1991 Protocol on Environmental Protection.*

LEFT *Framed by the sun's parhelion, which is also referred to as a 'sun-dog', a modern field party camps at 80°S using a pyramid tent, skidoos, sledges and a distance-measuring wheel to aid navigation. The sun's rainbow-coloured halo is caused when the sun shines through a thin cloud of hexagonal ice crystals which refract the light by exactly 22°.*

Antarctica, remote and pristine, provided the ideal natural laboratory for much of the scientific research, particularly in atmospheric physics and earth sciences. Nearly 60 research stations were established, the greatest number being on the Antarctic Peninsula. Scientists from the IGY then set out to establish international scientific cooperation for future research activities there. The Special (and later Scientific) Committee on Antarctic Research (SCAR) was formed in 1957 for this purpose. In 1958, the 12 IGY nations proposed that Antarctica should be set aside solely and permanently for peaceful purposes and cooperative scientific research under the protection of the Antarctic Treaty which was signed on 1 December 1959 and ratified in 1960. There are currently 42 Treaty members (see panel). Today Antarctica, its surrounding islands, seas and unique wildlife, are largely protected by the Antarctic Treaty and its various conventions. Yet the impacts of a burgeoning world population and its increasing demand for food and resources could threaten even this last wilderness.

Perhaps the most fundamental problem now facing Antarctica and its living resources, as well as the earth as a whole, is climate change due primarily to human activities. Future global warming is now thought to be probable, while the 'ozone hole' has become a reality. Associated with the former is the possibility of sea-ice retreat while evidence for a rise in sea level, primarily as a result of the thermal expansion of the oceans, is accumulating. Ozone depletion and the corresponding increase in UV radiation

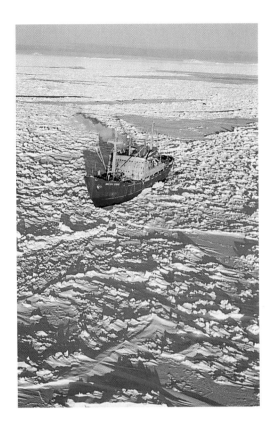

ABOVE *Polar resupply vessels service many of the Antarctic and subantarctic scientific bases.*

BELOW *Neumayer Base is built on the ice shelf and boasts high-tech equipment and comfortable living quarters. Steel tubes house the scientific and living areas, which become covered with drifting snow.*

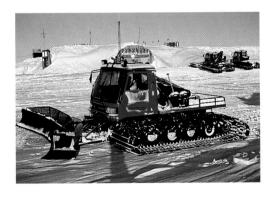

may have profound effects on biological systems. Antarctica, the Southern Ocean and their living resources are not only sensitive to climate change but Antarctica's polar ice dome, sea-ice distribution, ocean circulation patterns and biological processes in the ocean may themselves regulate global climate and that of southern hemisphere countries in particular. These issues challenge not only the world's scientists and politicians but particularly those of the 42 member nations to the Antarctic Treaty. If Antarctica and the Southern Ocean are to remain one of the last natural and relatively pristine environments for the heritage of our children, then we must face these issues squarely and honestly now.

ANTARCTIC TREATY MEMBERS

ORIGINAL CONSULTATIVE PARTIES (1960–61)

Britain*
Norway*
France*
New Zealand*
Argentina*
Australia*
Chile*
South Africa
Belgium
Japan
United States of America
Russia (formerly the Soviet Union)

LATER CONSULTATIVE PARTIES (1977–90)

Poland
Brazil
Germany
Uruguay
People's Republic of China
India
Italy
Spain
Peru
Sweden
Finland
Netherlands
South Korea
Ecuador

NON-CONSULTATIVE PARTIES (1962–92)

Czech Republic
Slovakia
Denmark
Rumania
Bulgaria
Papua New Guinea
Hungary
Cuba
Greece
North Korea
Austria
Canada
Colombia
Switzerland
Guatemala
Ukraine

* claimant states

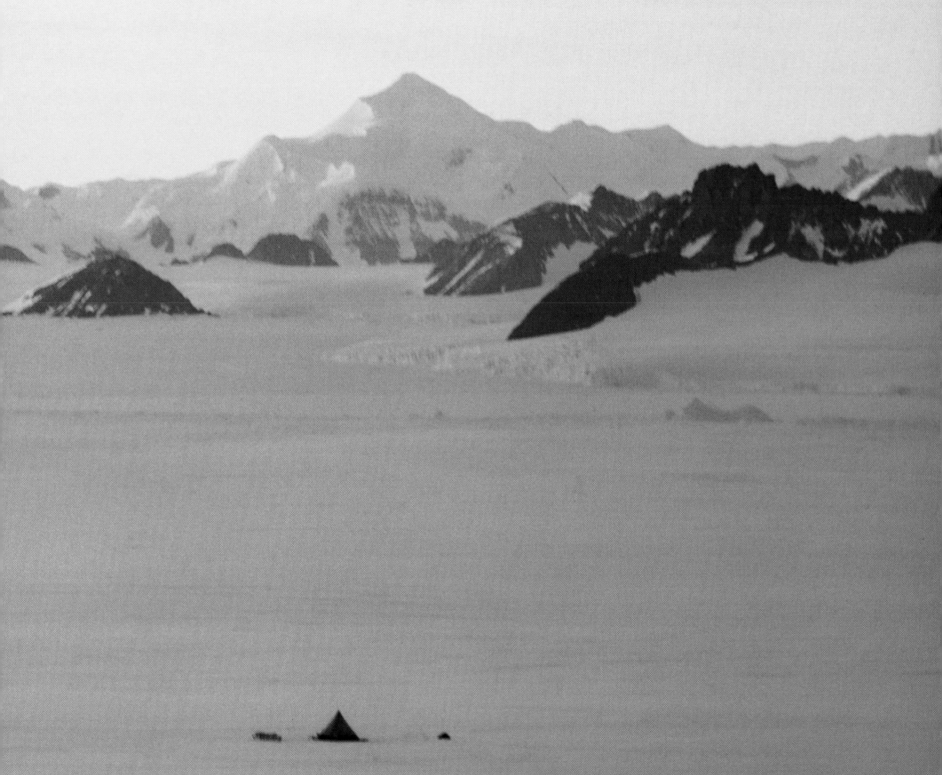

THE FROZEN CONTINENT

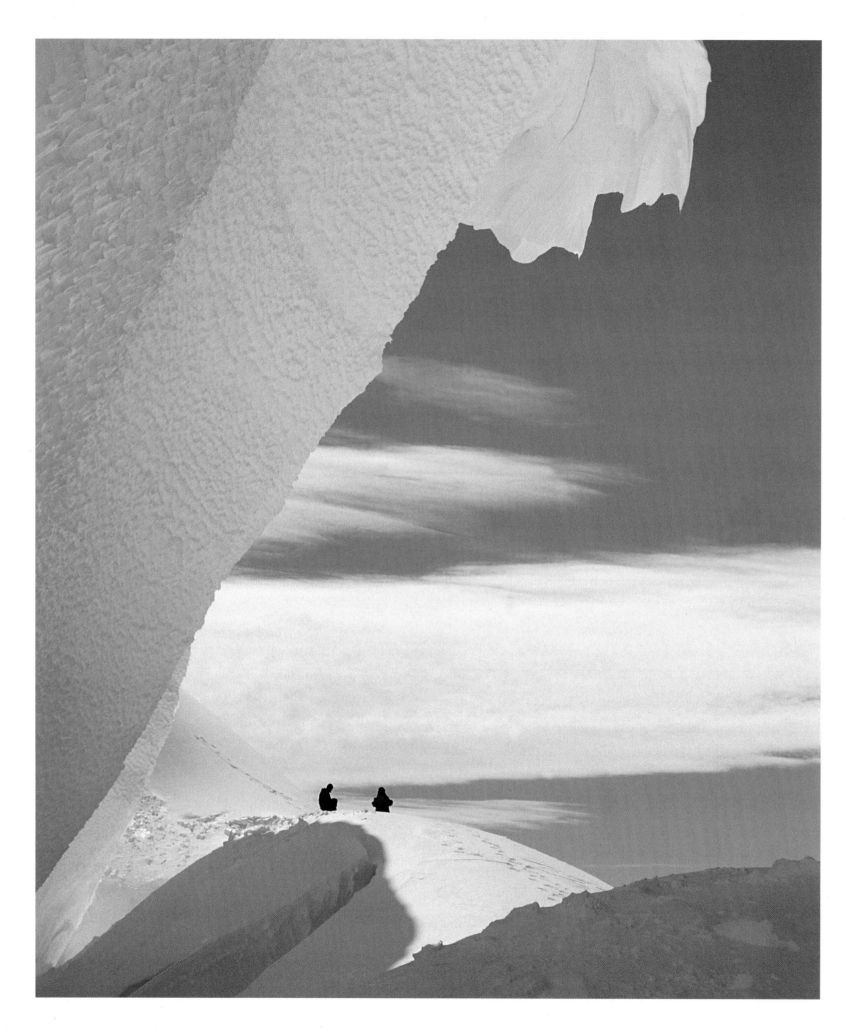

THE FROZEN CONTINENT

Antarctica's white desert

This stark, cold, white desert is mesmerizingly beautiful. Icy, desolate solitude amidst the utter silence of limitless space alternates with the raging fury of howling winds and blinding snow on the high polar plateau. It is here that the endless crevasse-ridden ice sheets and wind-sculpted ice ridges known as 'sastrugi' are found. Rocky outcrops called 'nunataks', and the majestic Transantarctic Mountains, glowing fiery orange in the low spring sun, reach through the enveloping ice sheets while above, in the cold blackness of the Antarctic night, the eerie lights of the *aurora australis* play across the sky.

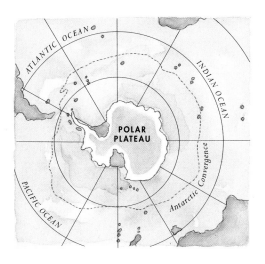

Antarctica's polar ice sheet is the highest, coldest, windiest, driest and most unforgiving place on earth. Dry as the Sahara Desert, with less than 5cm (2 in) of precipitation falling annually in the form of snow, it is also numbingly cold. The average temperature near the South Pole is −49°C (−56.2°F) and winds can reach over 200kph (125mph). The combination of wind and low temperatures produces 'wind chill' which dramatically lowers the temperature as heat is sucked from one's body. The lowest temperature ever recorded (−89.6°C; −129.28°F) was measured at Russia's Vostok Station in July 1983. Skin sticks to steel and ice forms in one's breath. Free water, the essence of life, is scarce.

Life within the harsh and desolate interior of the Antarctic continent is extremely sparse and confined to the mostly coastal nunataks. These are actually the jagged peaks of mountains which protrude through the 4km- (2.5 mile-) thick ice sheet.

Mites, primitive flightless insects called 'collembolans', and fleas are amongst the few invertebrates found here. All three are extremely small and, except for blood-sucking fleas carried by birds, feed on bacteria, fungi, algae and lichens. They also possess antifreeze substances in their tissue which enable them to withstand temperatures of −30°C (−22°F). Up on the high exposed plateau, however, the ice sheet produces conditions that are simply too harsh for even these organisms to survive.

Stretching 3400km (2100 miles) from the Weddell Sea to the Ross Sea, the Transantarctic Mountains separates the East and West Antarctic ice sheets. A number of peaks achieve heights between 3000 and 4000m (9800 and 13,100ft) with the highest, the Vinson Massif in the Sentinel Range, rising to 5140m (16,864ft). At 2300m (7550ft), Antarctica's average height is three times that of any other continent, due mostly to its covering ice sheet of up to 4.7km (2.9 miles) in thickness. The weight of the ice depresses the earth's surface, pushing parts of the land below sea level.

The ice sheet locks up more than 90 per cent of the earth's ice-bound freshwater reserves and, if it were to melt, sea levels around the world would rise by about 76m (250ft). Indeed, much of the West Antarctic ice sheet lies below sea level and is considered to be unstable and sensitive to break-up and melting should global warming become significant. For the East Antarctic ice sheet, however, this scenario is extremely unlikely as it is contained within a surrounding mountain barrier.

PREVIOUS PAGES *High on the polar ice sheet, a solitary tent is dwarfed by the distant Transantarctic Mountains. Field parties of scientists may spend two to three months in these lonely outposts, linked to home bases by radio. In emergencies, they are able in most cases to call on helicopter support but, when blizzards rage, they may be forced to remain tent-bound for a week or more.*

LEFT *A wind-blown 'cornice' of snow hangs from an ice cliff above two vulnerable explorers. Captain John Davis was perhaps the first man to set foot on Antarctica in 1821; until then, Antarctica had eluded human discovery for more than 2500 years.*

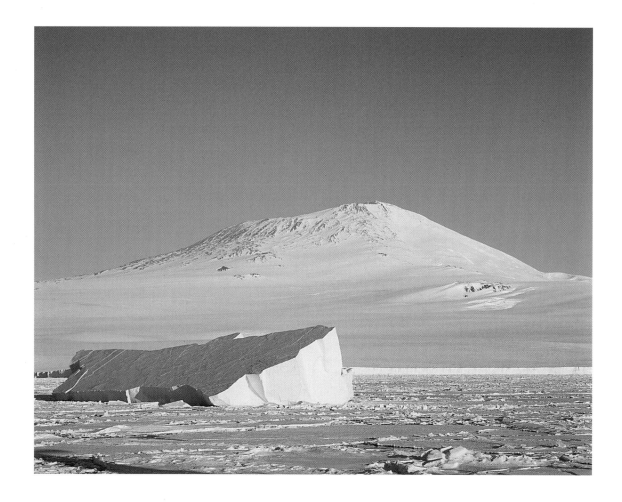

ABOVE *Mt. Erebus is the only active 'mainland' volcano in Antarctica. A smaller volcano, Mt. Terror, lies to the east. Erebus was first climbed in 1907, when it was found that the crater was 270m (886ft) deep and 800m (2625ft) wide.*
OPPOSITE *A pressure-crack in the pack ice leads towards the volcanic dome of Mt. Erebus, 3794m (12,448ft) high.*

The land beneath the ice

Geologically the older East Antarctic continent bears great similarity to ancient crustal rock formations in Western Australia, parts of the Indian Peninsula, Sri Lanka and the KwaZulu-Natal region of South Africa, providing evidence of the Gondwana supercontinent. The Transantarctic Mountains form a boundary between the older East Antarctic crustal bedrock and the younger, tectonically more active sedimentary, volcanic and granite formations characteristic of West Antarctica. Volcanic activity is widespread along the Antarctic Peninsula, in West Antarctica and in the Ross Sea sector of the Transantarctic Mountains. Volcanoes such as Mt. Erebus are still active and hot springs at various locations along the Antarctic Peninsula provide steaming baths amid a frozen landscape.

The sedimentary rocks of West Antarctica were deposited mainly in the Jurassic period from 213 to 144 million years ago when warm shallow seas, teeming with life, existed before the fragmentation of Gondwana began 150 to 160 million years ago. Vegetation was abundant and reptiles roamed the earth, leaving behind a rich fossil record. As a result of these sedimentary deposits, one question which has frequently been asked is whether or not the Antarctic continent hides mineral, coal and oil wealth. Some exotic and valuable minerals do exist and coal seams are visible in some regions of the Transantarctic and Prince Charles Mountains, but oil reserves are unconfirmed and based largely on speculation. However, none of these potential resources is of economic value since the logistics and costs of tapping rock-based resources hidden beneath 4km (2.5 miles) of ice are prohibitive. In addition, the ice cover is moving inexorably towards the coast while the underlying bedrock remains stationary. Furthermore, in terms of the 1991 Madrid Protocol on Environmental Protection to the Antarctic Treaty, all potential mineral and oil resources are protected from exploitation for the next 50 years.

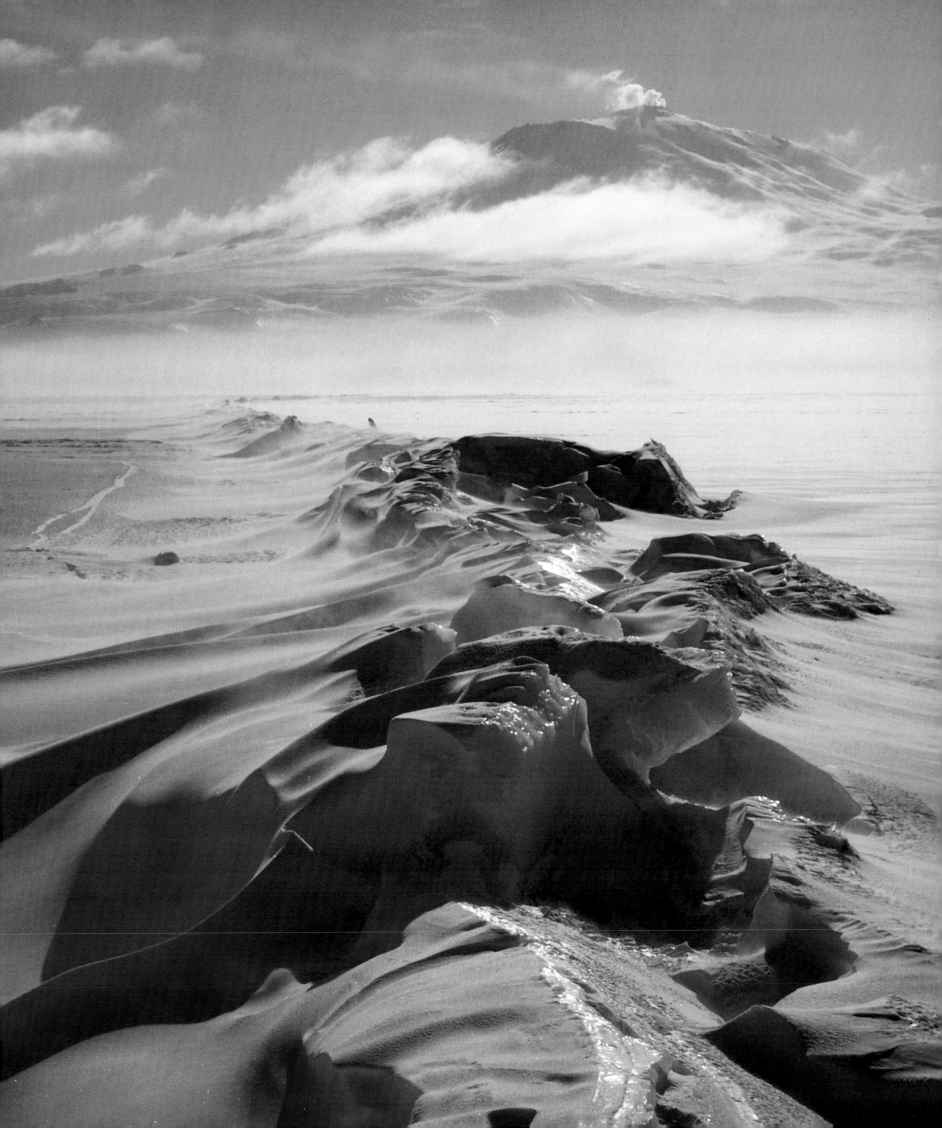

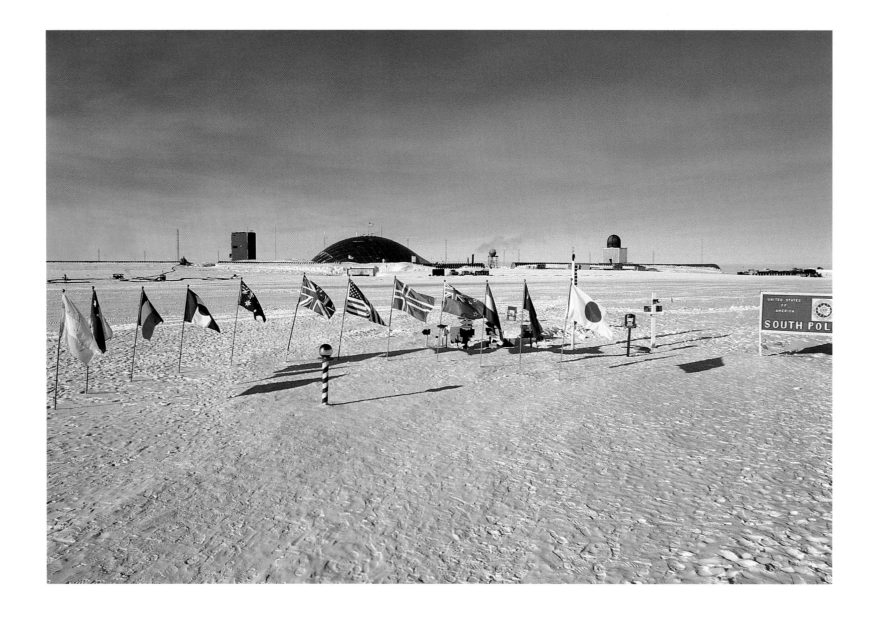

Ice cover also affects the construction of research bases on the ice sheet. In 1957, only 46 years after Scott's tragic attempt to reach the South Pole, the United States built a permanent station there.

Originally the Amundsen-Scott Station consisted of several huts built on top of the ice, but within 20 years it had melted its way 10m (30ft) down into the ice and had shifted with the ice sheet by just over 1km (0.6 mile) from its original position at the geographic South Pole. This experience is typical of all bases built on the polar ice sheet as it is continually flowing towards the sea.

In 1975, partly to overcome these problems and also in an effort to create a more hospitable climate, the Americans covered the base with a huge dome, 50m (164ft) in diameter. Regular flights of Hercules aircraft fitted with skis service the base, considerably lessening the sense of isolation. In less than a lifetime since Scott and Amundsen's day, the South Pole has become accessible to scientists equipped with the latest in modern technology. However, the movement of the ice sheet still necessitates the replacement of bases built on it every 15 to 20 years or so.

ABOVE *Flags of the Antarctic Treaty nations surround the South Pole. In the background, the Amundsen-Scott base is visible. Its position at the South Pole makes this base uniquely suited to study the earth's magnetic field.*

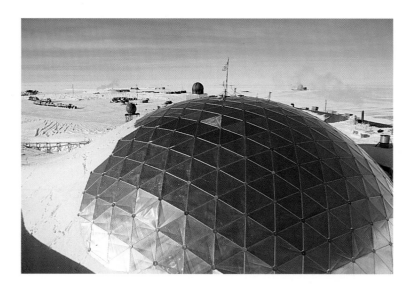

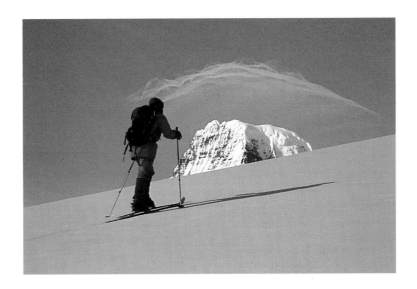

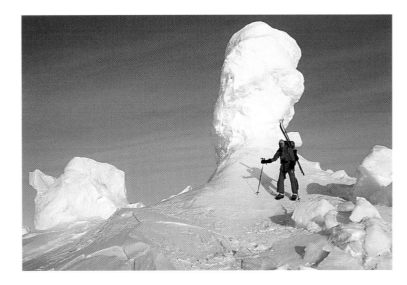

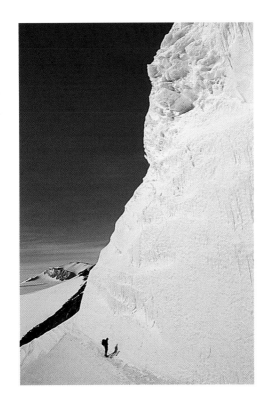

ABOVE *Moisture in the air condenses, creating clouds of ice crystals as it rises over a nunatak.*

BELOW *As glaciers descend through mountain passes to the coastal maritime region, ice flowing over the bedrock becomes deformed, cracking the surface into crevasses 30–40m (100–130ft) deep.*

OPPOSITE BOTTOM *Beneath the huge dome over the Amundsen-Scott Base, the living quarters and scientific laboratories have sunk 10m (30ft) below the ice. Inadequate ventilation and fire hazards pose potentially serious problems, while isolated and cramped quarters demand cooperation and tolerance from the scientists. The routine of scientific research is broken by films, videos and books, while mealtimes take on a sacred importance.*

ABOVE *Rather like a stalagmite, these ice fumaroles, or 'towers', grow when water vapour rising from Mt. Erebus's crater condenses into ice crystals. These, in turn, pile one on top of the other, gradually reaching higher and higher.*

LEFT *Lost in time and space, Antarctica still has the ability to dwarf humankind, despite the many years of discovery and scientific exploration.*

BELOW *Skis remain the most practical means of human-powered transport across the frozen snow and ice fields of the Antarctic continent. By evenly distributing one's weight over a larger area, hidden snow-bridges stretching across crevasses that would otherwise have yielded to the weight of a person without skis can often be safely traversed.*

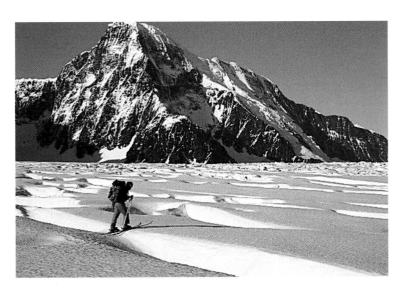

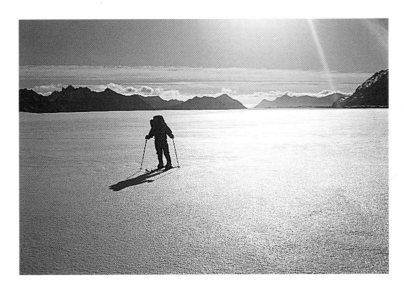

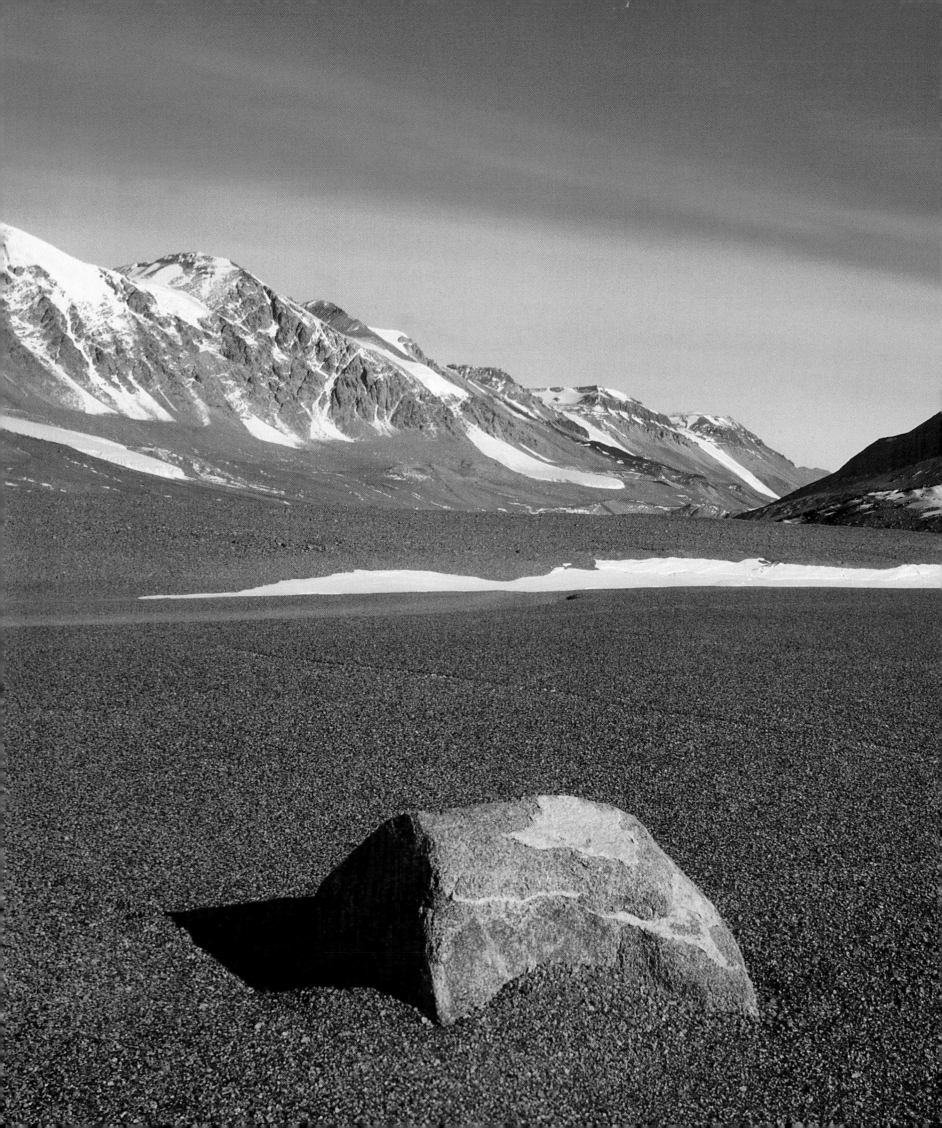

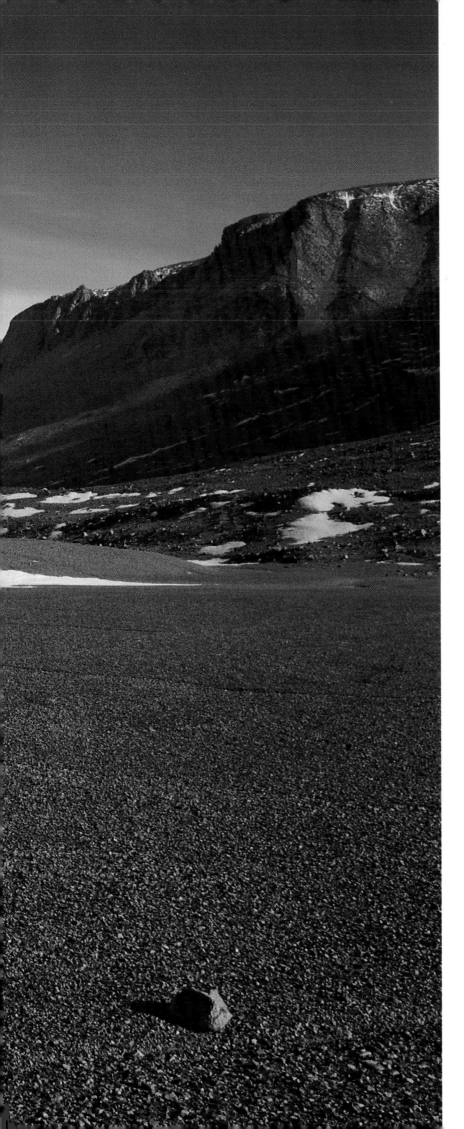

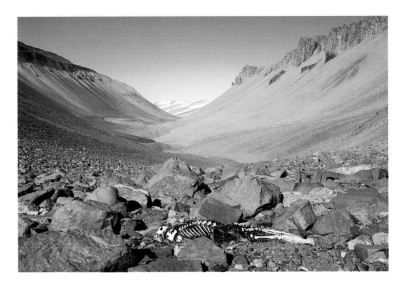

Valleys that escape the ice

Less than one per cent of Antarctica is ice free and, of this, the remarkable Dry Valleys must be considered one of the continent's most unusual phenomena. The largest are found just to the west of McMurdo Sound, on the western side of the Ross Ice Shelf. Here, the Transantarctic Mountains form an almost impenetrable barrier to the flow of glaciers to the Ross Ice Shelf. Nevertheless, at some time prior to 20–25 million years ago, during one of the earth's extensive glacial periods, huge glaciers draining the East Antarctic ice sheet carved the Dry Valleys through the Transantarctic Mountains. As global temperatures warmed again during the current interglacial period, the ice sheet retreated to expose them. Today, the valleys are absolutely ice-free places of bare bedrock. Katabatic winds which blow down them from the high plateau carry no moisture because the air has literally been freeze-dried, and any moisture or snow falling in the valleys is quickly evaporated. Only in the summer when the sun can briefly warm up the rocks do seasonal meltwater streams and lakes appear. In some of the Dry Valleys, no rain has fallen for two million years and the rocks have become sculpted into fantastic shapes by the wind alone. Without water, both decomposition and erosion are extremely slow processes and this has provided scientists with an ideal opportunity to study the bedrock formations and learn something of the geological processes which formed the Antarctic continent.

ABOVE *From time to time, seals and penguins have managed to stray far inland into these Dry Valleys where they died. Their corpses have been dried out and perfectly preserved in this mummifying atmosphere for thousands of years.*

LEFT *Dry Valleys occur mainly in Victoria Land, Queen Mary Coast and Queen Maud Coast and were scoured out of the bedrock 20–25 million years ago with intense glacial erosion. When the ice retreated, bare valleys were left exposed.*

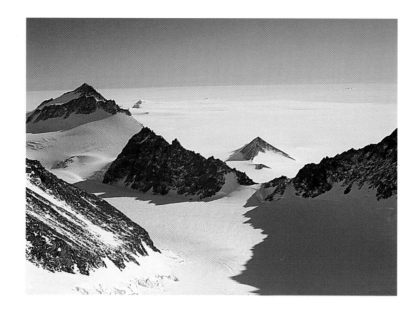 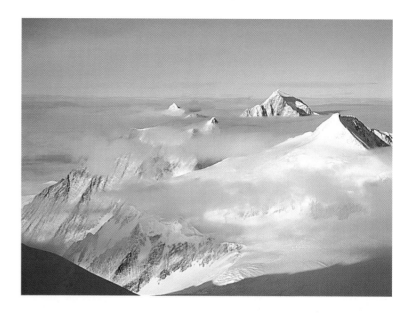

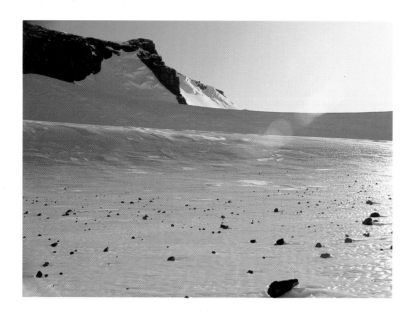 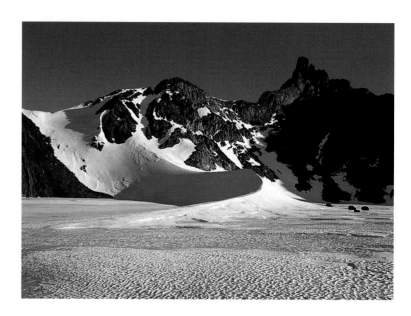

TOP LEFT *Vinson Massif, at 5140m (16,864ft), is the highest peak in the Sentinel Range. Lying adjacent to the western corner of the Ronne Ice Shelf, this imposing mountain guards the route south across the polar plateau, seen in the distance.*
TOP RIGHT *From Vinson's summit, Mts. Epperly, Tyree and Shinn peep through a misty blanket. These peaks lie at the Weddell Sea end of the Transantarctic Mountains which separate East and West Antarctica.*

ABOVE LEFT *Freeze-thaw cycles split rocks from the tops of the nunataks. Tumbling into ice-filled windscoops below, these sun-warmed black rocks melt pits in the ice that surrounds them. These pits are further shaped by the katabatic winds.*
ABOVE RIGHT *Wind-scour patterns of snow and ice reach out from the leeward side of Rumdoodle Mountain. This peak, which forms part of the Framnes Range, lies inland from the Mawson Coast in the Australian sector of Antarctica.*

OPPOSITE *Two skiers traverse warily along the crest of a gaping crevasse while crossing a slow-moving glacier. The loud, cracking reports emanating from active glaciers tauten already stretched nerves and set pulses racing wildly. Note the seasonal layering of snow in the walls of the crevasse, which becomes compressed and thinner with depth.*

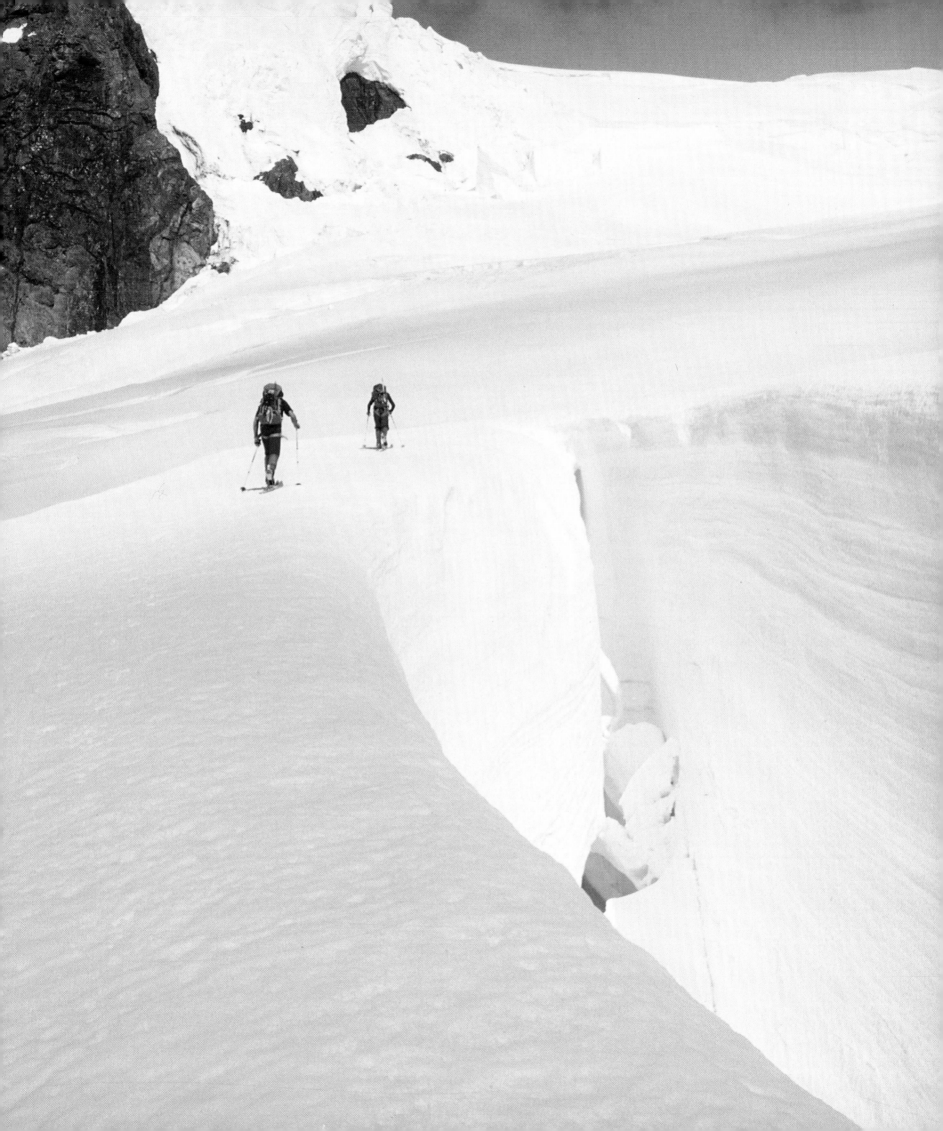

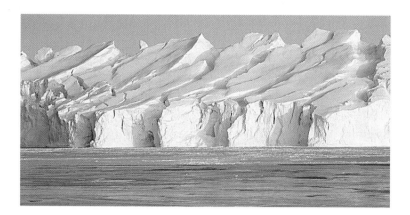

Ice on the move

Eight major glaciers drain the East Antarctic ice sheet through the Transantarctic Mountains to the Ross Ice Shelf and the Ross Sea. Most are named after the great explorers who used these glaciers as hazardous gateways up to the high plateau. It was over the Beardmore Glacier that Scott and his team passed on their ill-fated trek to the South Pole while Amundsen used the Axel Heiberg Glacier, to the west.

No two glaciers are alike. The Byrd Glacier has the distinction of being one of the fastest known valley glaciers in Antarctica, discharging 19km³ (4.5 cubic miles) of ice annually onto the Ross Ice Shelf. Another, the Shirase Glacier in Queen Maud Land, moves at an incredible 2km (1.25 miles) annually. The Beardmore Glacier is 200km (125 miles) long, 23km (14 miles) wide and moves at about 1m (3ft) per day, while the largest glacier is the East Antarctic Lambert Glacier which winds its way for 400km (250 miles) through the Prince Charles Mountains and down the Mawson Escarpment into the Amery Ice Shelf and Prydz Bay.

Such movement creates enormous pressures which buckle the ice into chaotic ice fields of house-sized blocks. Crevasses split the ice surface into huge fissures, some up to 10m (30ft) wide, some open, some concealed by fragile snow bridges. They are a dangerous obstacle, capable of swallowing people and machinery with often little hope of survival.

As the glaciers grind over the bedrock, the huge forces and weight combine to scour rocky material from the underlying rocks. This becomes entrained in the rivers of ice and, when the glaciers eventually reach the sea and break off as icebergs, grey streaks can often be seen in the ice. In this way scientists have the chance to examine rocky material that may have been covered by up to 4.7km (2.9 miles) of ice far inland.

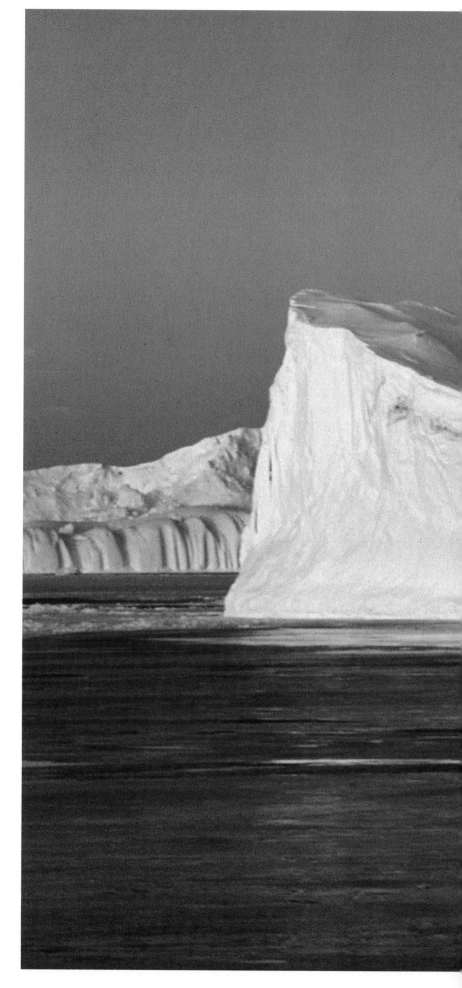

ABOVE *Aground in the shallow coastal region at Kapp Norwegia and wrought with fissures, perhaps 1000 years of frozen history crumbles into the sea.*

RIGHT *Glowing salmon-pink in the soft autumn light, the shelf edge near Kapp Norwegia drops precipitously into the freezing Southern Ocean.*

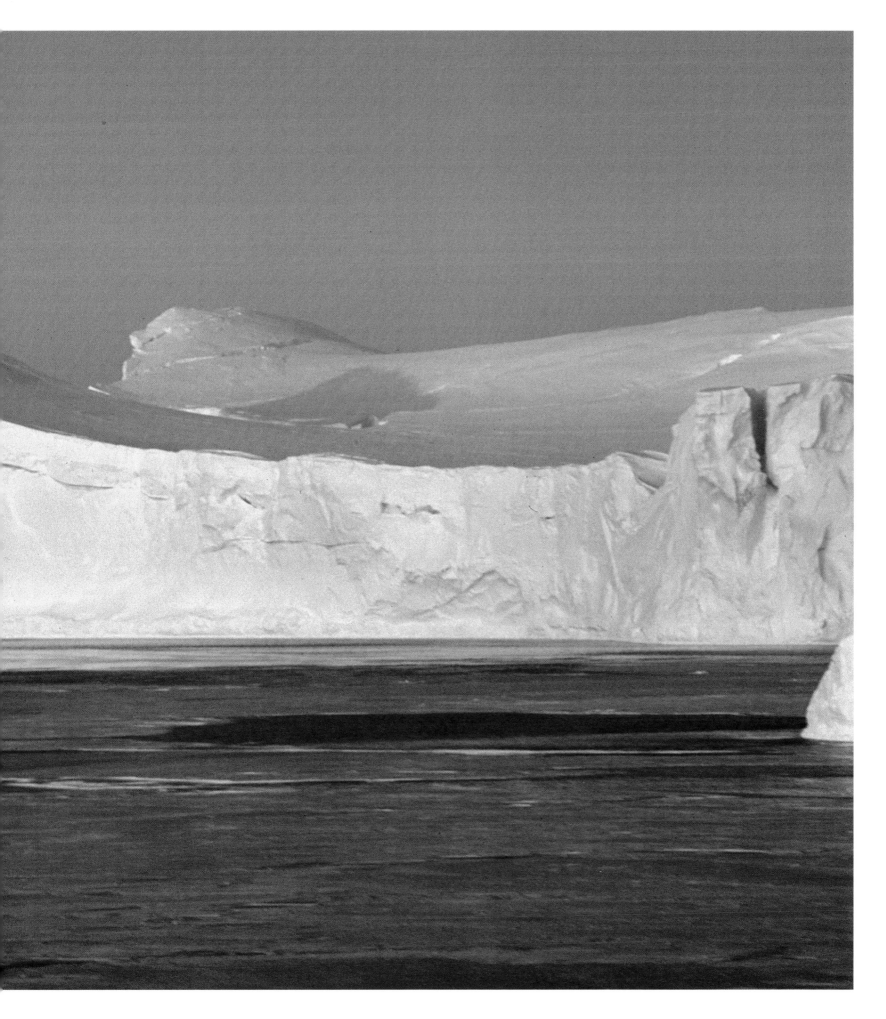

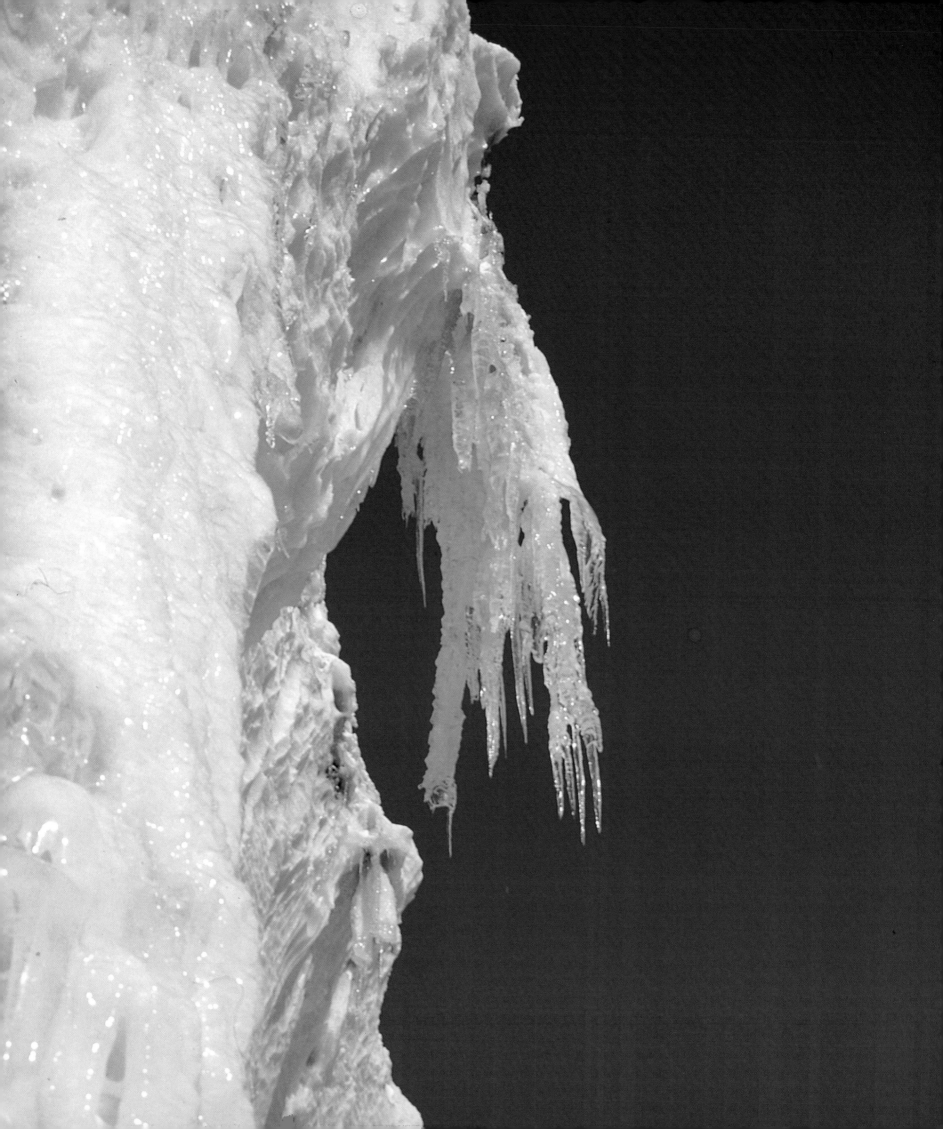

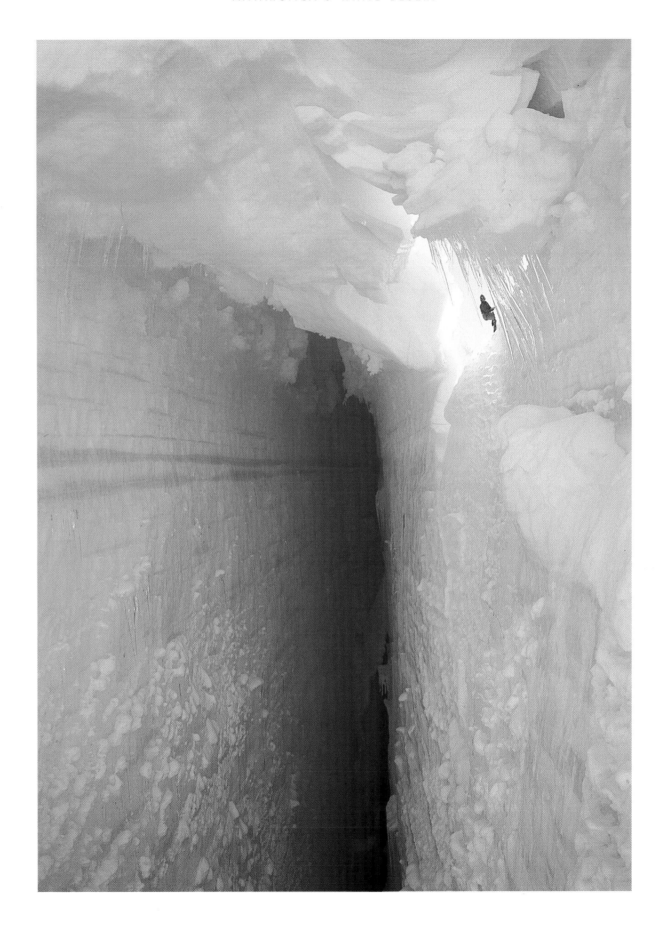

ABOVE *Stunningly beautiful but treacherously dangerous: a climber is dwarfed by the cavernous entrance to the blue interior of a huge crevasse. Wind-blown snow has formed a recently and partially collapsed snow-bridge across its gaping maw.*

OPPOSITE *Meltwater icicles hang like crystal stalactites from the glistening face of the Solas Glacier.*

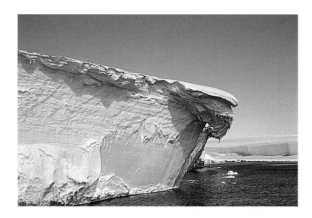
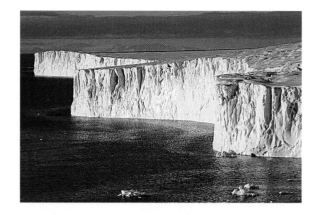
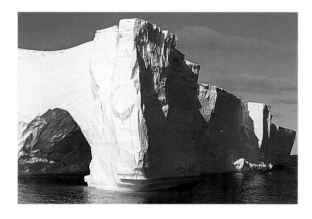
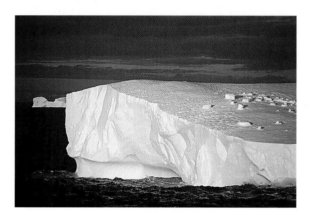

ABOVE *Contrasts of light and shadow, sky and sea play on the forms of the floating shelf-edge cliffs which rise 20–30m (65–100ft) from the sea. Overhanging snow cornices are sculpted by the wind while caves are formed as a result of the sea's erosive action.*

OPPOSITE *Mt. Byrd Glacier, Ross Island. Black layers of atmospheric dust, perhaps accumulating from past volcanic eruptions or rocky debris gathered up by the advancing ice sheet, become trapped in the ice. When the ice melts or collapses into the sea, this material is left behind as piles of 'moraine', providing geologists with insights into the evolutionary history of the continent.*

Climate and the ice sheet

Over geological time scales, the size of the ice sheet has altered cyclically through the great Ice Age periods. The earth's climate is controlled primarily by rotational changes in the earth's solar orbit which affect the way heat is received from the sun. During the last Ice Age, there were also changes in the earth's oceanic circulation patterns which, together with orbital changes, caused global temperatures to fall by 5–6°C (9–10°F). This caused both the Antarctic and Arctic ice sheets to grow until the latter covered most of northern and central Europe. Evidence of Antarctica's icecap growth can be found at the tops of the Prince Charles Mountains where ice-erosion patterns show that the ice was up to 800m (2625ft) thicker than it is today. One consequence of this was that sea levels worldwide were about 120m (400ft) lower than they are currently.

A question on the lips of many people is whether the polar ice sheet will melt in the event of global warming. Despite the fact that the poles are likely to warm up more than the equator, it will only be by a few degrees and not enough to cause much melting. In fact, computer simulation models predict that the ice cover over the poles may even increase in the short term due to more precipitation occurring in the form of snow.

Nevertheless, there is some evidence that the glaciers are retreating around the warmer perimeter of some parts of Antarctica, particularly the Antarctic Peninsula and the floating West Antarctic ice sheet. Should the major floating ice shelves collapse, calving of land-fast continental ice into the ocean could raise the sea level substantially (by up to 6m; 20ft) over time scales ranging from decades to centuries.

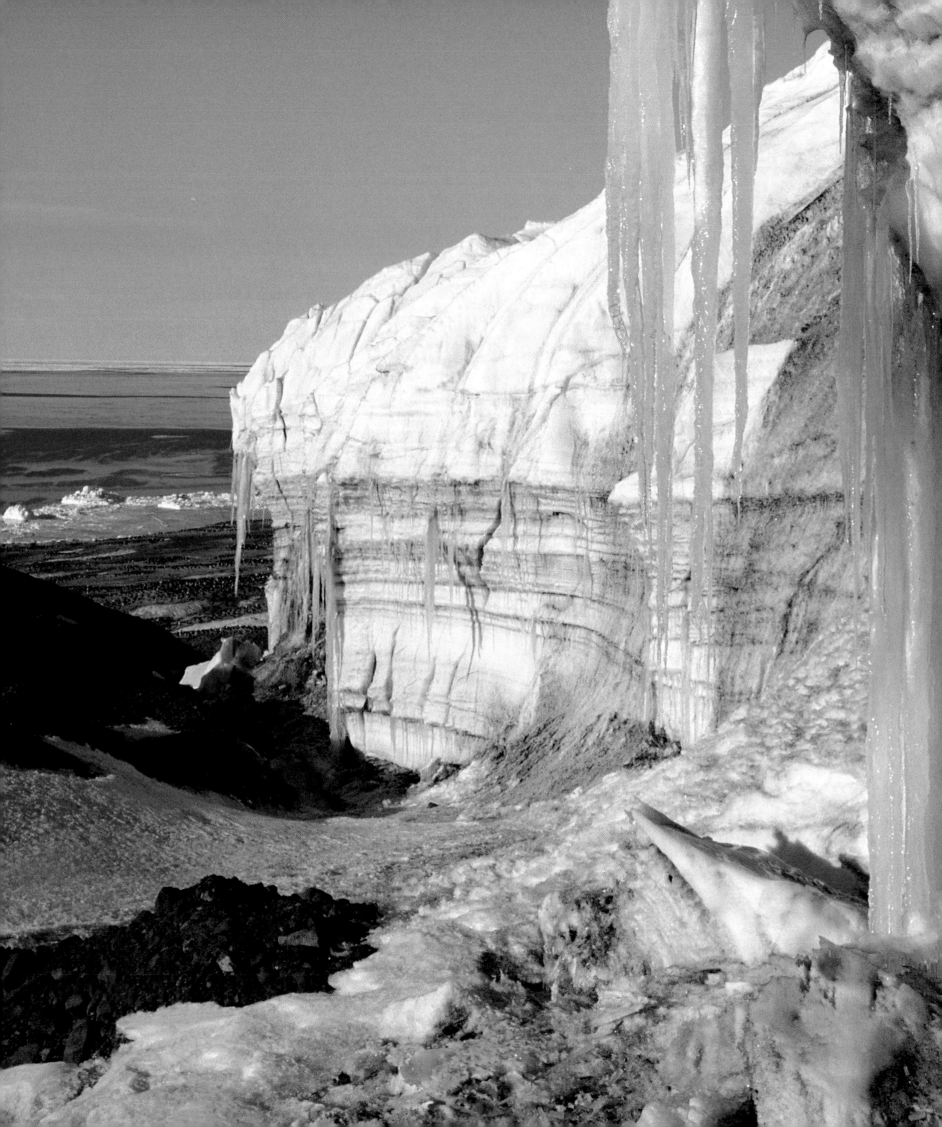

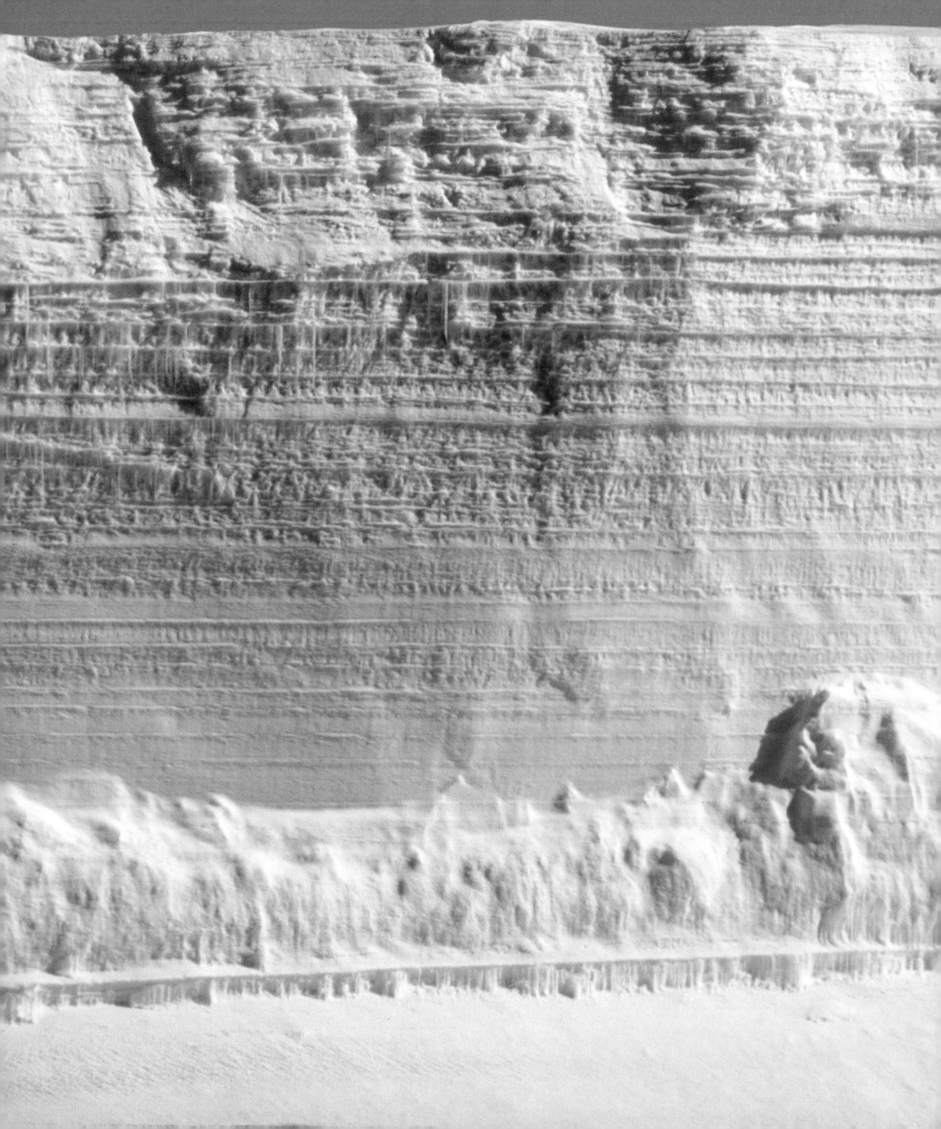

MARITIME ANTARCTICA

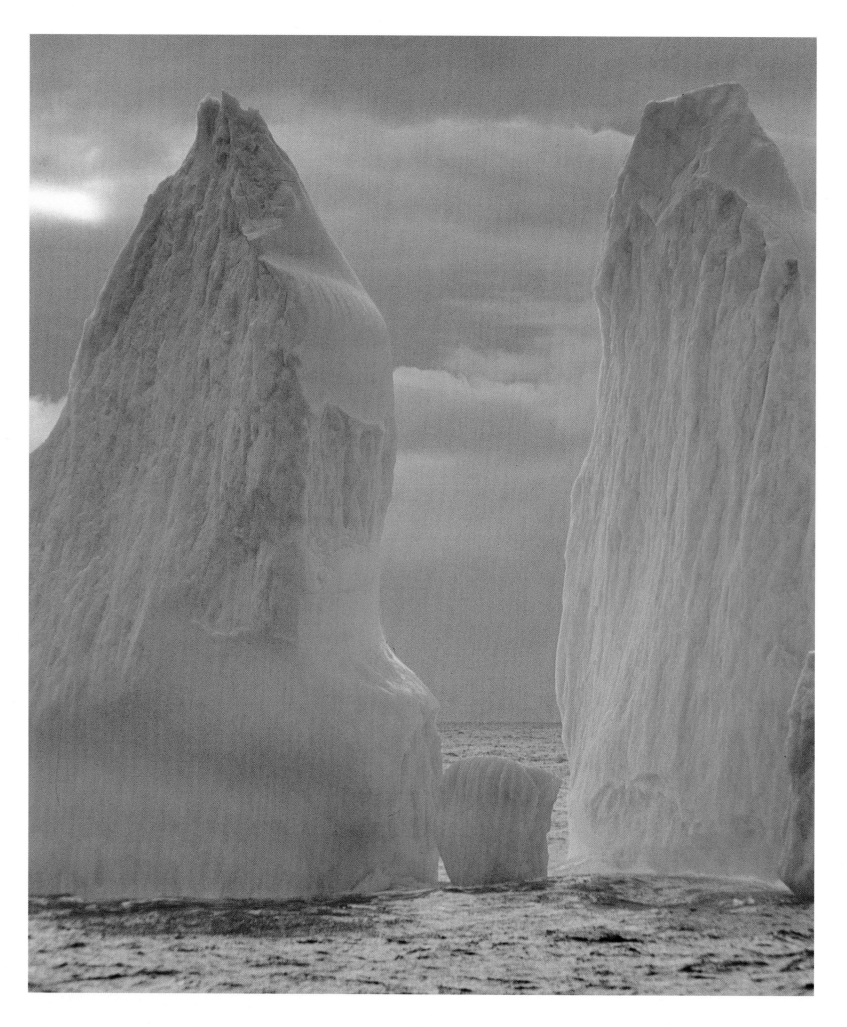

MARITIME ANTARCTICA

Where the ice meets the sea

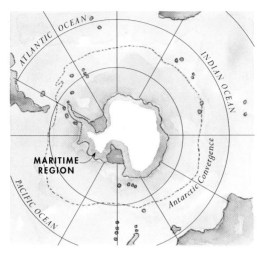

MARITIME REGION

Rising from 200m (650ft) beneath an azure sea, blinding white ice cliffs tinted with blues and greens and draped in icicles mark the 'barrier' between the ocean and the ice sheets of the interior. These forbidding cliffs can rise some 20 to 30m (65 to 100ft) high above the sea. Extending around half of the coastline, this barrier stretches for 10 to 20km (6 to 12.5 miles) beyond the continental landmass, a floating sheet of ice still attached to the ice sheet, rising and falling imperceptibly with the tides. At its edges, the seaward-moving freshwater ice sheets crack, crumble and break off into the ocean in the form of icebergs. Elsewhere active glaciers feed directly into the sea.

Some of the frozen blue icebergs are huge. In 1987, an American satellite spotted a gigantic flat-topped iceberg (nicknamed B-9) which had broken off from the Ross Ice Shelf; it measured 130km (80 miles) in length and was 30km (20 miles) wide. In 1963, a giant iceberg of 110 x 75km (70 x 50 miles) broke off the Amery Ice Shelf. Carried westerly in the East Wind Drift, a coastal oceanic current, the iceberg travelled around Antarctica over a four-year period until it collided in 1967 with Trolltunga, a northerly extension of Antarctica's Finbul Ice Shelf. The force of the impact broke off a second giant berg and together they moved into the cyclonic Weddell Sea Gyre current. The icebergs were discharged into the South Atlantic, close to the South Shetland Islands, 10 years later. For many bergs, progress is interrupted by running aground or by being trapped in the winter pack ice.

Newly formed icebergs are very angular but, as waves and warm winds erode and melt their surfaces, they become rounded and smooth or attain fantastic cathedral-like shapes. Travelling north into warmer water, the bottom of the bergs may melt faster than their tops, causing them to roll over. Finally, they disintegrate into smaller bergs and dangerous 'growlers', invisible to a ship's radar because of their small size and smooth shape. Rare green icebergs take their colour from phytoplankton and other particles which may become trapped in the bottom of the advancing shelf edge. The blueness of some bergs is due to the way they absorb and reflect light of differing wavelengths.

Some thought has been given to the idea of towing icebergs to those southern hemisphere countries in need of additional fresh water supplies, but the logistics are formidable. Furthermore, in the three to four months it would take them to reach their destination, half of each berg would either have melted or broken off.

Not all of Antarctica is surrounded by ice cliffs, however. In summer, the rocky beaches and towering snow-covered mountains of regions such as the Antarctic Peninsula reach out into the icy ocean, surrounded by jostling, melting ice floes. By contrast, in the long dawn light of winter, a steely ring of thick ice locks the edge of the continent to the frozen ocean. This boundary between land and ocean, 3000m (9800ft) lower than the polar plateau and experiencing a more temperate climate, provides a foothold for much of Antarctica's wildlife in the summer months.

PREVIOUS PAGES *The Amery Ice Shelf marks the end of the journey for East Antarctica's largest glacier, the Lambert Glacier, which winds its way for 400km (250 miles) through the Prince Charles Mountains. Distinctive, recent seasonal layers of snow are clearly visible. But, as more snow accumulates, the underlying layers are crushed; eventually dense ice is formed, obscuring the deeper layering.*

LEFT *Weathered, partly melted and perhaps two years old, a tooth-like iceberg drifts at 60°S off the South Orkney Islands. Probably originating from the Ronne Ice Shelf, it has been ejected into the open ocean to the north end of the Antarctic Peninsula.*

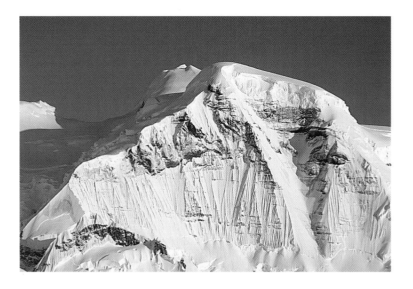

ABOVE *Broken, plutonic peaks and ice-plastered mountain faces are typical of the Antarctic Peninsula's rugged yet breathtakingly beautiful west coast.*
BELOW *Bright but stormy conditions prevail as wind-smoothed glaciers and a shining sea contrast with a jagged peak and its drifting ice-cloud plume.*

The Antarctic Peninsula

One of the few regions of the Antarctic continent that manages to break free from the polar ice sheet is the Antarctic Peninsula. This long mountainous chain is separated from South America's most southern tip, Tierra del Fuego, by Drake Passage, 625 nautical miles of some of the stormiest seas in the world. To the west lies the Pacific Ocean and to the east, the South Atlantic. Early explorers in their small wooden boats, followed by the great four-masted grain ships of the early 19th century and modern round-the-world racing yachts, have all plunged through this wild passage from the Pacific to the South Atlantic, turning north to Europe, or west across the Southern Ocean to the East, Australia and New Zealand.

For those early seamen, a small gold earring worn in the left ear was a badge of seamanship and courage which, at the same time, served as useful currency to pay for their funerals! Furling frozen and heavy canvas sails on those lofty, heaving spars was a dangerous occupation where one slip meant a forlorn and doomed plunge into the icy seas. At 2°C (35.6°F), survival time is measured only in minutes.

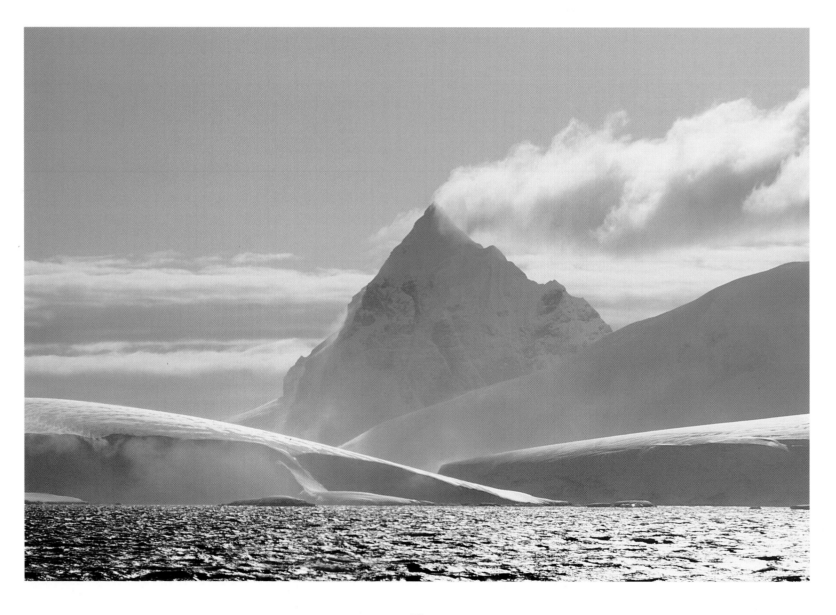

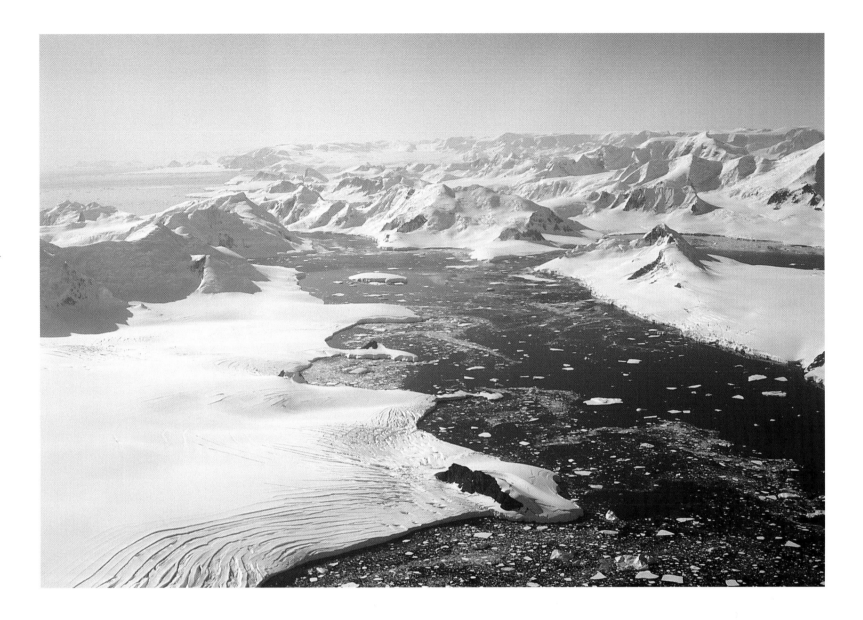

ABOVE *This aerial view taken in summer and showing Adelaide Island on the left and the Antarctic Peninsula mountain chain highlights the dramatic fjordland quality of the West Antarctic archipelago. Glacial flow-fields are apparent from lines of crescent-shaped crevasses in the foreground.*

Since the Antarctic Peninsula with its associated island groups extends to nearly 60°S, it is by far the most temperate region of Antarctica, attracting a host of wildlife, scientists and tourists. Coronation, Signey and Laurie islands make up the most northerly group, known as the South Orkney Islands. Further south lie Elephant, King George, Snow Hill, Deception and Anvers islands. The region has a history of volcanic activity and Deception Island and several of the South Sandwich Islands are still volcanically active; some even have hot springs in which to bathe. The soils are considerably better than on the peninsula itself and peat deposits on Elephant Island provide elephant seals with magnificent, muddy seal-wallows to snooze in! Along the western edge of the peninsula there are a myriad channels and navigable inlets which are increasingly frequented by cruise ships and intrepid yachtsmen from around the world.

Although winters are harsh, the summer thaw reveals more land and free water than anywhere else on Antarctica. Because of this, the region contains the richest diversity of plant and animal life found anywhere on the continent. As it lies further to the north, it also contains both truly Antarctic as well as subantarctic species which take advantage of the more clement conditions and the longer breeding season. In summertime, patches of a grass, *Deschampsia antarctica* and a small herb, *Colobanthus quitensis*, the only flowering plants in Antarctica, grow alongside the green, yellow and orange clumps of lichens and mosses. These are extremely slow growing; some of the 25 species or so of lichen are estimated to be several hundred years old. Yet, not a single flowering plant species has been found south of 70°S, in contrast to the flowering meadows of the Arctic tundra which extend to beyond 80°N.

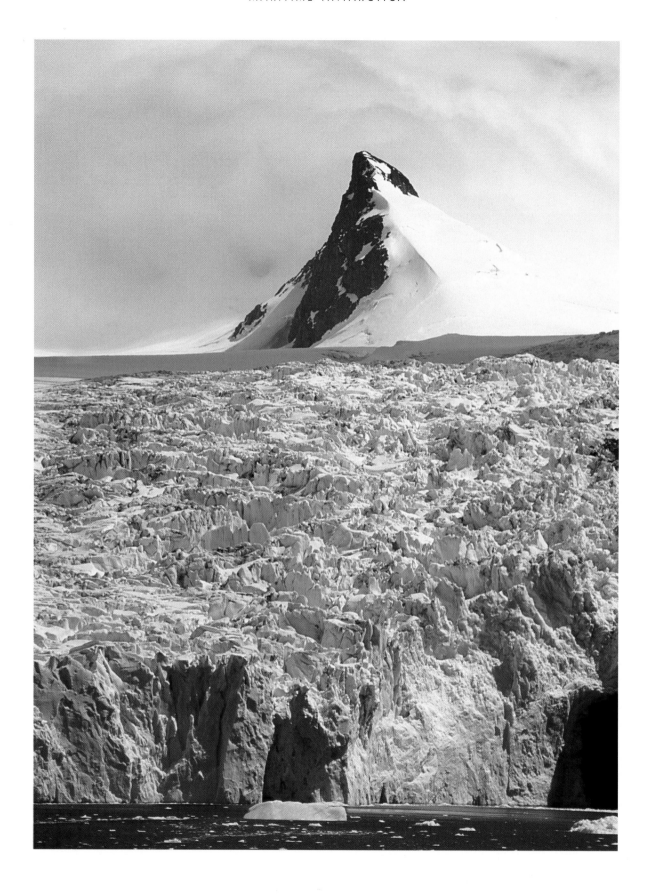

ABOVE On the Antarctic Peninsula, an active and chaotic glacier broken up by the underlying rocks
crumbles into the sea, carrying with it the rocky history of Antarctica's geological evolution.

RIGHT The mountainous arc of the West Antarctic archipelago and the Antarctic Peninsula was thrust
upwards partly by the clashing of the Pacific and Antarctic crustal plates 248 million years ago.

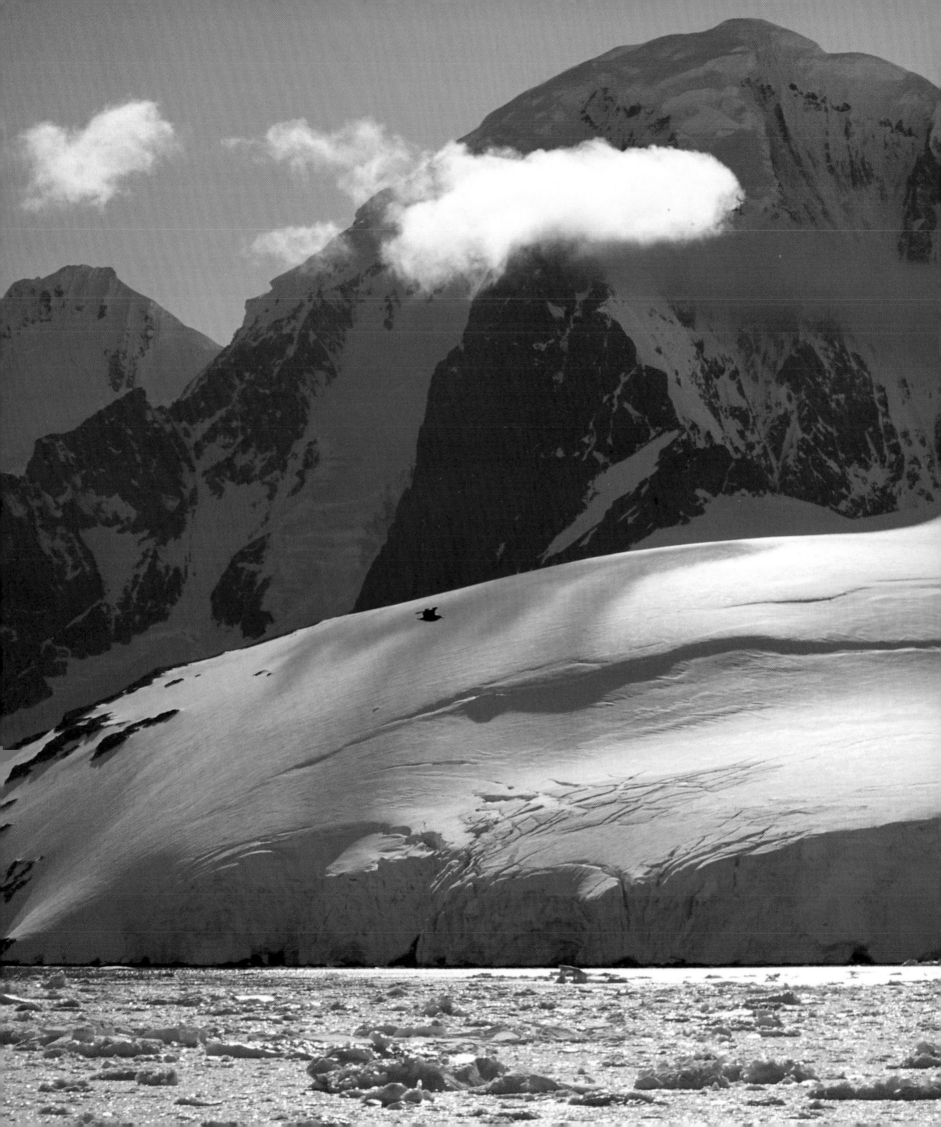

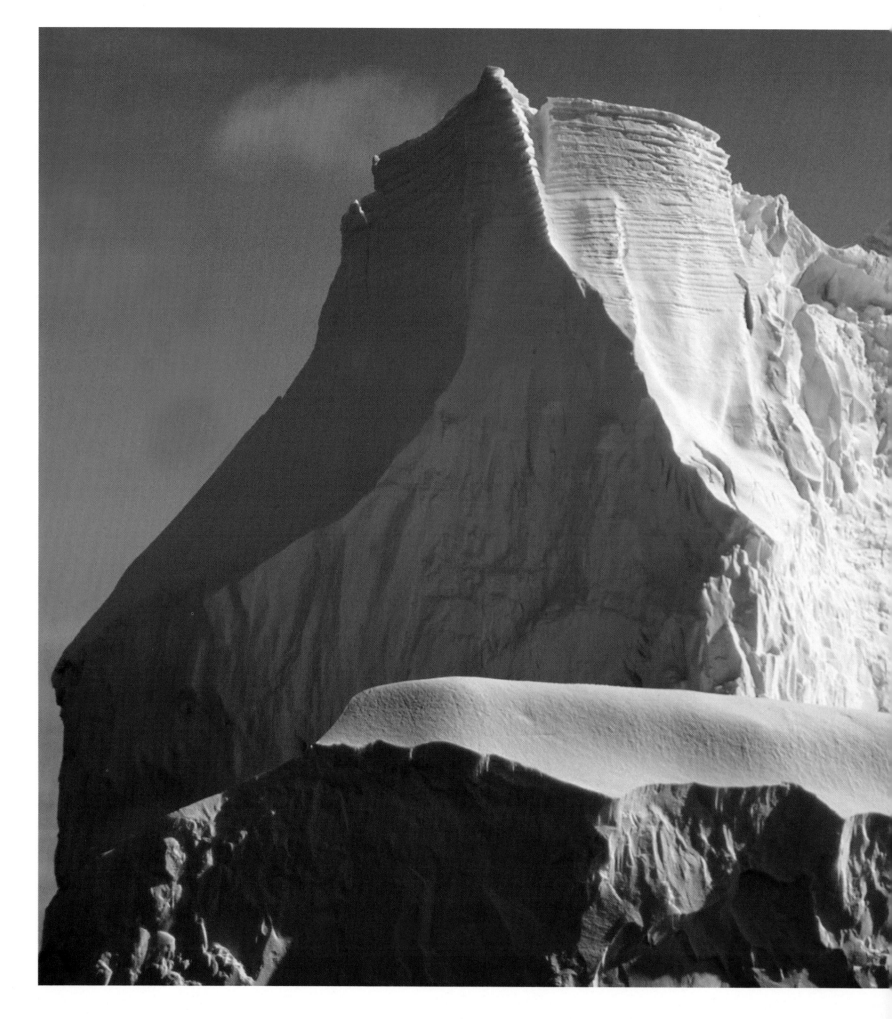

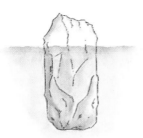

ABOVE *Most of an iceberg's volume lies below the sea's surface – usually about 80 per cent, depending on the density of the ice. As bergs can frequently extend to as much as 200–300m (650–1000ft) below the surface, they may run aground in shallow coastal areas close to the ice shelf. However, most escape into deep open water where, if the bottom melts faster than the top, they will eventually become unstable and topple over.*

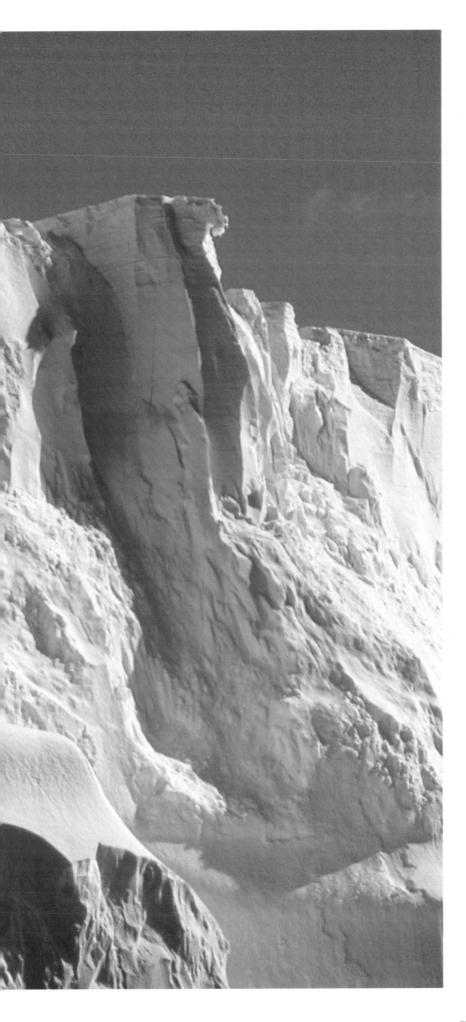

LEFT *A tabular iceberg in Prydz Bay off the Mawson Coast. Smooth slopes at the base are polished by surging seas. Icebergs such as these pose no serious threat to shipping equipped with radar; in fact, their immense size can even provide shelter during storms, while their stately progress through the pack ice can provide ice-free leads, or 'inlets', for ships to exploit. Some bergs have taken 10 years to travel westwards from Prydz Bay to Dronning Maud Land, nearly a quarter of the way around Antarctica's circumference.*

BELOW *Locked together during the icy months of the previous winter, iceberg and pack ice continue their odyssey in the late summer sun.*

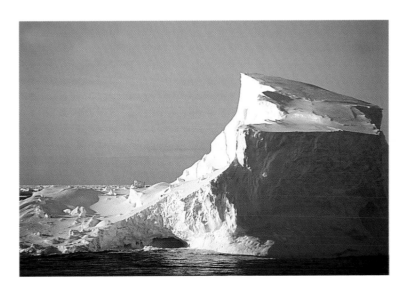

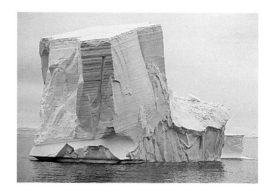
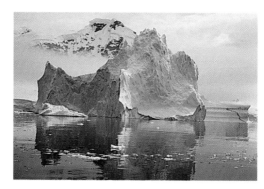
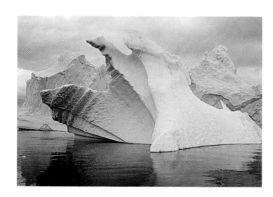

ABOVE *Various stages in the life of an iceberg: the angular features of a small but majestic tabular berg (left) reveal the seasonal layering of snow as well as the iceberg's youth, while (centre and right) smoothed and sea-sculpted bergs give away their advancing age to finally become mere shadows of their former glory.*
BELOW *Adrift in a clear blue ocean and driven by capricious winds and currents, this berg's days are clearly numbered as it melts in warmer, more northerly seas.*

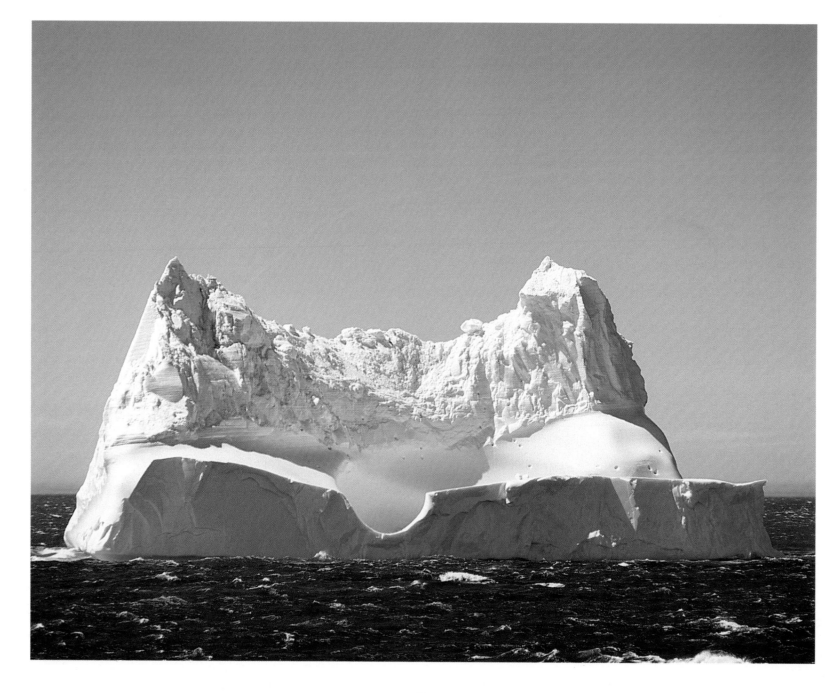

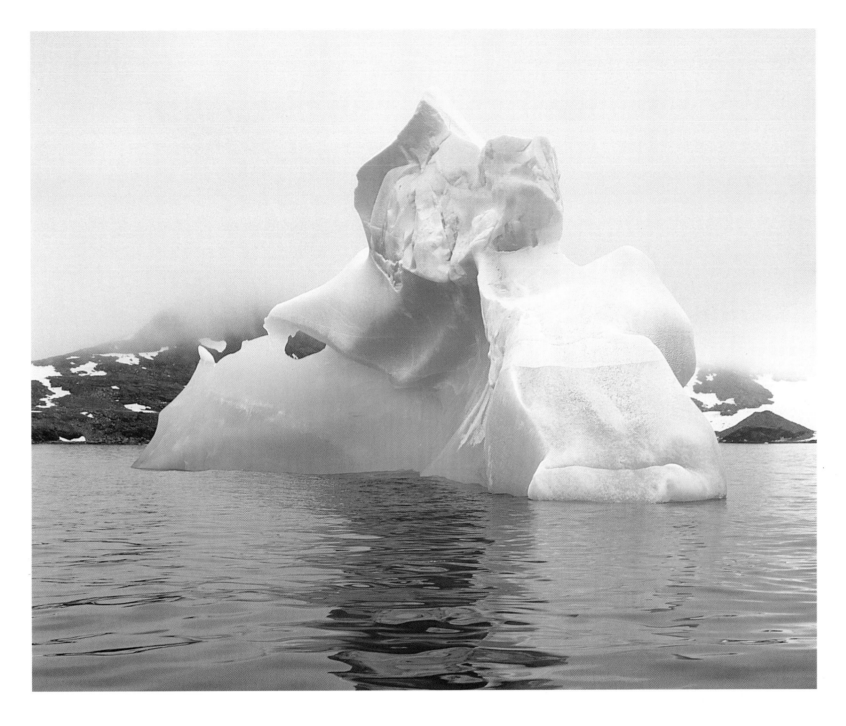

ABOVE *A rare blue iceberg lying just off Coronation Island, one of the South Orkney Islands, has a story to tell. Squeezed by the immense weight of more than 4km (2.5 miles) of overlying ice before calving into the sea, the berg's steely hardness and great density teases out and reflects blue light.*

RIGHT *A growler drifts peacefully in the calm waters off the Antarctic Peninsula; in foul weather these are particularly dangerous to shipping. Invisible to radar because of their smoothness and low outline, they conceal their malevolence beneath the waves. It is noticeable that icebergs often appear in groups. This is because ocean currents such as the outflow of the Weddell Gyre have a tendency to concentrate them in that region, while in some particularly shallow coastal regions many of the bergs will run aground to form an iceberg 'graveyard'.*

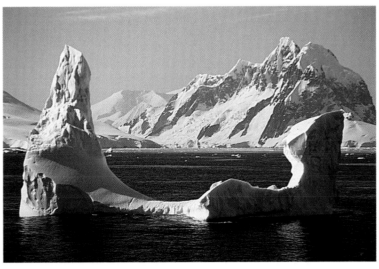

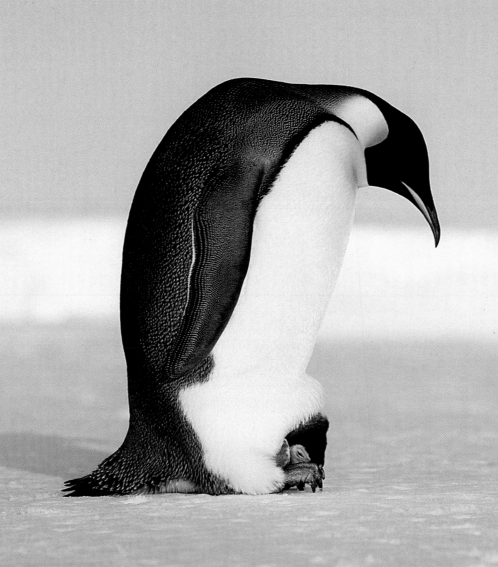

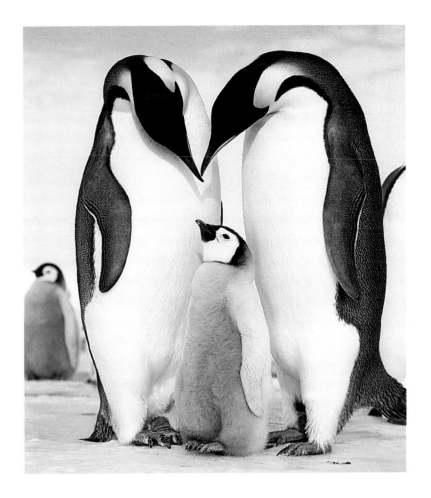

Life on the ice

Maritime Antarctica plays host to huge numbers of penguins and oceanic birds. These migrate south in the summer, following the retreating ice edge where food, especially Antarctic krill, is abundant. In the brief summer months, the truly Antarctic species come here to breed, particularly to the Antarctic Peninsula where beaches and land become exposed with the seasonal retreat of the snow. Subantarctic birds and penguins, in the meantime, migrate north to the numerous outlying islands to breed.

There are 11 species of Antarctic and subantarctic penguin: emperor, king, Adélie, chinstrap, gentoo, macaroni, royal, rockhopper, erect-crested, Snare's crested and yellow-eyed. Emperor, Adélie, gentoo and chinstrap penguins inhabit the coastal maritime region; the others are primarily inhabitants of the subantarctic islands and the northern parts of the Antarctic Peninsula. All are extremely proficient swimmers, using their stubby but powerful flippers to 'fly' through the water at surprising speeds of up to 30kph (19mph) in bursts. Their prey is dominated by Antarctic krill, squid and fish and their stubby tails and webbed feet allow them to twist and turn acrobatically to make their catch and, at the same time, elude their principal enemy, the powerfully sleek leopard seal.

Apart from swimming underwater, penguins may frequently be seen 'porpoising' along the surface, leaping into the air at intervals as they swim. They are also prodigious divers, with differing species of penguin diving to different depths. Some also forage further out to sea than others. This prevents them from competing for the same food resources.

On land, most are clumsy and walk or hop with apparent difficulty, although they may cover huge distances and overcome significant obstacles if necessary. If frightened or in a hurry, emperors, Adélies and some other penguins flop onto their stomachs and toboggan across the snow and ice at speed. Downhill slopes become a chaotic roller-coaster ride.

OPPOSITE *At the end of a long dark winter, a young emperor penguin chick peeks out from under the adult female's warm brood pouch. Recently returned from feeding at sea, she is fat and sleek with a waterproof coat that is her key to survival in this hostile world.*

ABOVE *Doting emperor penguin parents with their older chick. Warm blood is carried to the penguins' feet in small arteries; these lie next to small veins which return cold blood to the body which warms up the returning blood, so that neither bodies nor feet get cold.*

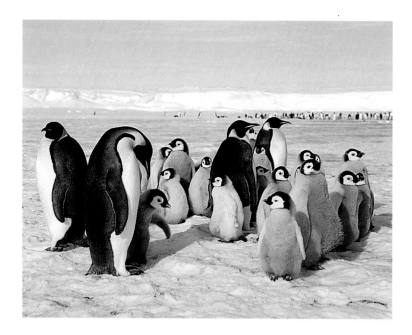

ABOVE *Emperor penguin adults and chicks dot the Lambton Glacier in East Antarctica during the spring. The downy chicks will later moult into their waterproof adult coats before they can finally venture into the sea.*

Despite the individual differences, there is one particular problem that all penguin species share: arranging their breeding cycle so that they can mate, lay eggs and rear their chicks before summer ends and the harsh winter closes in. It is a race against time which only the fittest survive. The larger birds are most at risk since their chicks take the longest to rear, a dilemma that the emperor penguin has ingeniously overcome.

The largest of the penguins, the emperor penguin occurs mainly in the Weddell Sea, Dronning Maud Land, Enderby and Princess Elizabeth Lands and the Ross Sea, where it breeds on ice shelves or frozen ice at the base of the ice cliffs. Standing nearly 1m (3ft) tall and weighing over 25kg (55 lb), it is unique amongst all of Antarctica's wildlife in choosing to breed during the harsh winter season. This is to make sure the chicks hatch at the very end of the winter, so that they have a whole summer of feeding in which to grow and fatten up. There would not be sufficient time if they were to start breeding in spring.

A single egg is laid in May or June and handed over to the male. He then incubates it on his feet which he covers with a warm brood pouch. In the meantime, the female makes the long trek back to the sea to feed. This march may be 100km (60 miles) or more because, by now, the ice

RIGHT *Emperor penguin chicks huddle in a crèche during a late spring blizzard. By this age, chicks have no natural predators on the ice and can regulate their own body temperature allowing the adults to leave them and forage for food.*

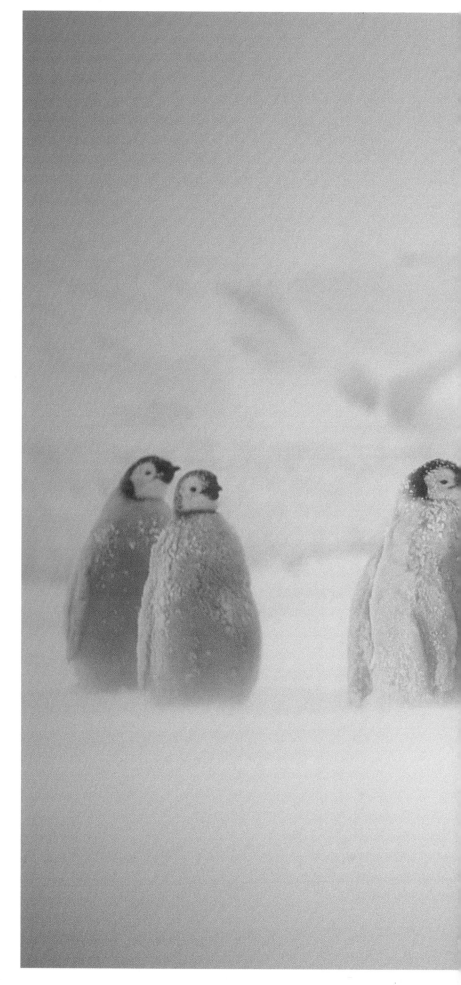

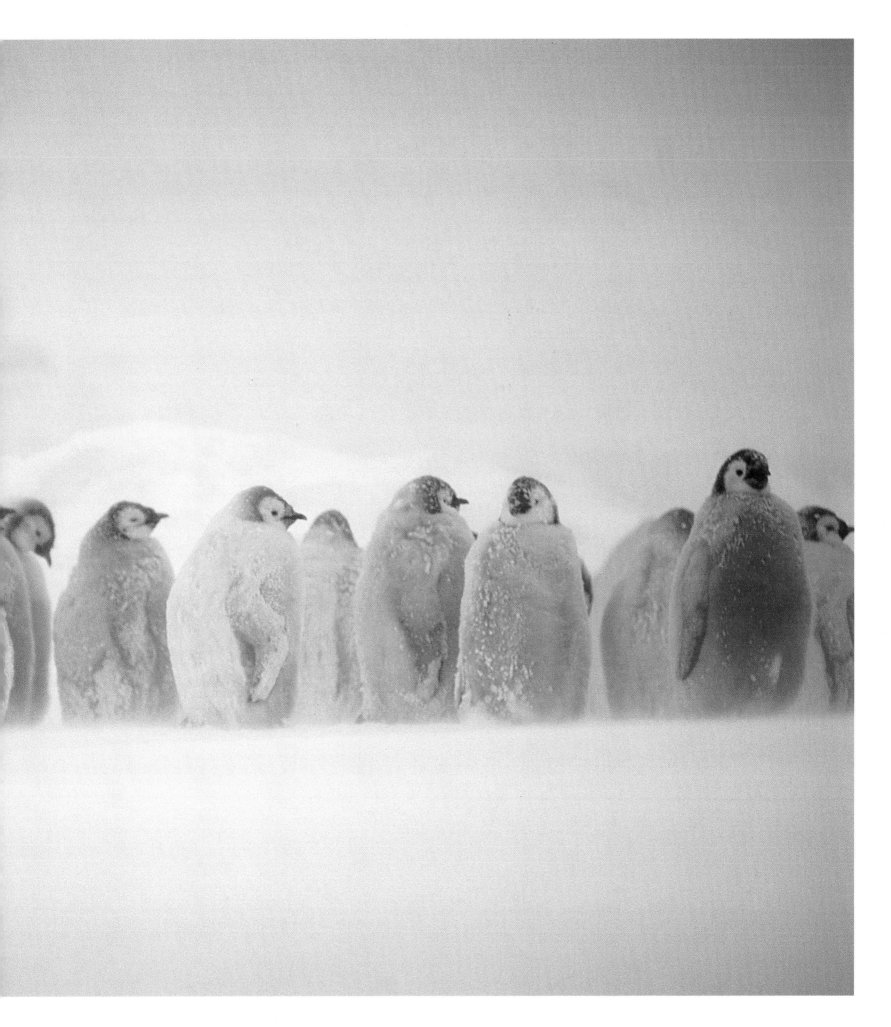

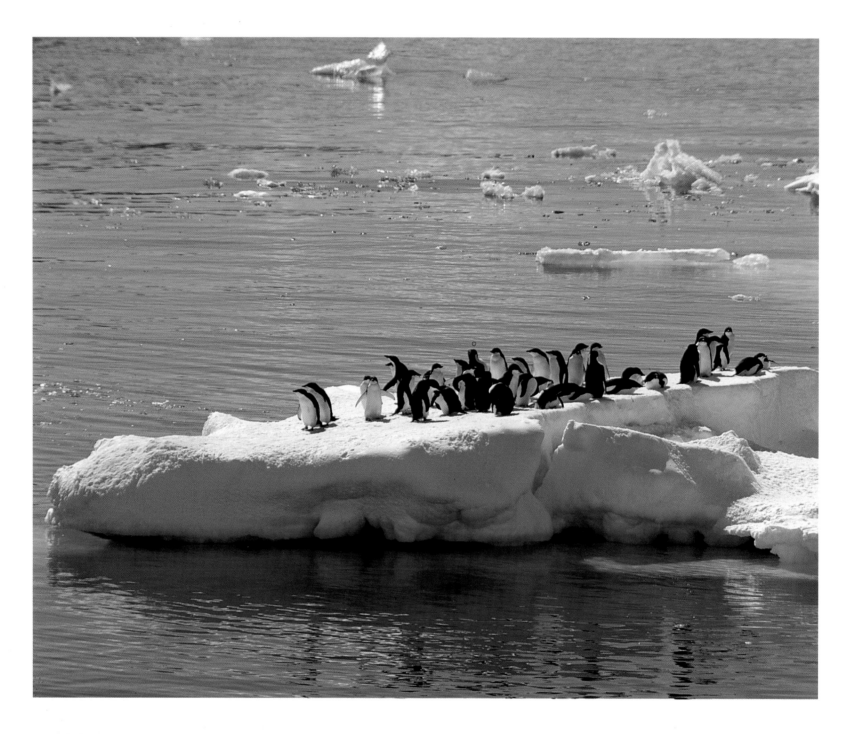

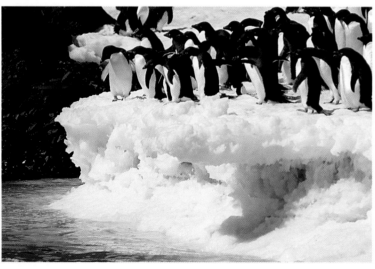

ABOVE *Adélie penguins crowd together on an ice floe. Such floating islands greatly increase the birds' foraging range and also provide a refuge from the unwanted predatory attentions of leopard seals and killer whales.*

LEFT *'Look before you leap' seems to be the motto for these Adélies; food and danger lurk in the icy waters but they must take the risk in order to survive.*

OPPOSITE BOTTOM, LEFT AND RIGHT *Looking at these Adélie penguins, it is easy to understand Apsley Cherry-Garrard's comment that: '[Adélie penguins] are extraordinarily like children, these little people of the Antarctic world, either like children, or like old men, full of their own importance and late for dinner, in their black tail-coats and white shirt-fronts... and rather portly withal.'*

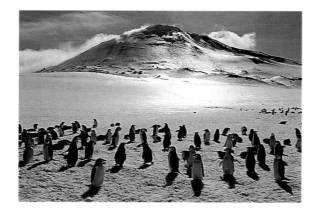

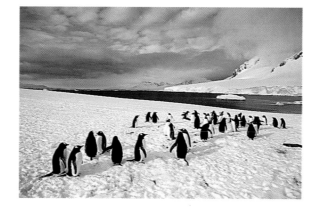

ABOVE *Chinstrap penguins congregate in breeding groups on the slopes of Mt. Curry on Zovodovsky Island in the South Sandwich Islands. Chinstraps are an exclusively southern species. These penguins derive their name from the narrow band of black-tipped feathers running under their chins.*

ABOVE *Southern gentoo penguins (*Pygoscelis papua ellsworthii*), seen here coming ashore in early November in order to breed on the Antarctic Peninsula, differ only slightly from their more northerly gentoo cousins (*Pygoscelis papua papua*), which breed on subantarctic islands.*

edge will have extended far out to sea. After nine weeks the chicks hatch, usually in July or August. In all of this period, the male has been fasting and living off his fat reserves. During the dark winter months, temperatures can plummet to −40°C (−40°F) or more with winds of over 200kph (125mph). To keep warm, the colony of penguins huddles together against the wind. Those on the outside and on the windy side of the colony continually shuffle downwind so that they get a turn to be in the warm centre. And so the process continues throughout the long winter, each penguin taking its turn to bear the brunt of the weather.

After the chick hatches, the male feeds it with a special secretion, but it is imperative that the female returns and finds her mate and chick. It is an epic journey, covering vast distances to return to exactly the same spot. No one is entirely sure how the female finds her way across the featureless wastes, but it seems more than likely that she navigates using the earth's geomagnetic field as do many species of migrant bird.

If, however, she fails to return within 10 days of the chick hatching, the male will abandon it, if it has not already died. He simply cannot wait any longer. His fat reserves have been used up and he must go to sea to feed and regain his strength. After a diet of mainly squid and fish obtained from depths of as much as 300m (1000ft), this is soon achieved.

The total breeding population of emperor penguins is about 195,000 pairs located in 42 colonies. However, a population census of emperor penguins is always a difficult task to undertake because of the logistics involved in reaching them in their virtually inaccessible colonies during winter. As a result, some colonies have not been re-counted in several decades, but it is believed that colonies in East Antarctica and on the Ross Ice Shelf are increasing in numbers and most others appear to be stable. Nevertheless, some are diminishing in size, which scientists attribute to the disturbance or longer-term retreat of some of the ice shelves on which the emperor penguins breed.

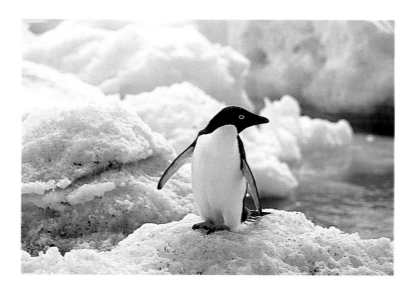

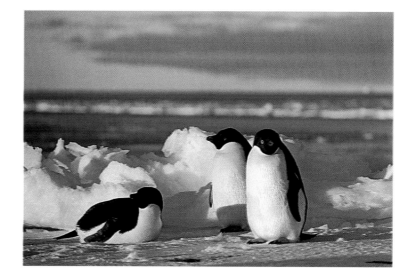

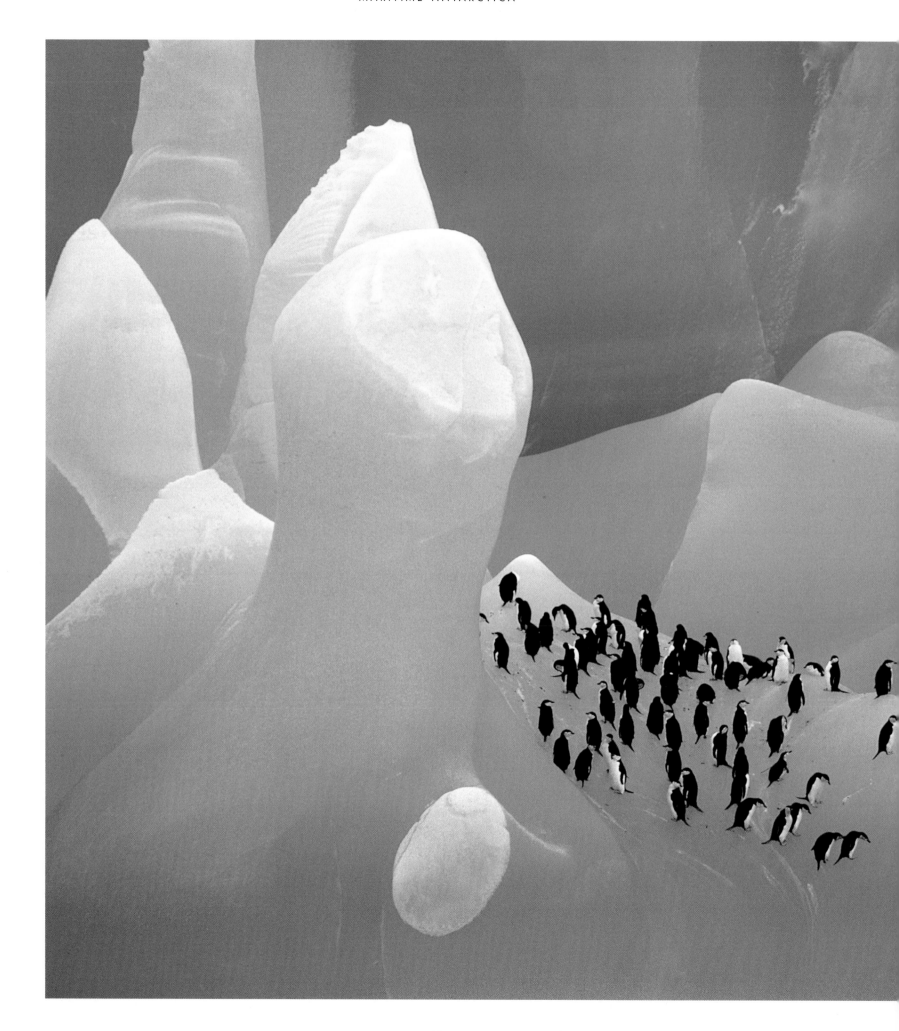

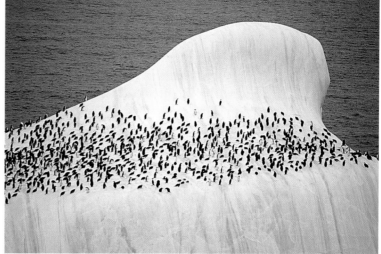

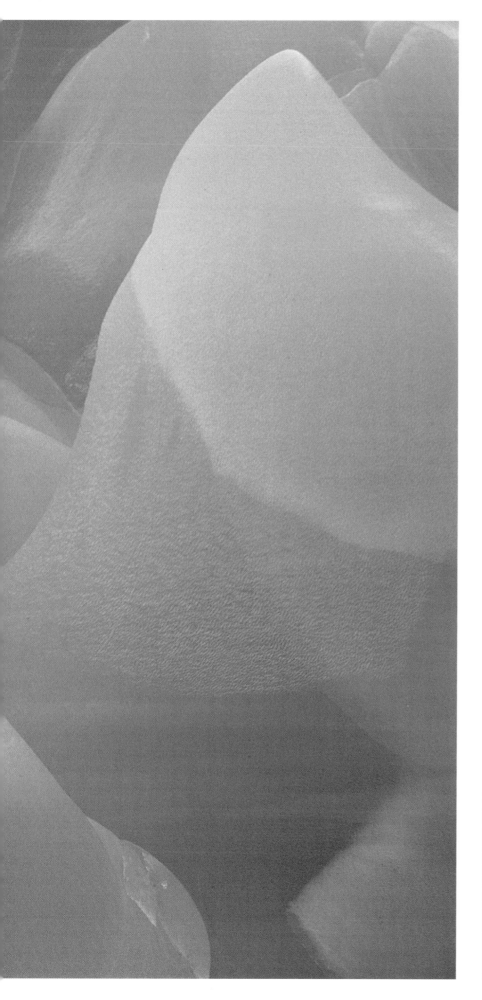

Another of the southern penguin species is the diminutive and comically inquisitive Adélie penguin which numbered about two million pairs in 1983 when the last major census was completed. Although the most widely distributed, it is not the most numerous of the Antarctic penguins; this distinction belongs to the extravagantly yellow-tufted macaroni penguin numbering about 11.8 million breeding pairs. The chinstrap penguin, numbering 7.5 million pairs, and the gentoo complete the list of penguins who choose maritime Antarctica as their breeding ground. Closely related to Adélie penguins, chinstraps are confined almost entirely to the Antarctic Peninsula and Scotia Sea region although vagrants can be found on some of the more southerly subantarctic islands.

ABOVE *Adélie penguins huddle together on an old iceberg that has gradually been worn smooth as a result of its constant exposure to the sea's waves.*
LEFT *Chinstrap penguins hitch a ride on a rare blue iceberg. It is only a matter of time, however, until they are forced to abandon their melting 'raft'.*
BELOW *Emperor penguins queue on the fast ice off Dronning Maud Land.*

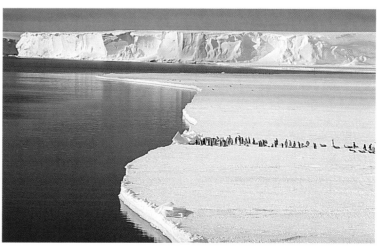

Of the oceanic birds to be found in the maritime Antarctic region, petrels are by far the most important. Perhaps the most beautiful and endearing of these is the snow petrel, a delicate and graceful bird with pure white feathers and a slender black bill. When the sunlight strikes these birds against a backdrop of dark grey storm clouds, black rocks and calm seas, they are reminiscent of butterflies dancing in sunbeams. Against the snow, however, they are almost impossible to see, especially if settled on a floe.

Weighing just under 300g (0.75 lb), snow petrels are usually found south of 63°S as they forage only where there is some ice cover. Endemic to Antarctica, they breed in the crevices of exposed nunataks throughout the maritime region. Their nests have been found further south than those of any other bird – sometimes as far as 300km (186 miles) inland. After the summer breeding season, snow petrels disperse across the ocean, but remain at the fringe of the advancing pack ice as winter returns.

Other important flying oceanic birds of this region are the Antarctic (or southern) fulmar, the Antarctic petrel, the southern giant petrel, Wilson's storm petrel and the south polar skua; the latter is not a member of the petrel family and is a voracious predator of eggs and chicks.

RIGHT *South polar skuas, seen bathing here in freshwater melt pools which collect on the sea ice in summer, are bold, aggressive predators and scavengers. Migratory birds, they fly from Antarctica in autumn to the North Pacific and North Atlantic oceans in the northern summer. The skua is the only bird ever to have been recorded at the South Pole's Amundsen-Scott Station.*

BELOW *One of only six petrel species to make its home on the Antarctic continent, this snow petrel is seen at its nest among the rocks of a remote nunatak. Guano and feathers enrich the meagre soils around the nests.*

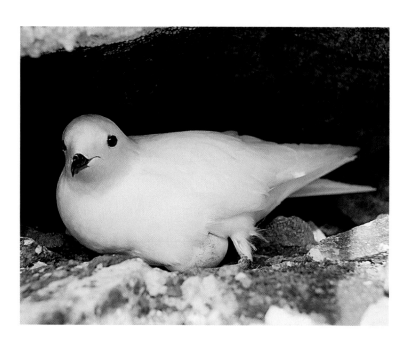

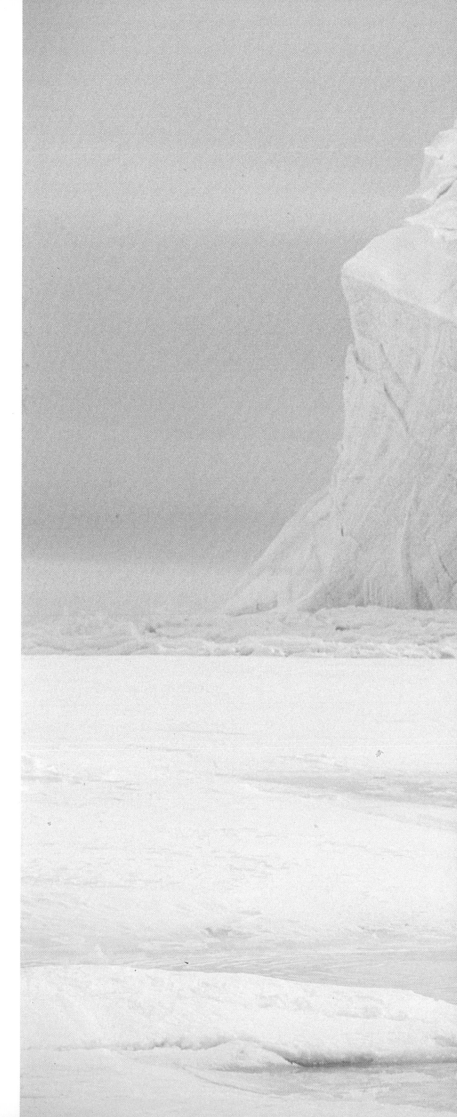

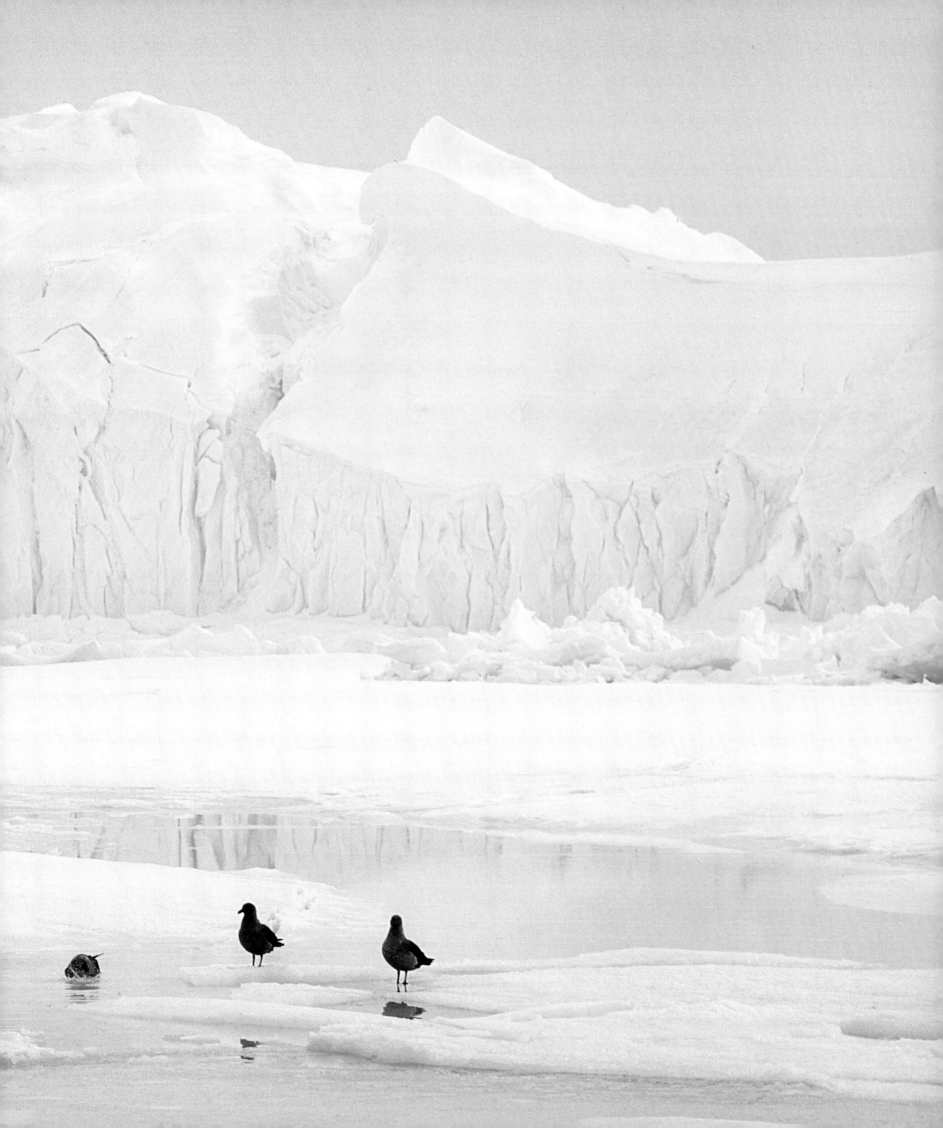

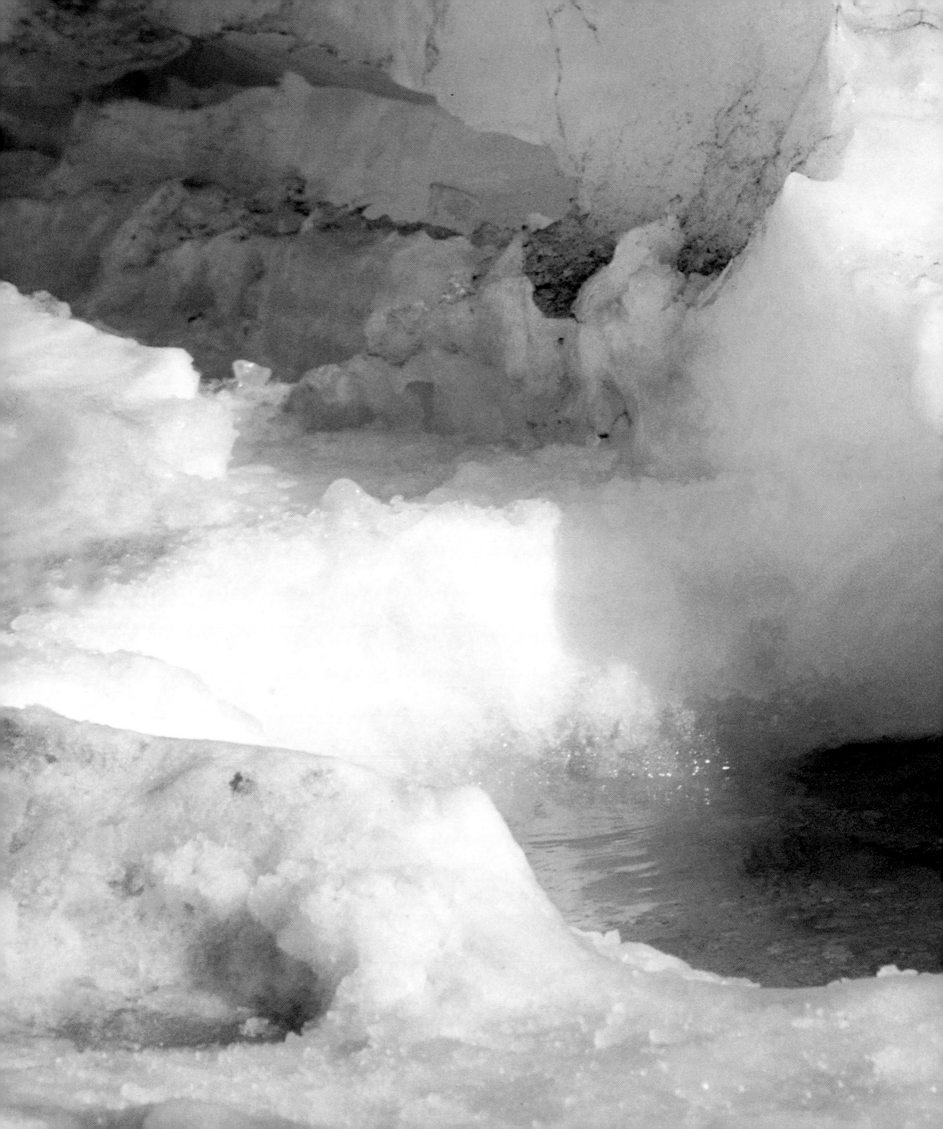

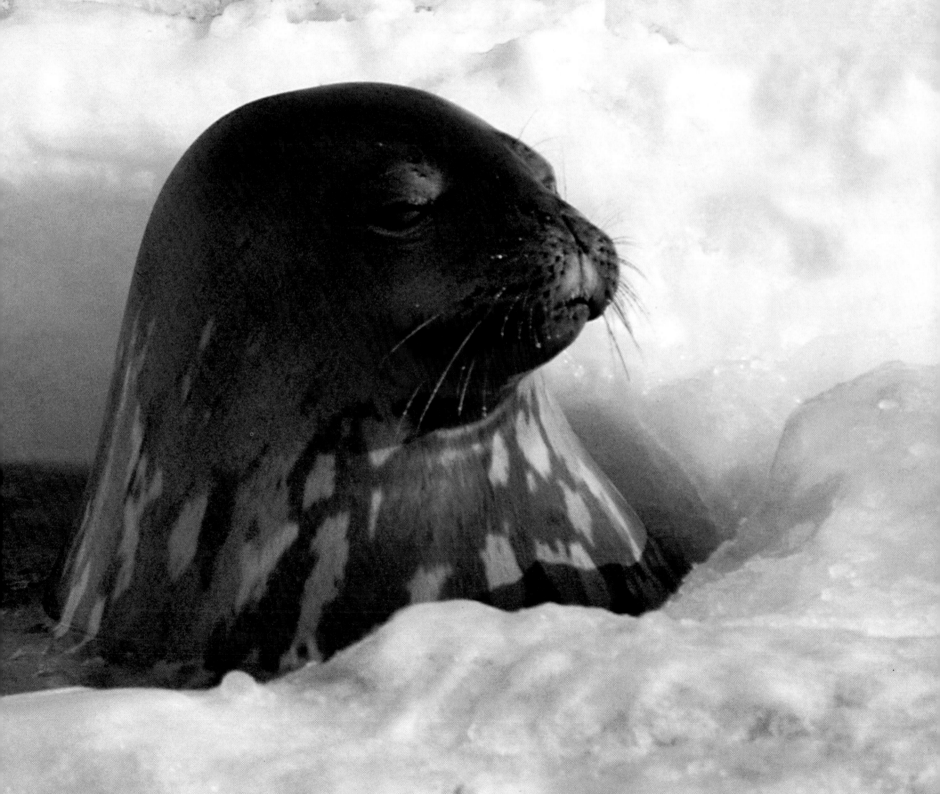

FOSTERING LIFE ON SEA ICE

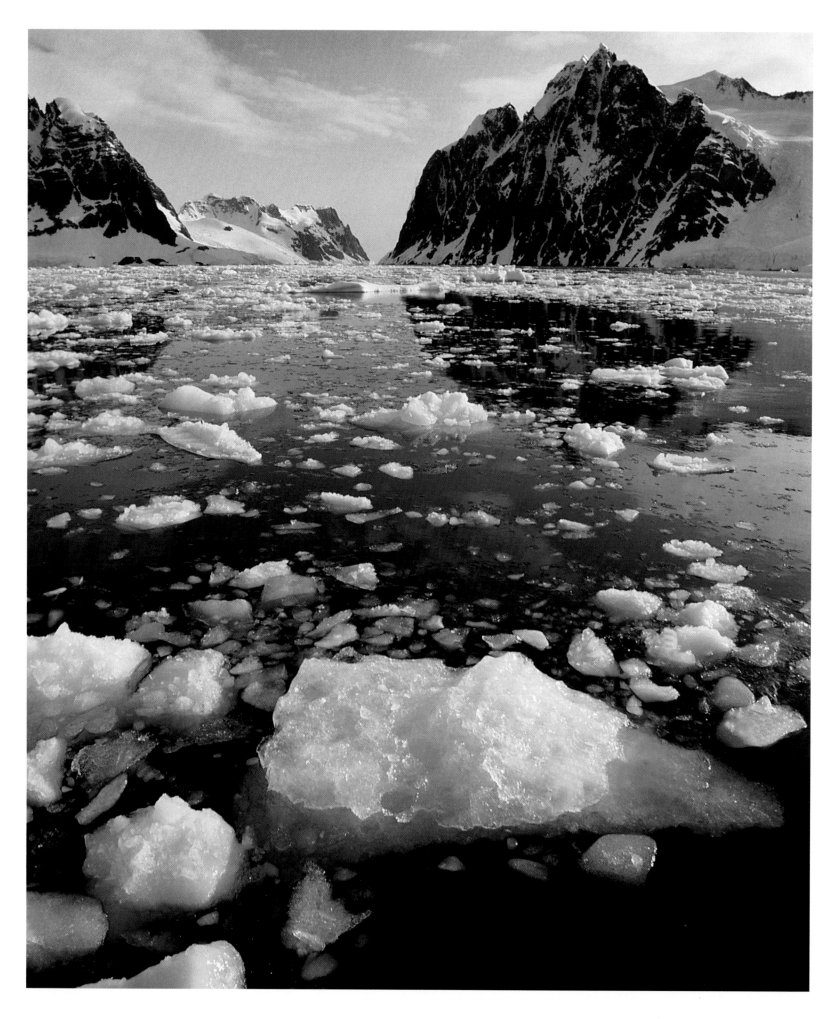

FOSTERING LIFE ON SEA ICE

A place to live, breed and seek refuge

When the sea is curiously calm (despite the cold wind that blows from the west) and clouds appear brilliantly white in the grey gloom: these are signs that sea ice is forming. As the short austral summer draws to a close over the Southern Ocean, the 24-hour sun sinks lower on the horizon and temperatures start to fall. May has come and the sea has started to cool progressively from the south. At −1.8°C (28.76°F) it freezes. Reflected light from the ice brightens the clouds and the ice-covered ocean deadens the sea's swell into an eerie tranquillity. Interspersed with small icebergs, or growlers, the wintry sea is now covered with 'pancakes' of ice, bumping and jostling each other as far as the eye can see (in fact, extending more than 1000km [600 miles] from the ice shelf). The weather worsens and more frequent snowstorms and gales sweep across the ice fields. Soon the plates of ice consolidate and buckle into tortured shapes covered by powdery dry snow which becomes fluted by the freezing polar winds.

The process of ice formation is a slow but fascinating one. Ice crystals forming at five to 10m (15 to 30ft) in depth float to the surface and coalesce into a thin layer of frazil (or 'splintered') ice before gentle wave action causes this to accumulate as pancake ice. Pancakes slide over each other and, inexorably, grow in size. In a matter of days, they freeze together and thicken into larger ice floes as more ice accumulates and snow covers their surface – this is the pack ice, home to thousands of seals and penguins.

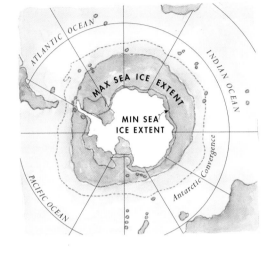

In cold, clear and absolutely windless conditions, however, sea ice forms in a different way. Ice crystals float to the surface and, in the absence of wind, form delicate sheets of smooth 'nilas' ice encrusted with salt crystals and ice 'flowers'. As the sheets grow, they slide over each other to create delicate 'fingering' patterns in the ice. Soon these fragile sheets grow in thickness and gather snow, just as pancake ice does. From now on, the process is the same: the ocean has frozen over and the ice edge advances northwards. The ice thickens and expands, causing unimaginable pressures to build up as the ice sheets force themselves against each other. Pressure ridges of buckling ice tumble into frozen blocks to be sculpted into tortuous shapes by driving winds, and travelling by foot or sledge across these chaotic ice fields becomes an exhausting and virtually impossible task.

This immense, and seemingly empty, expanse of pack ice is increased by the presence of 'shore-fast' ice, also known as 'fast ice'. Unlike pack ice, which occurs seasonally – 2.5 million km² in summer growing to 20 million km² in winter (1 million to 7.7 million square miles) – fast ice consists of frozen sea that is semi-permanently attached to the land or shelf ice. It is often found in the sheltered 'buktas' (bays) which indent the perimeter of the shelf-ice cliffs. When the pack ice retreats in summer, the fast ice remains, becoming a sought-after platform for Weddell seals to haul out onto. Emperor penguins also take advantage of this platform and congregate in dignified groups.

PREVIOUS PAGES *A Weddell seal peeps from its breathing hole, kept open throughout the winter by rasping away new-formed ice from the edges with its canine and incisor teeth. Tidal cracks in the fast ice also provide the seals with access to the underlying sea.*

LEFT *Dramatic Lemaire Channel is filled with melting 'brash ice', all that remains of the pack ice which completely closes the channel in winter. The French scientist, Jean-Baptiste Lemaire, overwintered on Booth Island in 1904 while charting the region. Named after its discoverer, the channel is becoming an increasingly popular route for the many tour operators sailing to the Antarctic Peninsula.*

While physical changes are occurring during ice formation, a remarkable biological process also takes place. As the first ice crystals float to the surface, they trap microscopic life and phytoplankton into the chaotic top layer of frazil ice. This becomes the characteristic brown brine channel layer below which clear ice forms. During freezing, salt in the sea water is ejected into the underlying ocean. Pack ice is therefore not as salty as sea water, containing only about five parts per thousand (ppt) of salt instead of the usual 35 ppt that sea water contains. However, the concentration of salt can reach as much as 100 ppt in the water-filled brine channels, preventing them from freezing. Within these channels a fascinating sea-ice microbial community lives. It is a complete and self-supporting miniature world of bacteria, phytoplankton and minute protozoans that feed on these algae. A larger community of zooplankton (small crustaceans) and Antarctic krill feeds on unprotected algal mats found on the underside of older floes and fast ice. While the rest of the water beneath the ice is barren of microscopic life, as is the open ocean just to the north, this oasis sustains many of the sea's creatures during the long dark winter months.

The question of where the swarms of krill disappeared to in winter remained unanswered until only a few years ago when remotely operated submersible vehicles carrying video equipment showed pictures of krill moving around on the underside of the ice. Some authorities also suspect that many krill overwinter at extreme depths in the ocean.

POLAR ICE SHEET AND SEASONAL SEA ICE

A U T U M N / W I N T E R   F R E E Z E

| OPEN OCEAN ZONE | SEASONAL ICE ZONE | COASTAL MARITIME ZONE | INTERIOR |

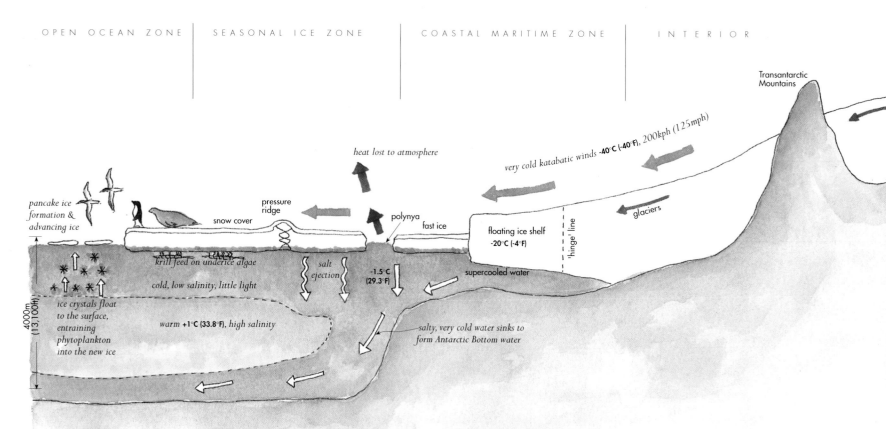

Transantarctic Mountains

heat lost to atmosphere

very cold katabatic winds -40°C (-40°F), 200kph (125mph)

pancake ice formation & advancing ice

snow cover

pressure ridge

polynya

fast ice

glaciers

floating ice shelf -20°C (-4°F)

'hinge' line

krill feed on under ice algae

salt ejection

-1.5°C (29.3°F)

supercooled water

cold, low salinity, little light

4000m (13,100ft)

ice crystals float to the surface, entraining phytoplankton into the new ice

warm +1°C (33.8°F), high salinity

salty, very cold water sinks to form Antarctic Bottom water

WINTER

Satellite imagery and ships' observations have revealed that the advancing pack ice, which averages between 1–2m (3–6.5ft) in thickness, extends to as much as 1000–1700km (600–1060 miles) offshore and reaches nearly as far north as 50°S. Most penguins, seals and birds follow the edge of the advancing ice, except the remarkable emperor penguin. Weddell seals also stay behind, relying on breathing holes in the ice to gain access to the water and food.

With little light, phytoplankton disappear from the water and krill no longer swarm in the open ocean. Baleen whales, fat after a summer diet of krill, migrate north to their spring breeding grounds in subtropical and equatorial waters. In the dark winter months the cyclonic Polar Vortex is at its strongest and bitingly cold katabatic winds blast across the pack ice. However, some areas of this otherwise frozen ocean – the 'polynyas' – remain free of ice due to the ocean's heat.

RIGHT *Seasonal sea-ice extent is shown, in shades of pink, by these false-colour satellite images. They are monthly averaged sea-ice concentrations for the minimum extent in February and the maximum extent in September. The images were taken by the USA's Defence Meteorological Satellite Programme Special Sensor Microwave Imager which is designed to 'see' through clouds. Images such as these are valuable for polar resupply vessels since they show areas of little ice cover, thereby making the ships' passage through the thick ice faster and safer.*

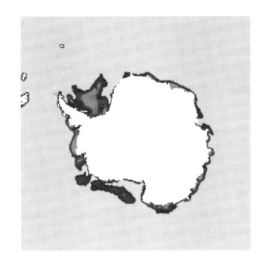
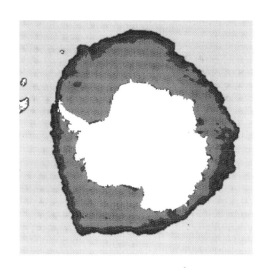

S P R I N G / S U M M E R   T H A W

INTERIOR | COASTAL MARITIME ZONE | SEASONAL ICE ZONE | OPEN OCEAN-ZONE

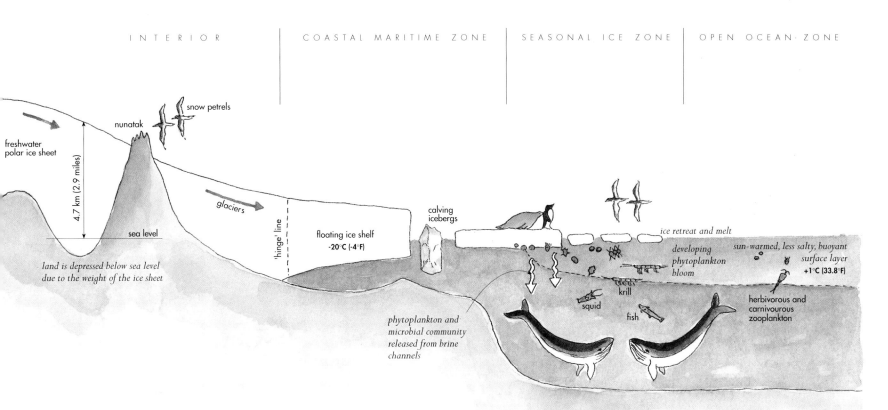

snow petrels

nunatak

freshwater polar ice sheet

4.7 km (2.9 miles)

sea level

glaciers

'hinge' line

floating ice shelf
-20°C (-4°F)

calving icebergs

ice retreat and melt

developing phytoplankton bloom

sun-warmed, less salty, buoyant surface layer
+1°C (33.8°F)

land is depressed below sea level due to the weight of the ice sheet

phytoplankton and microbial community released from brine channels

krill

squid

fish

herbivorous and carnivourous zooplankton

SUMMER

By late October, the pack ice slowly starts to retreat under the warming influence of the sun's rays which once more bring light to Antarctica. By December, the pack ice starts to break up and melt in earnest. The sea-ice microbial community and phytoplankton are released into the water initiating rich phytoplankton blooms which develop and follow the retreating ice edge. These single-celled plants initiate an explosion of life which ripples throughout the food chain.

Adult krill feast on the phytoplankton while juvenile krill, which hatched from eggs 1000m (3280ft) or more down, rise to the surface and join the adults in huge swarms. Baleen whales return to feed on the krill and in the short summer months, most of the birds, penguins and seals retreat with the pack ice. Where they can, many species move onto the now exposed rocky shores and neighbouring islands to breed and rear their young.

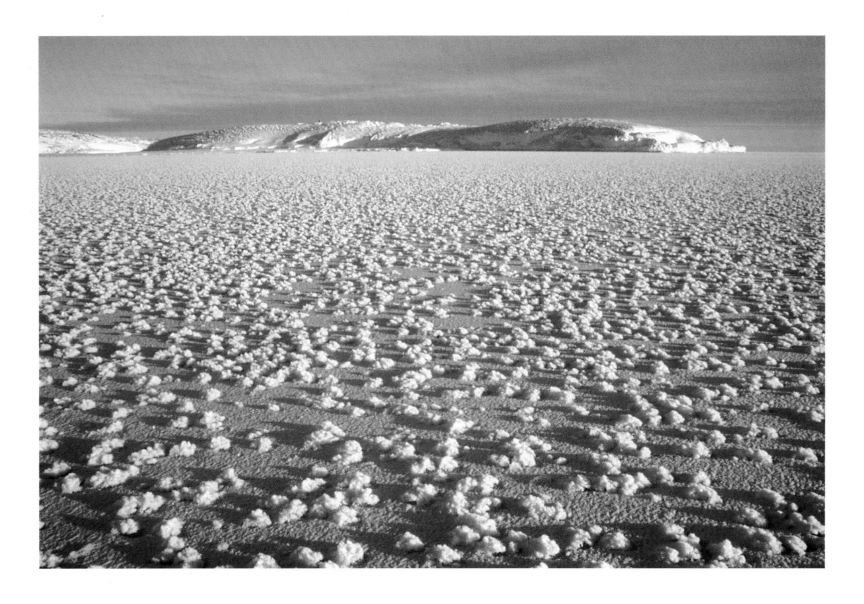

ABOVE AND BELOW *A field of rare 'ice flowers', or 'ice daisies', emerges only in winter's cold still air when an undisturbed ocean freezes over thinly. Over several weeks, the 'flowers' grow until they eventually reach up to 2cm (1in) in diameter.*

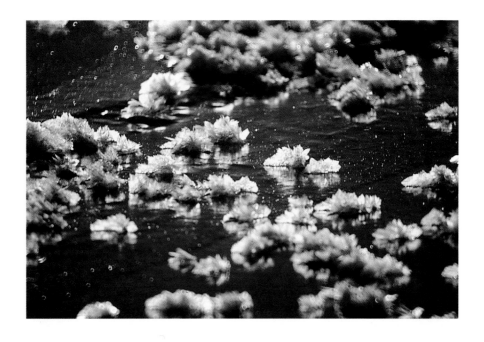

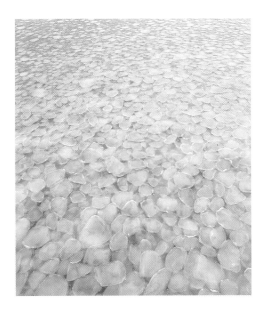

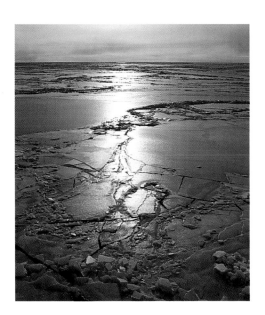

LEFT *Frazil ice forms in early winter when ice crystals float to the surface and coalesce into larger plates and spicules: this is the birth of 'pancake ice'.*
RIGHT *As nilas ice slowly consolidates and thickens, pressure ridges and cracks appear; these are often caused partly by currents and weak tidal forces.*
BOTTOM LEFT *Very new and thin pancake ice turns white as it gradually thickens and hardens.*
BOTTOM CENTRE *Nilas ice and slowly forming 'ice flowers' glow orange in weak early winter sun.*
BOTTOM RIGHT *A sea of pancake ice carpets the ocean. Jostling and bumping together, the pancakes will eventually freeze over to form solid pack ice.*

An explosion of life

By December, the thaw is well underway. With the returning sun, winter gives way to spring and the melting ice retreats southwards. Warmed from above and below, the pack ice breaks up into brilliant white ice floes which dot an azure and crystal-clear sea. Like rafts, they carry seals and Adélie penguins, but on a voyage to nowhere, for soon most of the floes will have melted completely. The nutrient-rich water beneath the ice becomes sunlit once more and the ocean's surface warms from −1.8°C to +0.5°C (28.76°F to 32.9°F), adding to the melting influence of the sun. As the pack ice breaks up, it becomes soft and honeycombed with melting cavities, releasing the microbial community which has been trapped in the narrow brine channels of the winter ice. An explosion of microscopic life follows as the oceans bloom with phytoplankton. This spring bloom frequently follows the retreating pack ice southwards signalling an awakening of all the animals of the Southern Ocean and Antarctica.

Indeed, the survival of many thousands of seals and penguins is largely dependent on the ever-changing pack ice and more permanent fast-ice habitats. Although the vast ocean provides living space for krill, fish and whales which do not depend on land for part of their life cycle, this is not so for birds and seals which cannot breed or give birth to their young in water. Penguins need to moult and replace their water-repellent feathers regularly if they are to survive constant immersion in the icy waters. This can only be done on land. Subantarctic bird and seal species solve the problem of where to live by using the subantarctic islands, while some of the truly southern Antarctic seals and penguins make use of the exposed land on the Antarctic Peninsula and other ice-free coastal areas in summer.

Access to the ice dome is available only to flying birds; for flightless penguins, the high cliffs of the shelf edge bar the way into the interior in most places. Sea ice is the only alternative for these creatures, and both pack ice and more stable fast ice are exploited to the full.

Even those creatures who choose to breed in maritime Antarctica make use of these sea-ice habitats. Although Adélie and chinstrap penguins breed on the beaches of the Antarctic Peninsula, they make extensive use of the ice cover and spend the winter out on the edge of the pack ice where they can forage amongst the open leads ('inlets') or ice-free polynyas ('lakes'). Emperors, unable to reach some of the ice shelves, make use of the newly formed ice in sheltered buktas to begin their breeding cycle in May and early June when eggs are laid, while snow and Antarctic petrels also use the sea ice as a platform from which to forage.

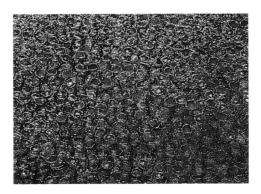

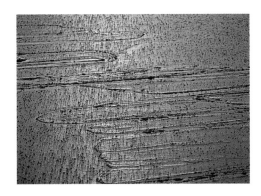

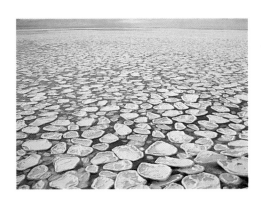

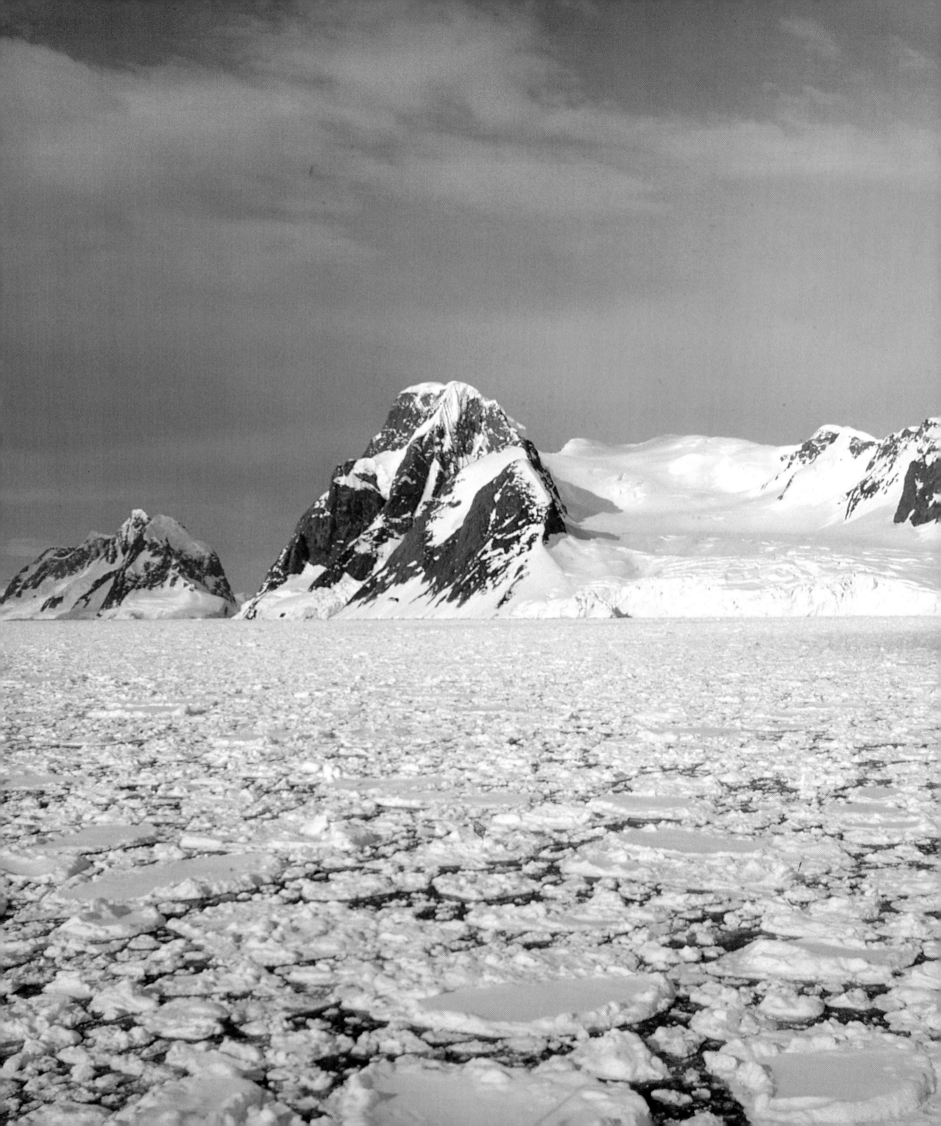

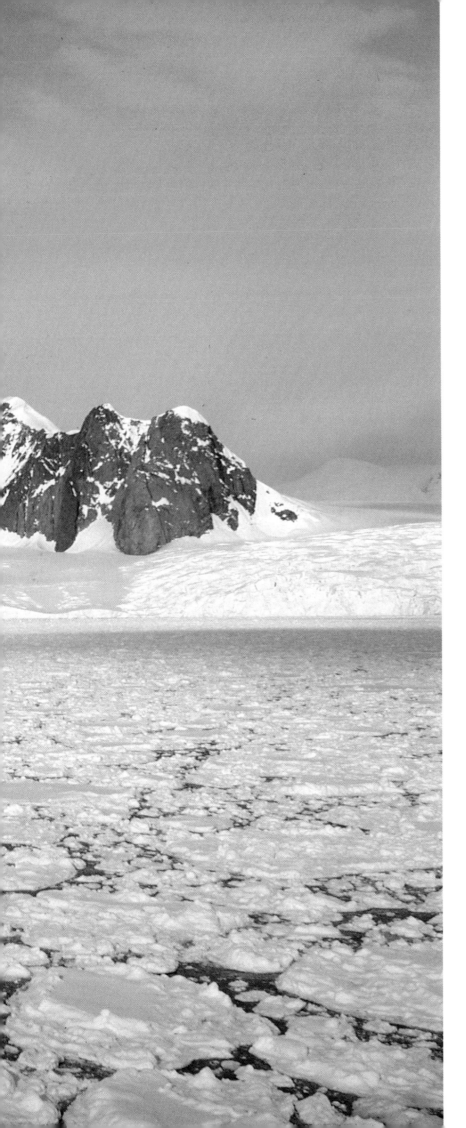

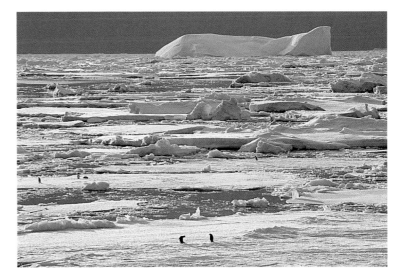

ABOVE *Adélie penguins often tend to disperse far and wide across the pack ice in winter but, as the summer thaw sets in, they will follow the retreating ice.*

LEFT *Floes of pack ice crowd the sea in summer, close to the Antarctic Peninsula. Seen like this, it is easy to understand how pack-ice cover can profoundly affect the earth's climate by reflecting heat, in the form of sunlight, back into space and also by controlling the exchange of gases between the ocean and atmosphere.*

BELOW *Some of the larger ice floes of the pack ice provide a haven for many of Antarctica's seals, particularly the elusive Ross, crabeater and leopard species.*

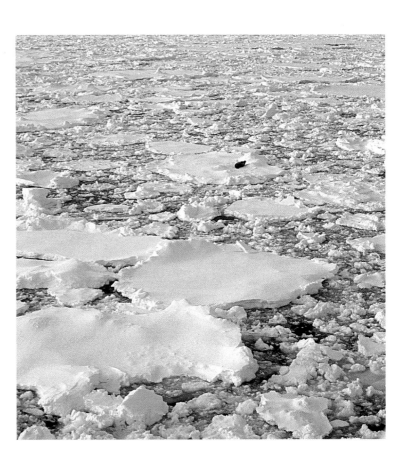

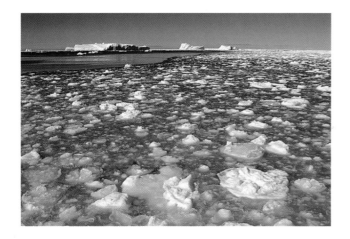

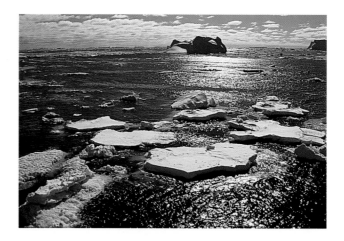

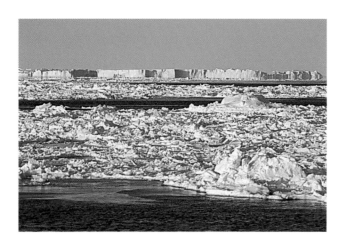

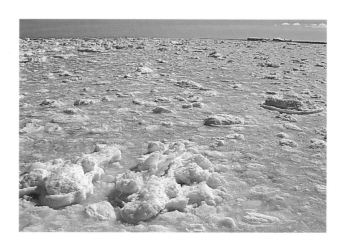

ABOVE *In summer, as the ice starts to retreat, solid pack ice slowly gives way to melting brash ice, open water leads and ice floes. In its wake, an explosion of microscopic plant life develops.*

BELOW LEFT *A glassy sculpture is all that remains of a growler.*
BELOW CENTRE *When tipped over onto its side, broken sea ice reveals brown layers of ice algae trapped in the brine channels.*
BELOW RIGHT *Worn into smooth, fluted shapes by the sea, these melting ice floes drift placidly on a quiet ocean.*

OPPOSITE TOP *An ice-breaker forges its way through broken pack ice. The ice will soon close in behind again, obliterating the trail.*
OPPOSITE CENTRE *Robert Swan's ship, the Southern Quest, follows an opening lead in the ice through McMurdo Sound. The vessel eventually became trapped in the ice, however, and foundered.*
OPPOSITE BOTTOM *Large table-topped icebergs make a good floating quayside. Here, a Russian ship unloads its cargo 150km (90 miles) from Australia's Davis Base. Helicopters will fly the cargo the rest of the way in nets slung beneath the aircraft.*

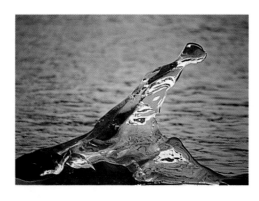

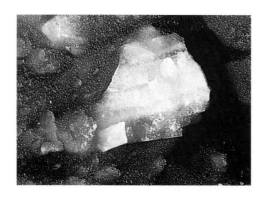

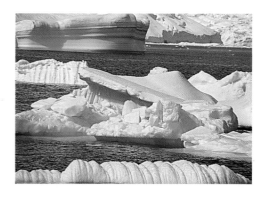

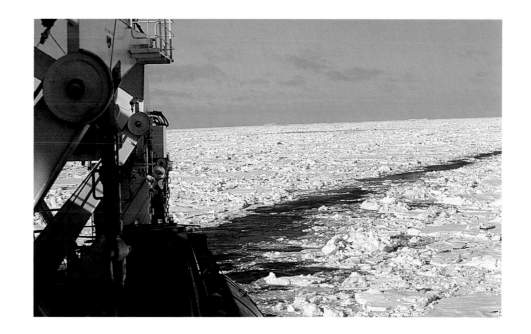

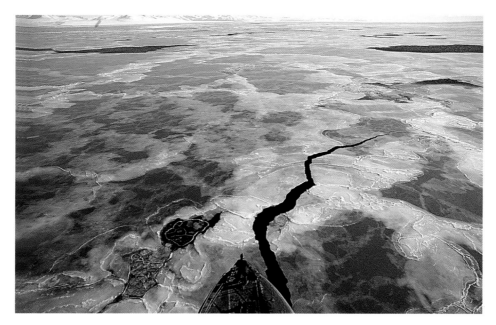

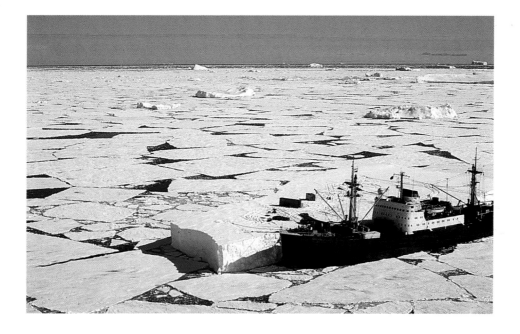

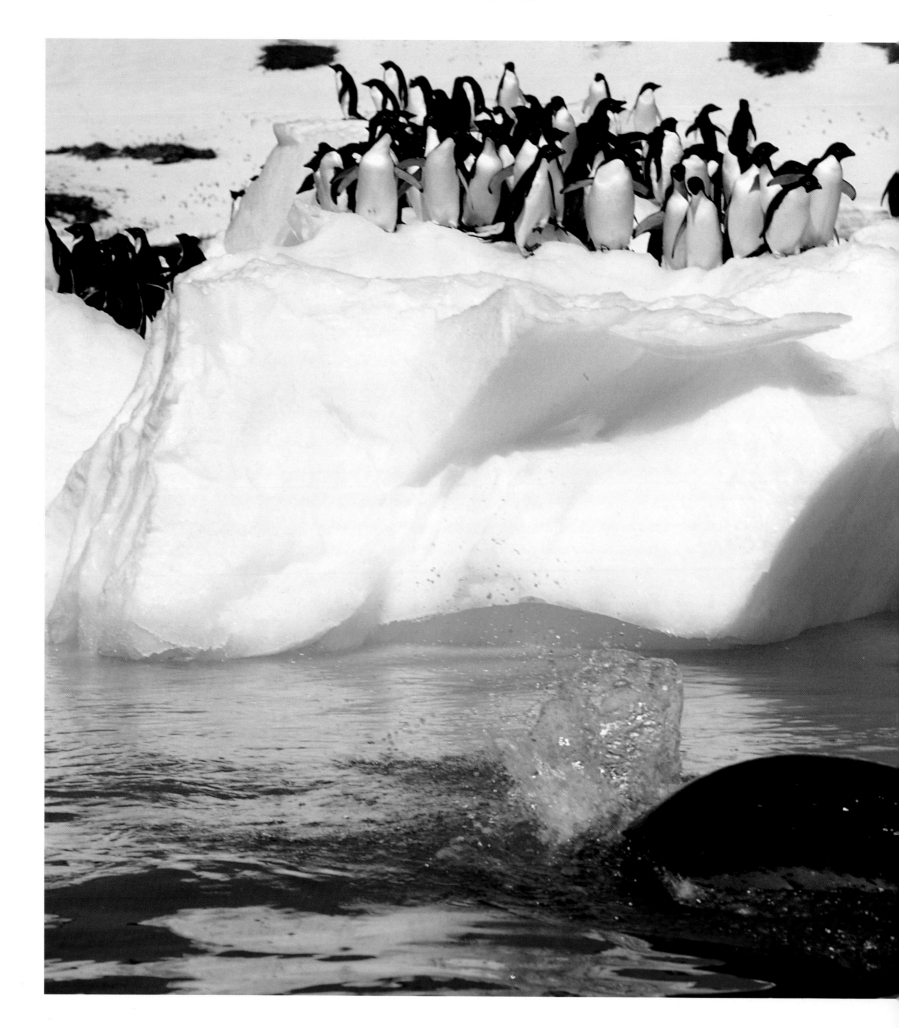

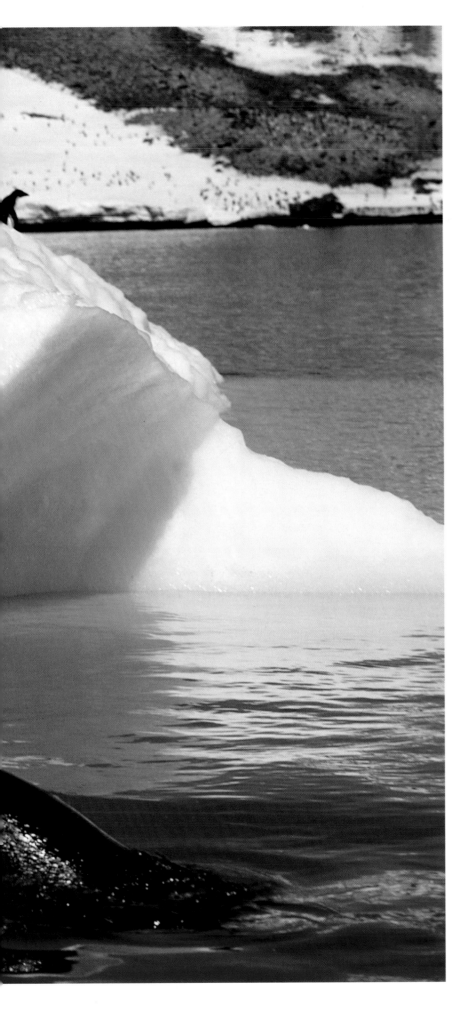

An icy refuge

The pack ice surrounding Antarctica contains at least 50 per cent of the world's population of seals. Of the six Antarctic seal species, four inhabit the Antarctic pack ice all year round, following the seasonal advance and retreat of the ice edge. These are the crabeater, leopard, Ross and Weddell seals. These so-called true seals are characterized by having no external 'pinna', or 'flap', to their ears (unlike fur seals). Instead of fur, they depend on a thick layer of blubber to provide insulation against the cold. However, it is worth remembering that it is usually much warmer in the water than out of it where temperatures can often be less than −40°C (−40°F), or even colder, when wind chill is taken into account.

Crabeater seals are large (± 220kg; 485lb) specialist feeders on krill and the most numerous of all the seal species, numbering about 35 million according to 1989 figures. However, the latest estimates (1993) have revised this figure downwards to about 15 million. Females are slightly larger than males and give birth to a single pup on ice floes in September to October. At this time they are joined by a male to typically make a party of three. Because crabeaters inhabit the pack ice, they are difficult to study and, consequently, relatively little is known about them.

Leopard seals are unmistakable, large (± 500kg; 1100lb), slender seals which include krill, young crabeater seals, penguins and fish in a cosmopolitan and often opportunistic diet. Adélie penguins seem to be a particular favourite. Lurking beneath the water in ambush at the edge of

LEFT *Adélie penguins cluster anxiously together on an old ice floe, all too aware of the fact that a hunting leopard seal has gastronomic designs on them!*

BELOW *Three-metre (10ft) leopard seals are sleak and fast in the water. The hindflippers provide propulsion, while the foreflippers help to manoeuvre at speed.*

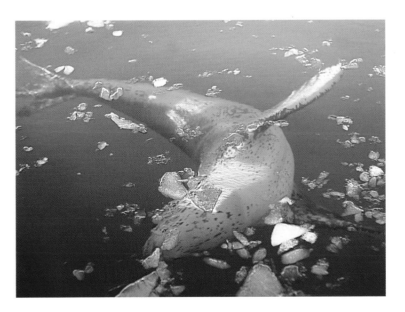

the ice floes, leopard seals wait until the Adélies dive into the water before pouncing on an unsuspecting victim. Typically, the penguins are then caught and tossed around on the surface until the skin and feathers come off, before being devoured. Leopard seals occupy the same habitat as crabeaters. However, they can be found much further to the north and are frequent visitors to subantarctic islands such as South Georgia and Macquarie. Vagrants are even occasionally found as far astray as South Africa. The world population is estimated to be 220,000.

Ross seals are the rarest of the Antarctic seals, numbering fewer than 200,000. They are medium-sized ($\pm$ 200kg; 440 lb) and are confined to the heaviest pack ice close to the continent. Here they dive down some 300 to 500m (980 to 1640ft) in search of invertebrates, squid and fish. They are dark grey in colour and have prominent large eyes for seeing prey in the dimly lit depths where they hunt.

Weddell seals normally pup on fast-ice from September to November. However, they can be found throughout the pack-ice region. These large fat seals, weighing in at 400 to 500kg (880 to 1100 lb), feed primarily on fish of all sizes and have a total population of about 730,000 individuals. In the relative warmth of the ocean beneath the pack ice, Weddell seals seek temporary refuge from savage winter gales. Here, in a twilight, blue-tinged world that is silent save for their eerie whistles, these masters of the underwater environment glide effortlessly among the submerged blocks of ice seeking their prey of fish and Antarctic krill.

As Weddell seals live on the permanent pack ice, they must maintain breathing holes in the ice. These are kept open by the adults, who use their teeth to file away at the edges of the holes to prevent them from freezing over. But there is a price to pay. By using their teeth in this way, they cause them to erode faster than normal. Once they lose their teeth, Weddell seals are unable to catch their prey and die of starvation. As a result, they have one of the shortest life spans of all the seal species.

The largest of all the seals, the southern elephant seal, does not make use of the sea-ice environment. It, like the fur seals, normally occupies the ice-free oceanic region to the south of the subantarctic islands on which it generally breeds.

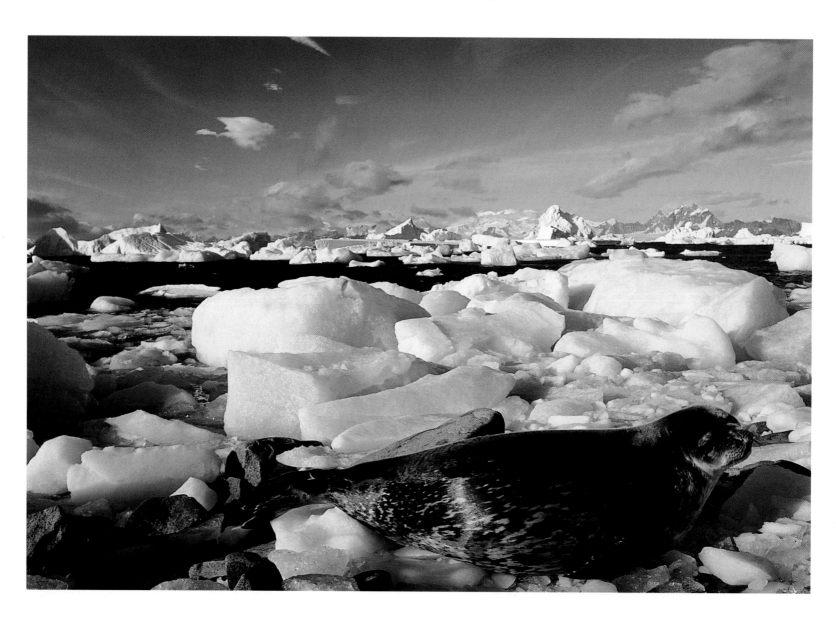

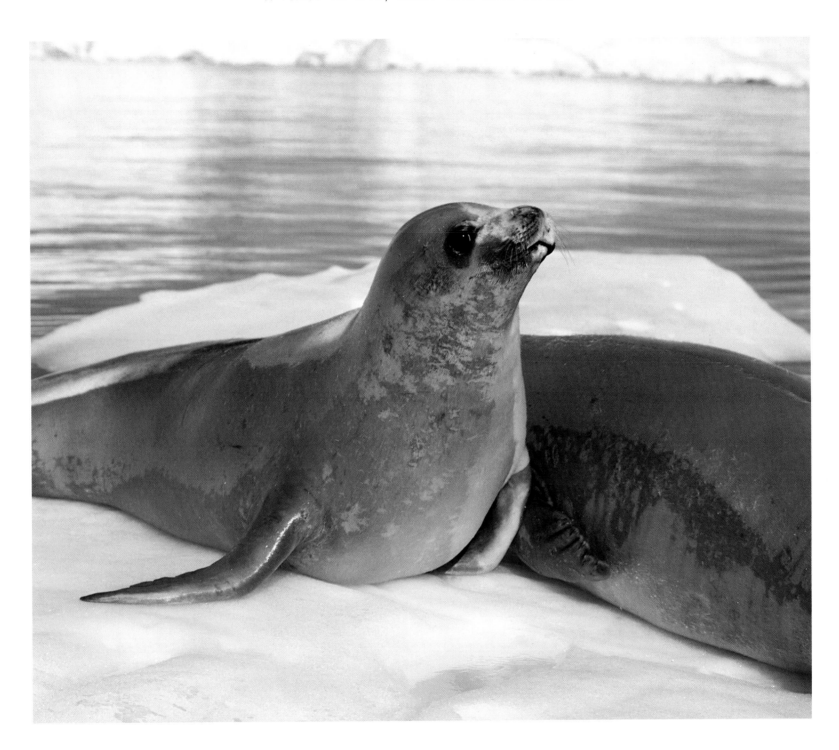

ABOVE *Ancestrally related to otters and bears, seals, like whales, are marine mammals superbly adapted to an aquatic life with their thick blubber providing insulation. Unlike whales, however, all seals are carnivores.*

RIGHT *Like all seal species, crabeater seals must haul out onto the ice, or land, to mate and pup. Crabeaters have very unusually cusped teeth which are used to strain Antarctic krill, their sole source of food, from the water.*

OPPOSITE *Crabeater seals were once thought to be rare because they can easily 'lose' themselves in their habitat of pack ice, making their numbers difficult to estimate. In fact, these seals are the most numerous of the pack-ice species.*

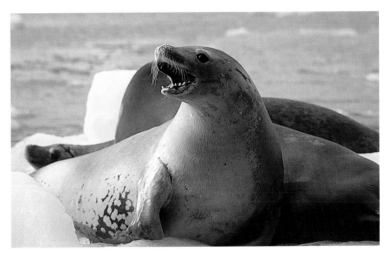

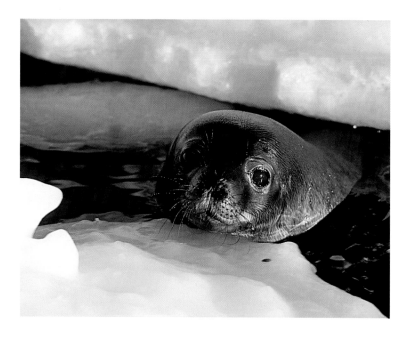

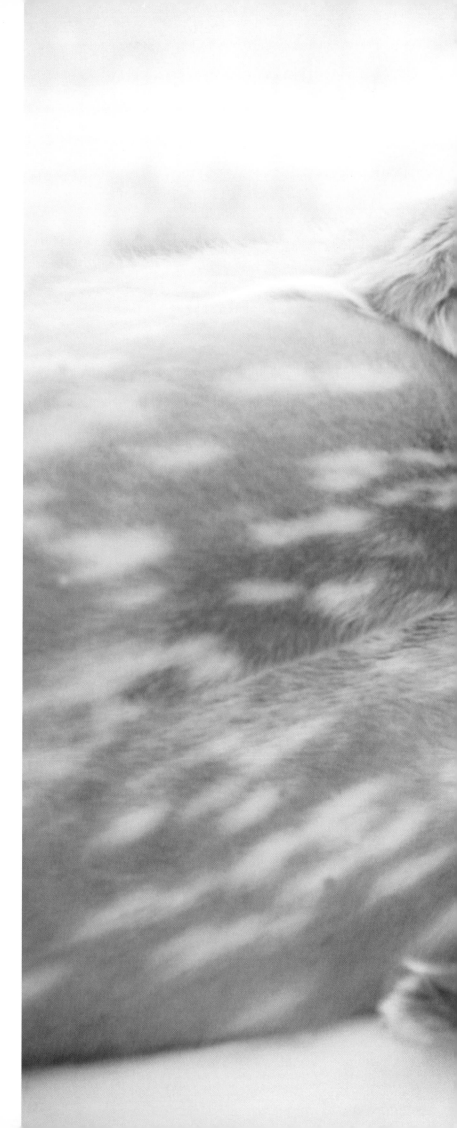

ABOVE *A Weddell seal gazes balefully from its watery world at McMurdo Sound.*

RIGHT *A juvenile Weddell basks on the ice at Signy Island. Seals belong to the taxonomic order Pinnipedia, derived from the Latin for 'wing-footed', a term which aptly describes the webbed feet of the seals. Pinnipeds are split into two main groups: the 'true' seals, like the Weddell seal, which have no external ear flap; and the 'eared' seals which include walruses, fur seals and sea lions.*

BELOW *Weddell seals doze peacefully around a breathing and access hole in the fast ice. These seals can dive to 700m (2300ft) and feed mainly on fish. Diving patterns and feeding frequency are measured with ingenious electronic sensors carried by the seals. 'Data loggers', given in the form of oral capsules which land up in the seal's stomach, record dive times, depth and direction. Any sudden drops in recorded temperature mark the capture of icy cold fish.*

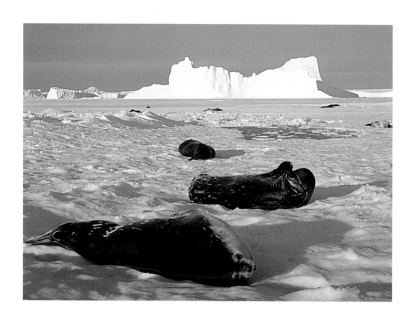

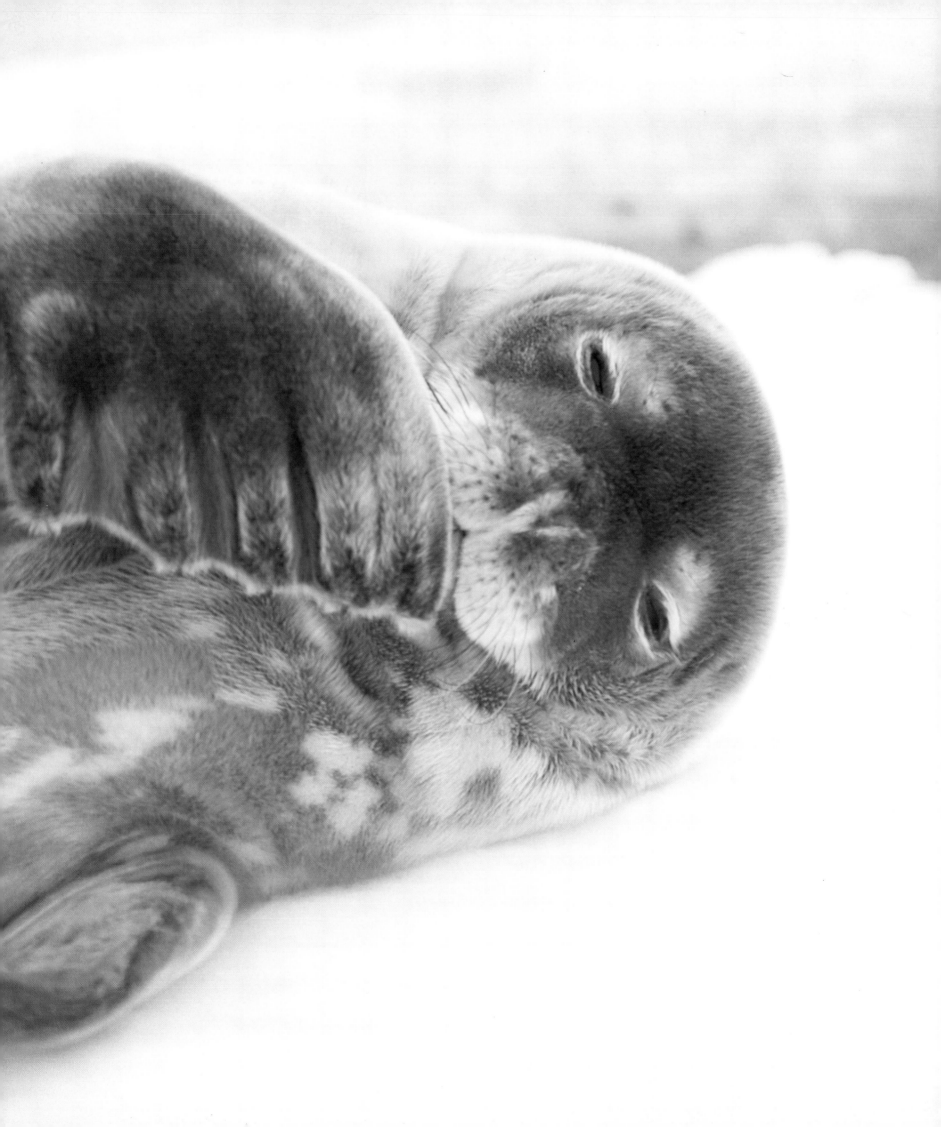

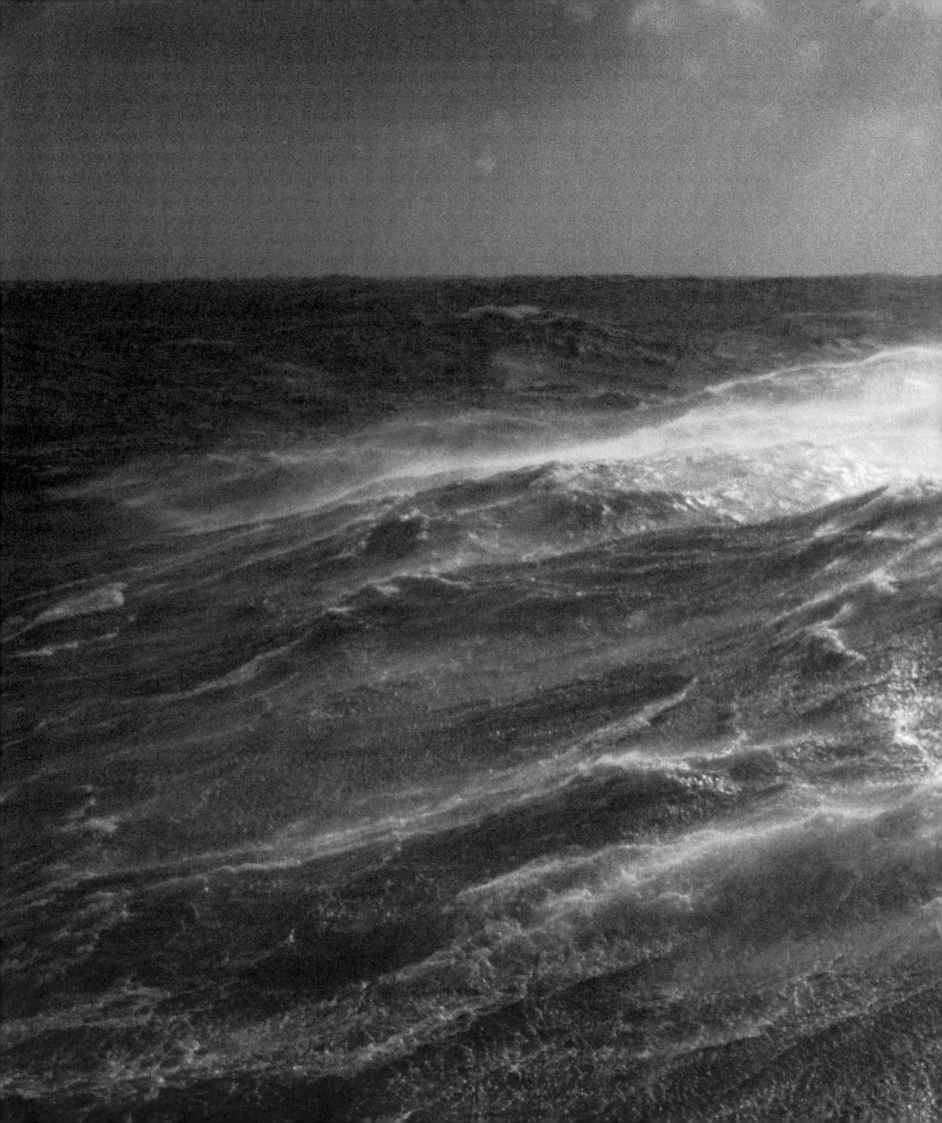

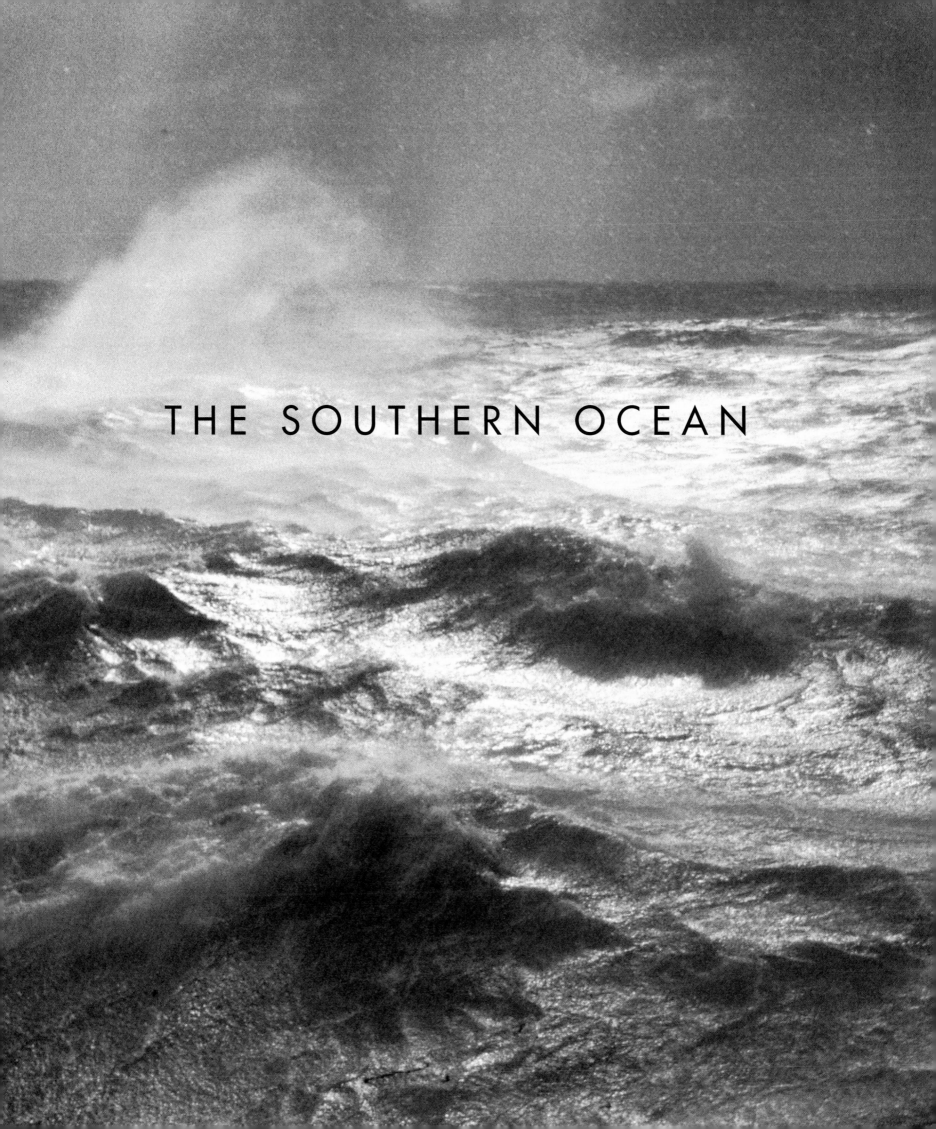

THE SOUTHERN OCEAN

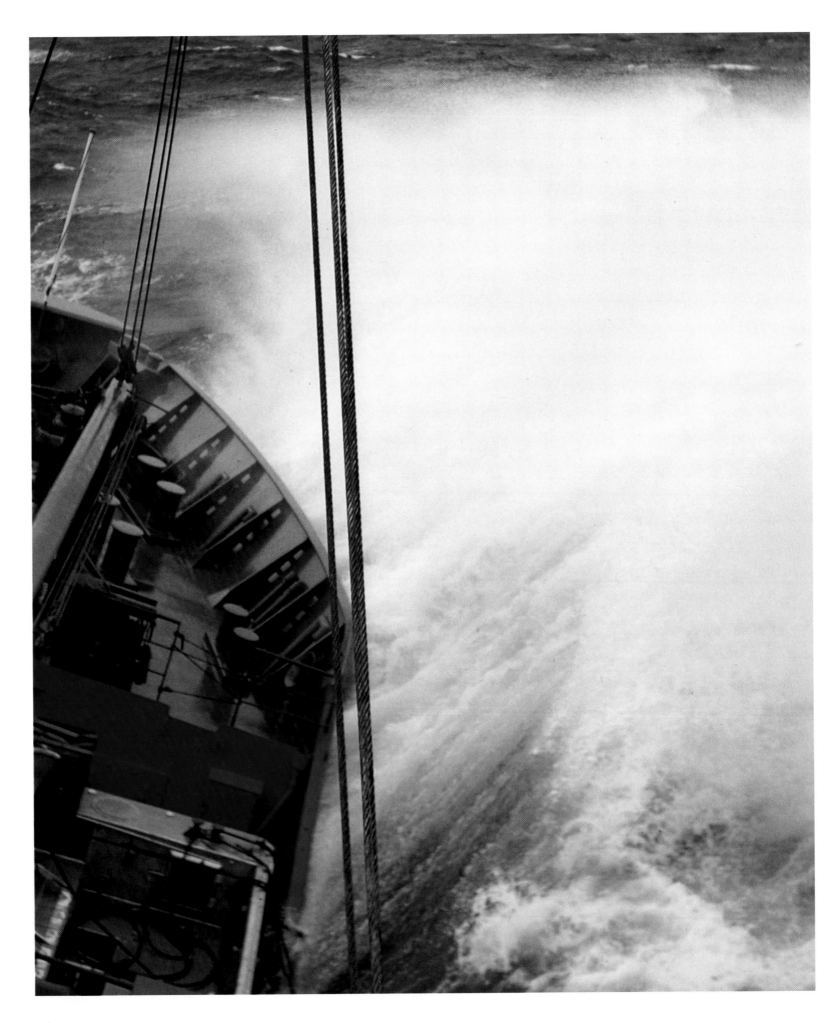

THE SOUTHERN OCEAN

Wild and restless seas

Vast and immensely powerful, the Southern Ocean is not to be trifled with. Yet, it can take on a beguiling, docile mood when gentle zephyrs blow and blue waves dance in the sun. Albatrosses and petrels soar on the breeze in effortless grace, while prions and storm petrels flit, bat-like, across the ocean crests. In the soft evening light, as the unhurried clouds take on an orange hue, bright Venus appears on the horizon and as the red sun sinks into the sea, reflecting silver and gold in the evening light, the Southern Cross emerges to point the way further south to where the pack ice reaches out across the ocean.

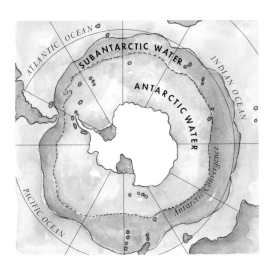

Defining the Southern Ocean's outer limits is a series of oceanic boundaries. Marking the ocean's northern limit is what is known as the Subtropical Convergence while the Antarctic Divergence, or Antarctic Slope Front, demarcates its southern extremity. Between these two boundaries, one of the world's major currents, the Antarctic Circumpolar Current, is driven ever eastwards by prevailing westerly winds. A slow, deep current, reaching almost to the bottom of the ocean, it is also called the West Wind Drift.

The Subtropical Convergence is clearly defined by sharp differences in temperature, salinity, chemistry and species of organism inhabiting the oceans on either side. The confluence of different water types at the Subtropical Convergence (and other similar boundaries) creates unusually productive regions rich in phytoplankton, microscopic single-celled plants which attract large concentrations of small herbivorous crustaceans (zooplankton), squid, fish, birds and various marine mammals. All to some extent depend upon each other and phytoplankton for food. As this oceanic boundary is crossed, a distance of 100 to 150km (60 to 100 miles), the sea temperature typically drops from about 15°C to 10°C (59°F to 50°F) and a noticeable chill appears in the air.

The presence of large numbers of albatrosses and other oceanic birds such as petrels, skuas and shearwaters provides the most visible sign of this boundary. All are attracted by the concentration of food which they know can be found here, mostly zooplankton, squid and fish which migrate up from the depths to the surface of the ocean to feed at night on phytoplankton. At dawn, they descend into the depths once more, hoping to minimize predation by concealing themselves in the inky blackness that envelops them below 200 to 300m (650 to 1000ft).

Although sunlight penetrates dimly to about 100m (330ft), the open ocean is 3000 to 4000m (9800 to 13,000ft), and sometimes as much as 5000m (16,400ft) deep, making much of the ocean interior dark and cold. Most life is, therefore, found on or near the surface of the ocean where phytoplankton can trap the sun's energy and convert it into plant material.

Since much of the Southern Ocean lies in the Roaring Forties and Furious Fifties, where winds are nearly always strong, some of the biggest waves in the world can be found here. At times they reach as high as 30m (100ft), topped by foaming crests and mixing the surface of the ocean down to a depth of about 100m (330ft).

PREVIOUS PAGES *In the empty Southern Ocean, the winds of the world assemble their might in a mad and frenzied dance. Shafts of light pierce cloud-laden skies to capture the turmoil of wild mountainous seas, wind-blown spume and furious raw power.*

LEFT *Pitted against the elemental power of the turbulent sea, a research and logistical resupply vessel crashes its way southwards towards a remote Antarctic base. The scientific stations eagerly await the arrival of these vessels as, to scientists who may have been away for a year or more, they can often signal the promise of a long-awaited return journey home.*

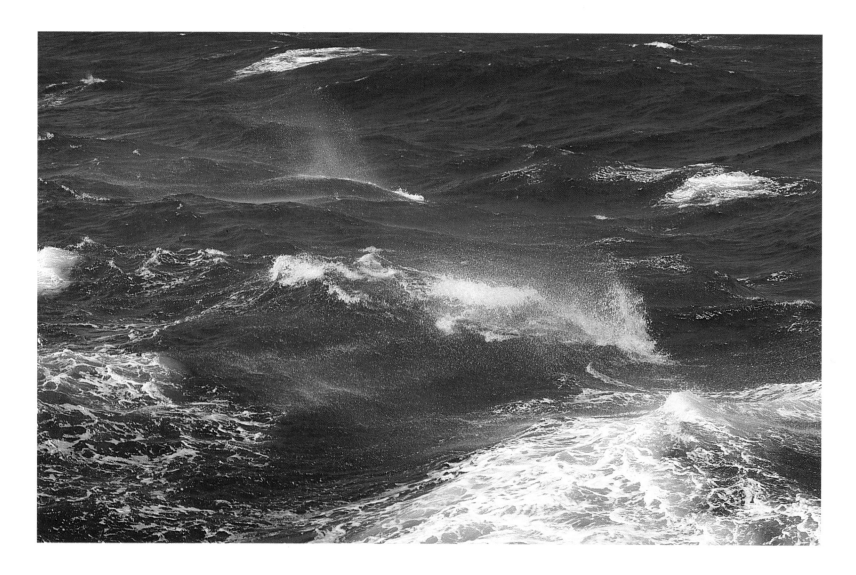

OCEANIC BOUNDARIES OF THE SOUTHERN OCEAN

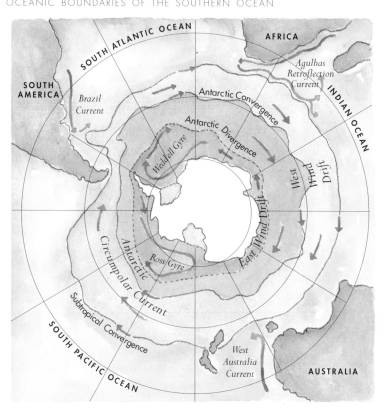

ABOVE *The foaming, turbulent surface of the ocean is one of the earth's 'lungs', where gases such as oxygen and carbon dioxide exchange with the atmosphere.*

OPPOSITE TOP, LEFT TO RIGHT *Beneath the leaden skies and racing clouds of the turbulent Southern Ocean, restless white horses run before the wind, racing past the scattered island outposts. In these stormy conditions the only calm is often to be found in the lee of towering bastions of ice — the giant icebergs.*
OPPOSITE BOTTOM, LEFT AND RIGHT *Wind-whipped spindrift fills the air while, in the eerie brooding light, seas rage against an iceberg.*

LEFT *The Southern Ocean completely encircles Antarctica and is marked by definite boundaries — referred to as 'fronts', 'convergences' or 'divergences' — which separate the different water masses. Driven by prevailing winds, two currents flood around Antarctica — the West Wind Drift and, closer to the continent, the East Wind Drift. The West Wind Drift, or Antarctic Circumpolar Current, is over 2000km (1240 miles) wide, moving at about 20km (12.5 miles) per day and carrying 165 million tonnes (162 million tons) of water a second. It is the greatest current on earth.*

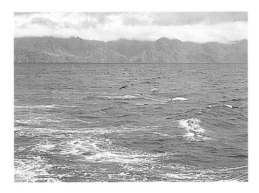

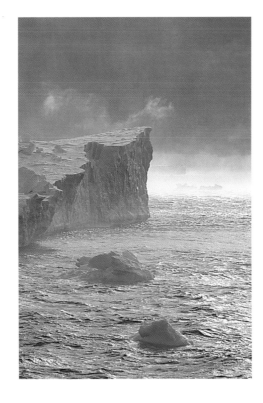

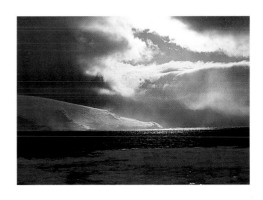

Six hundred nautical miles to the south of the Subtropical Convergence, at about 50°S, there is a second circumpolar oceanic boundary – the Antarctic Polar Front, or Antarctic Convergence, as it is otherwise called. The temperature drops here from about 4°C (39.2°F) to less than 2°C (35.6°F). To the south extends the huge expanse of the true Southern Ocean, 'Neptune's Kingdom', where majestic, sculpted icebergs are first sighted. Only rarely do they cross north of the Antarctic Polar Front and, when they do, they rapidly melt in the warmer waters. It is only in this region, south of about 58°S, that the seas freeze in winter to form the almost impenetrable pack ice that thwarted many of the early explorers. It is also in winter that storms born close to the Antarctic continent track northwards and eastwards across the ocean to reach the southern tips of South America, Africa, Australia and New Zealand. With them, they bring low, scudding grey clouds, rain and snow squalls as seas and sky merge into one amidst the flight of wind-whipped spray across the ocean surface. Days are short and bitingly cold, with only a few hours of sunlight, often marked by spectacular sunrises and sunsets. It is a wild, tumultuous sight. Huge, foaming rollers march relentlessly east before the wind, unimpeded by landmasses, until they eventually crash on

far-distant shores. Round-the-world racing yachtsmen sail south from Cape Town to harness the power of these winds, surfing on huge roller-coaster swells as they surge across the Southern Ocean to their next port of call in Sydney or Auckland. Further south, the ocean is trapped in the icy grip of the pack ice which will only be unlocked in the spring when the sun's warming rays return to this region once again.

With the heralding of spring and the prospect of long summer days, the pack ice melts, retreating southwards and allowing light to enter the ocean once more and phytoplankton to bloom along the retreating ice edge. Winter storms give way to the more clement conditions of summer. However, in these high latitudes, calm conditions seldom last for very long. The first sign of change may be a dizzying fall in the barometric pressure and within hours or less, an azure blue sea can give way to the full fury of another gale from the southwest. Nevertheless, a blue ocean flecked with white horses is a more frequent and playful scene in summer, occasionally even giving way to an oily calm where nothing stirs.

The dominance of the Southern Ocean in the southern hemisphere is of global and regional importance. On a global scale the Antarctic, its atmosphere, sea ice and the Southern Ocean interact to play a crucial role

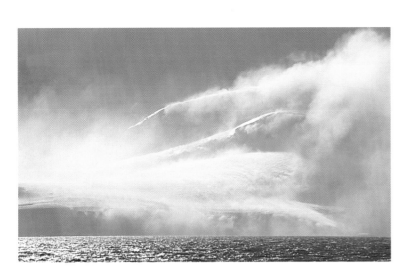

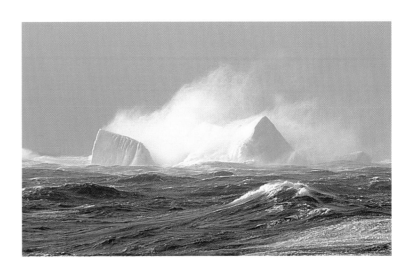

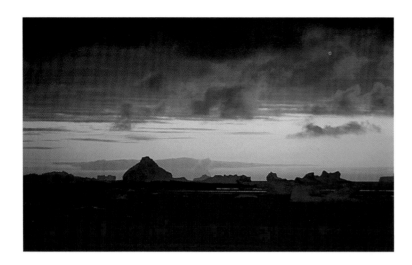

in maintaining the earth's climate system as we know it today. This cold ocean is currently the focus of international scientific scrutiny to see if it is capable of removing the excess carbon dioxide in the atmosphere which originates primarily from fossil fuel combustion and is the cause of global warming. Atmospheric scientists and climatologists have great interest in this region as well. Heat absorbed by the oceans at the equator is transported poleward into the Arctic and Southern Oceans where it can be dissipated into the atmosphere, setting up southern hemisphere atmospheric circulation patterns. These atmospheric circulation cells drive the weather systems which bring winter rainfall to southern Africa, Australia, New Zealand and South America.

ABOVE AND RIGHT *Silhouetted icebergs and rosy alto-cumulus clouds lace the sky above Arrowsmith Peninsula. When storms give way to calm, a world of subtle pinks and purples emerges to soften the harsh Antarctic landscape.*

BELOW *Pastel pink, blue and orange hues guild the evening sky as the sun slips quietly behind gathering clouds; such tranquillity is, however, only temporary.*

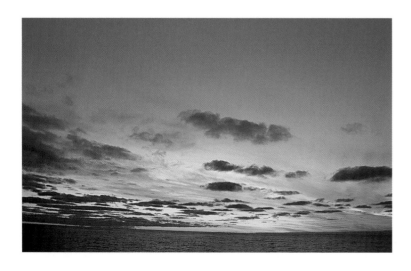

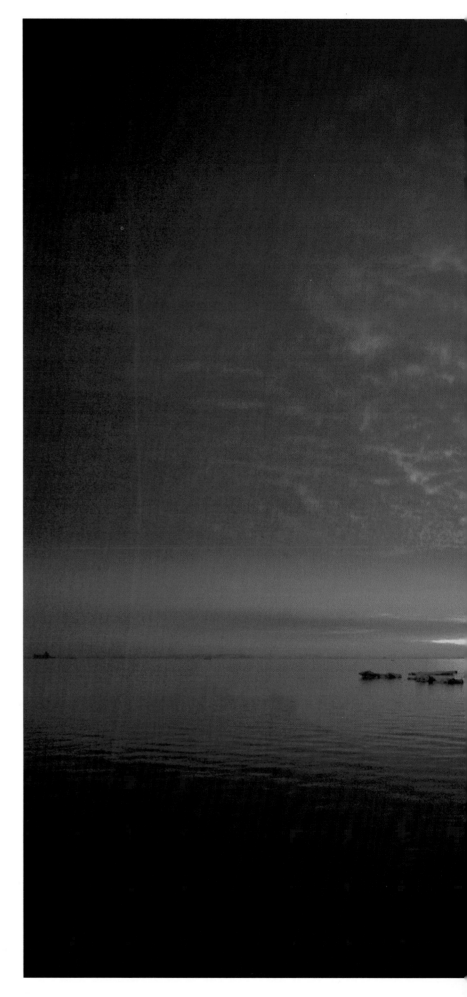

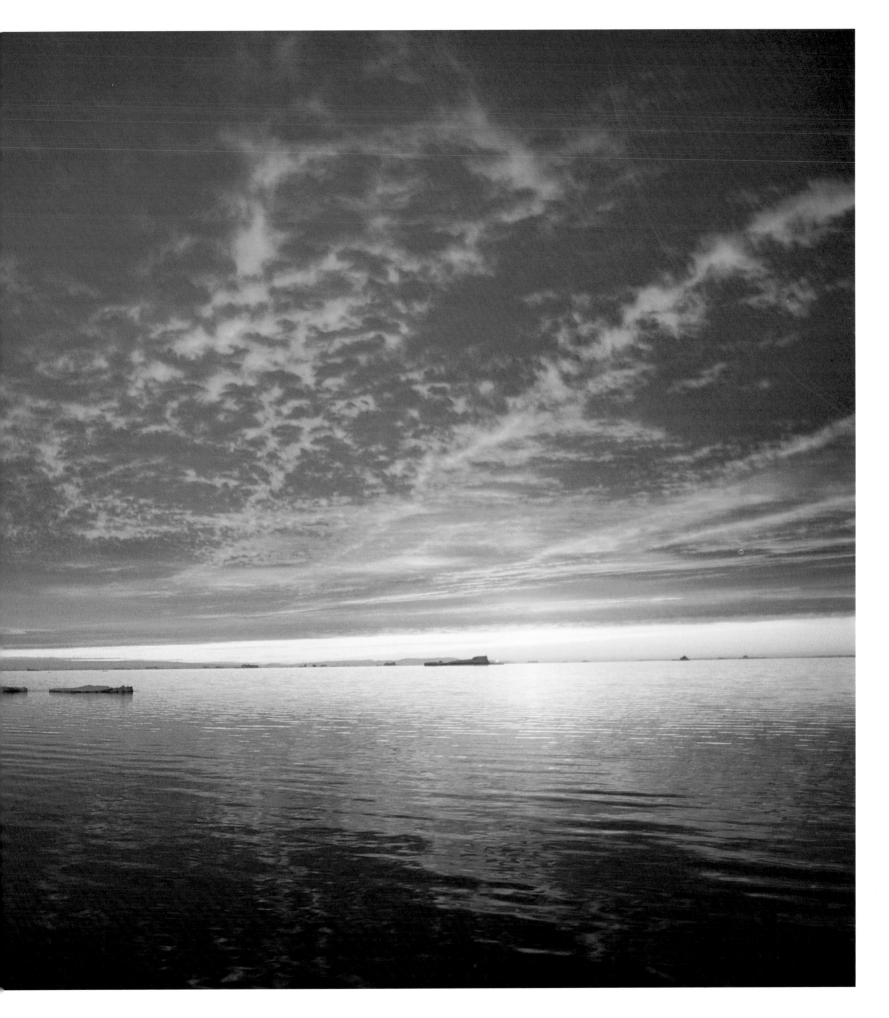

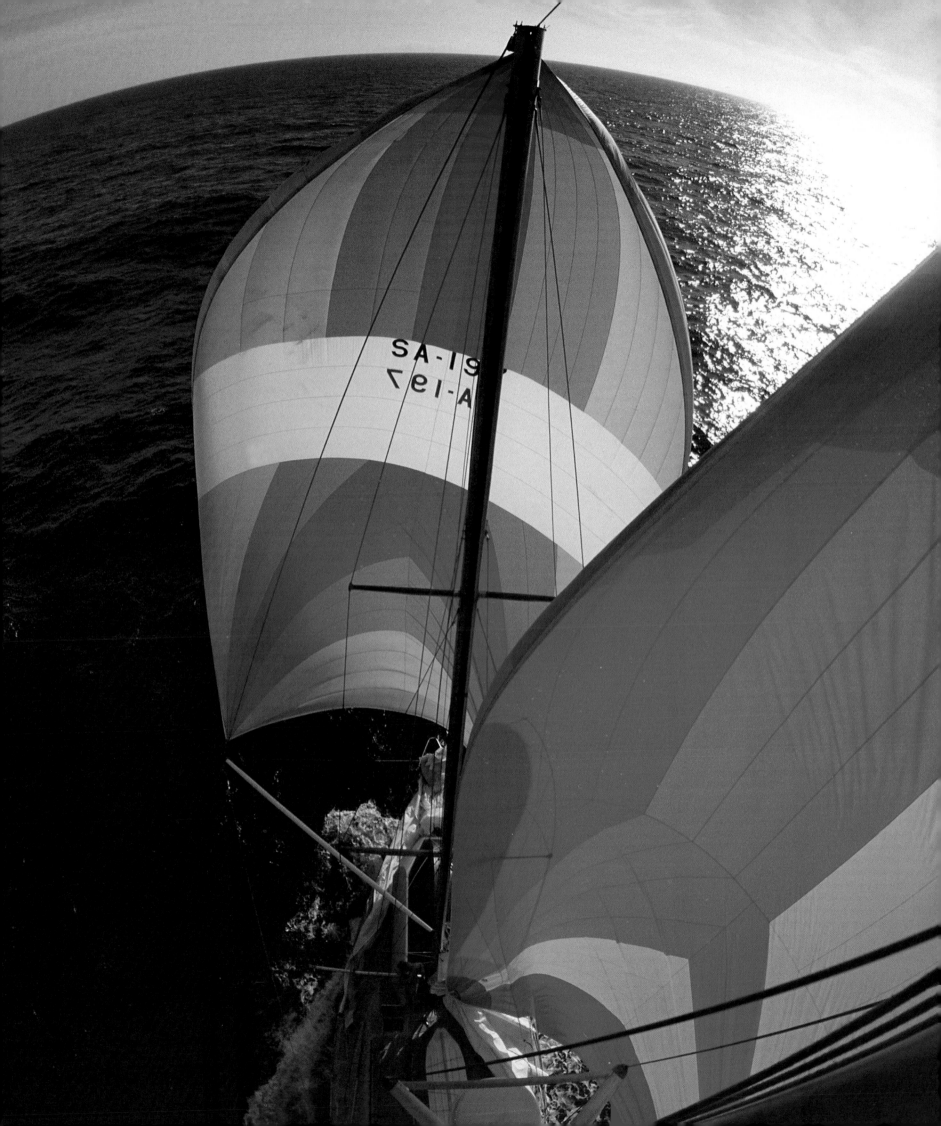

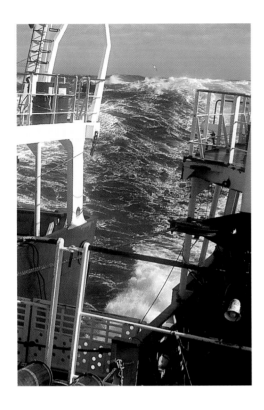

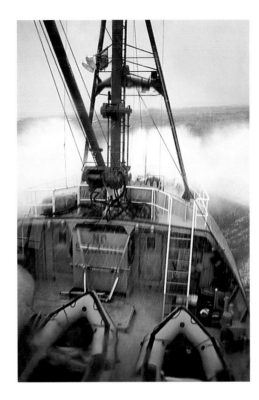

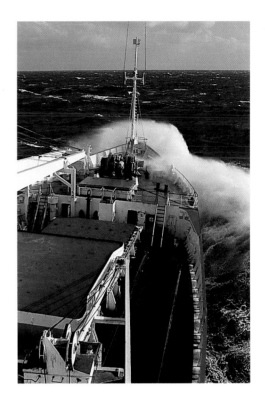

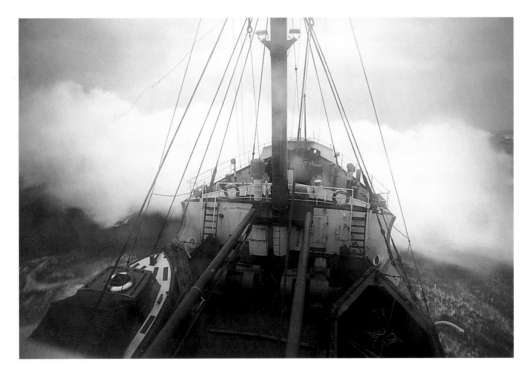

LEFT *Since David Lewis's pioneering voyage to Antarctica on* Ice Bird *in 1974, more and more yachts have braved the Southern Ocean to make landfall among the sheltered islands and inlets of the western Antarctic Peninsula.*

TOP *Rollicking along before Southern Ocean swells, or pounding and crashing into unchecked lines of crested rollers coming out of the west, the ship shudders along its entire length. Tons of water surge across the foredeck as the ship drops and plunges into a trough, before struggling to shake free and rise again as the next swell passes under.*

ABOVE *Occasional and terrifying, a 20m (65ft) rogue wave slams into the bow of a British Antarctic Survey ship.*

Sustaining the food web

In the ocean close to the Antarctic continent, surface water cooled by the extremely cold katabatic polar winds sinks to the bottom and spreads northwards into the depths of the world's oceans, keeping them cool. When some of these nutrient-rich oceanic currents reach the west or south coasts of South America, southern Africa, Australia and New Zealand, they stimulate the growth of huge blooms of phytoplankton which support important fisheries for anchovy and pilchard in particular.

Similarly, during the long summer days, these well-illuminated waters of the Southern Ocean stimulate the growth of phytoplankton at oceanic fronts and at the edge of the pack ice. Such blooms form the basis of a complex food web, dominated in the south by the unique Antarctic krill, which supports the fish, bird, seal and whale populations of the entire Antarctic ecosystem. The word 'krill' is actually a misnomer derived from the Norwegian word for a small fish, *kril*. Relatively large (5–6cm; 2–2.5in), shrimp-like crustaceans, Antarctic krill are adapted to feed on algae growing on the underside of ice in winter. In summer, they aggregate into huge swarms to filter-feed on phytoplankton blooms which now develop in the surface layer of some regions of the open ocean. Swarms may be 10km (6 miles) long and 50m (165ft) deep, containing millions of individuals that sweep the sea virtually clean of phytoplankton as they move through the ocean at speeds of 0.5kph (0.25 mph).

In almost all phytoplankton-rich oceans, small, fast-swimming, filter-feeding fish such as anchovy and pilchard dominate the food web, providing the link between plants and top predators such as large fish, squid, seals, birds and whales. However, the Southern Ocean has no such phytoplankton-feeding fish, probably because of the extreme cold of the environment. The average temperature of the ocean surface falls between +2°C to −1.8°C (35.6°F to 28.76°F). This creates problems for the ocean's

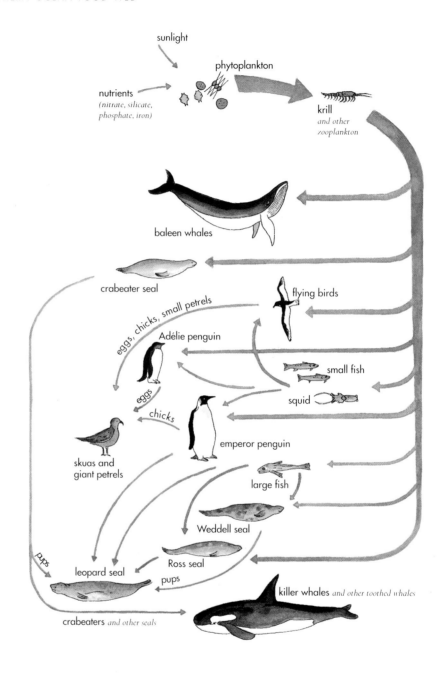

inhabitants, who require special adaptations to survive. Fast-swimming fish need a lot of oxygen. Normally, this is carried in the blood stream by red blood cells, but in the cold Southern Ocean blood containing red blood cells would be too viscous to pass along the blood vessels. Antarctic fish have solved this problem either by having few red blood cells or by dispensing with them altogether. The penalty, however, is that their blood cannot carry much oxygen, making these fish slow

ABOVE *This diagram of the Southern Ocean food web emphasizes the central role that Antarctic krill and other zooplankton have in the Antarctic ecosystem. During summer, the growth of single-celled plants (phytoplankton) provides food for Antarctic krill.*

Either directly or indirectly, all the other animals – ranging from 30m- (100ft-) long baleen whales to birds, fish and squid – depend on zooplankton. The arrows signify the direction in which food transfer takes place, while the thickness of the arrow indicates the relative quantative importance of the food consumed.

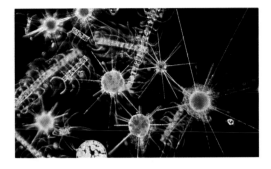

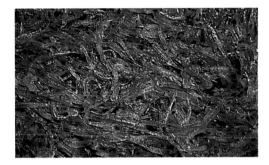

Captain Sir James Clark Ross of the British Navy was particularly intrigued by the question of what lay in the depths of the Southern Ocean. Could any animals survive in this freezing environment at pressures of about half a tonne per cm² (3 tons per sq in)? In 1839 Ross led an expedition of zoological discovery to Antarctica aboard his two ships, HMS *Erebus* and HMS *Terror*. Close to the continent, he dredged the ocean floor down to 730m (2400ft), discovering brittle stars, huge amphipods, brightly coloured sponges and fish. He and his team, including an enthusiastic young botanist, Joseph Hooker, made many important discoveries of life in these oceans; among them phytoplankton, zooplankton, fish, seals, penguins and whales. Two treatises describing plants of the subantarctic islands also emerged from the voyage, but many of the discoveries were not properly documented.

Now, 150 years later, Ross's name has been given to the British Antarctic Survey's polar research vessel, RRS *James Clark Ross*, which continues his pioneering scientific exploration.

The depths contain other surprises. Once the bottom of the ocean was thought to consist of flat, featureless plains devoid of life. But with the advent of sonar and satellite imagery, it has become clear that the ocean floor has greater mountains and deeper valleys than any found on earth. In the still solitude of the ocean depths, without the eroding forces of driving winds and rain, these submarine mountains remain untouched. The mid-ocean ridge in the South Atlantic, at the boundary of two of the earth's crustal plates, meets a third on which Antarctica rides, close to Bouvet Island. This mountain chain, rising more than 2000m (6500ft), continues for 50,000km (31,000 miles) around the world, making it easily the largest single geological feature on earth.

moving and unable to compete directly with fast-swimming krill for phytoplankton. Giving up the struggle, most of the approximately 120 Antarctic fish species are small and live on or near the bottom. The only important species living near the surface in coastal regions is the Antarctic silverfish.

Despite the cold, the vast Southern Ocean provides a stable and predictable environment and evolutionary processes have taken advantage of this. Although the temperature at the surface south of the Antarctic Polar Front is in the range −1.8°C to 2°C (28.76°F to 35.6°F), the presence of salt in the water prevents it from freezing at 0°C (32°F) as fresh water does. Curiously, it is warmer deeper down than at the surface, the reason being that the density of water is governed by both temperature and salt content. Saltiness dominates the density of the Southern Ocean's water, so warm water is denser and deeper than the cold, buoyant but considerably less salty surface water.

Temperature extremes in the ocean are only 1–2°C (1.8–3.6°F). By contrast, air temperatures can range from about −50°C (−58°F) in winter to 10°C (50°F) in summer. At times, wind chill can reduce the winter temperatures to as low as −70°C to −80°C (−94°F to −112°F). The ocean is thus warmer than the atmosphere in winter and steam can often be seen rising from the surface of polynyas, open areas of ocean up to several hundred kilometres in diameter: it is this heat flux to the atmosphere which keeps the polynyas ice-free. It may frequently be warmer for seals to get into the water than to stay on a gale-swept ice floe.

ABOVE *Spines on some phytoplankton may deter zooplankton consumers, enabling blooms to grow.*
BELOW *Antarctic krill is of vital importance to the food chain, forming a link between phytoplankton and higher animals such as seals and whales.*

ABOVE *Some krill swarms contain millions of animals and weigh over 100,000 tonnes (98,000 tons).*
BELOW *Virtually transparent because of the lack of oxygen-carrying red blood cells, this ice fish contains 'anti-freeze' to prevent its thin blood from freezing.*

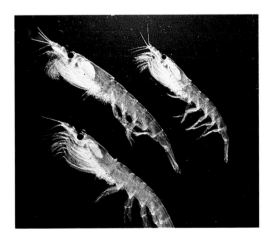

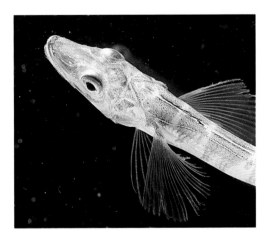

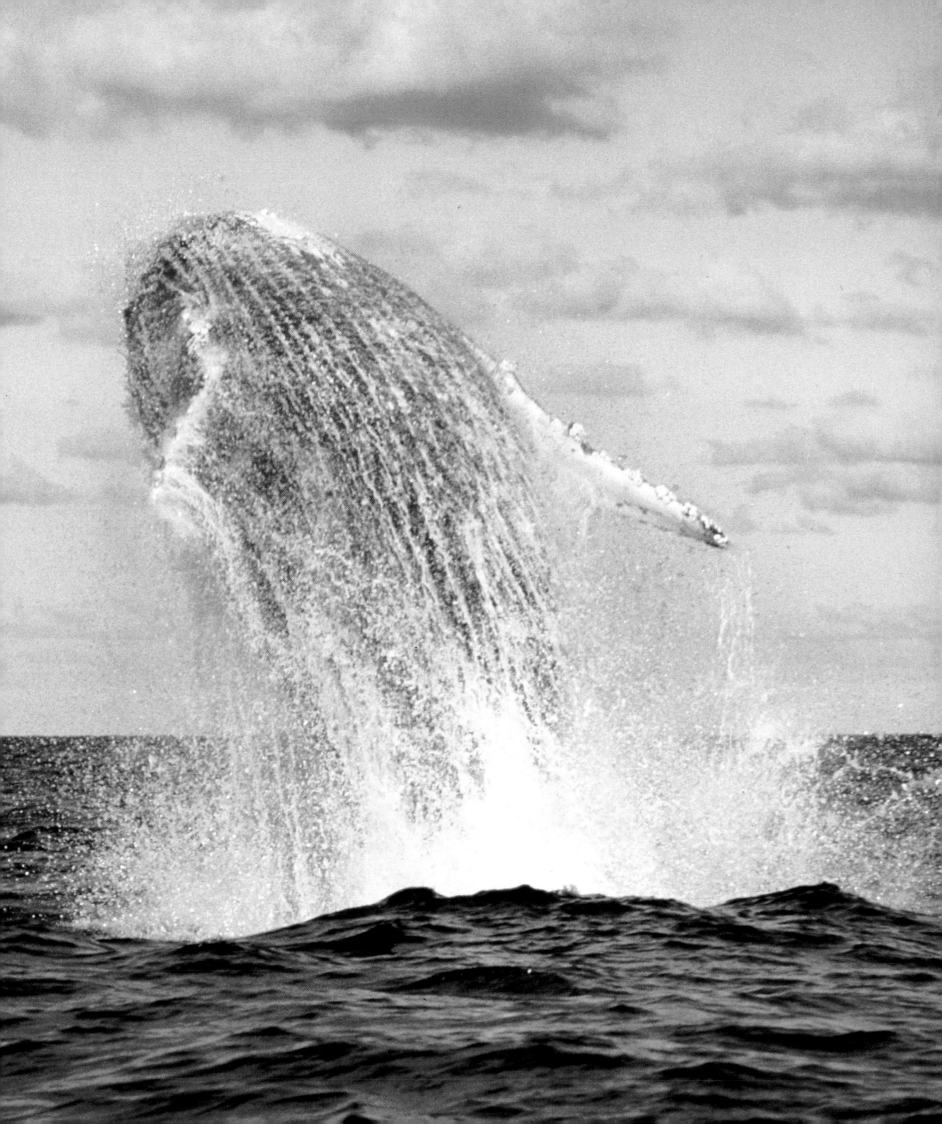

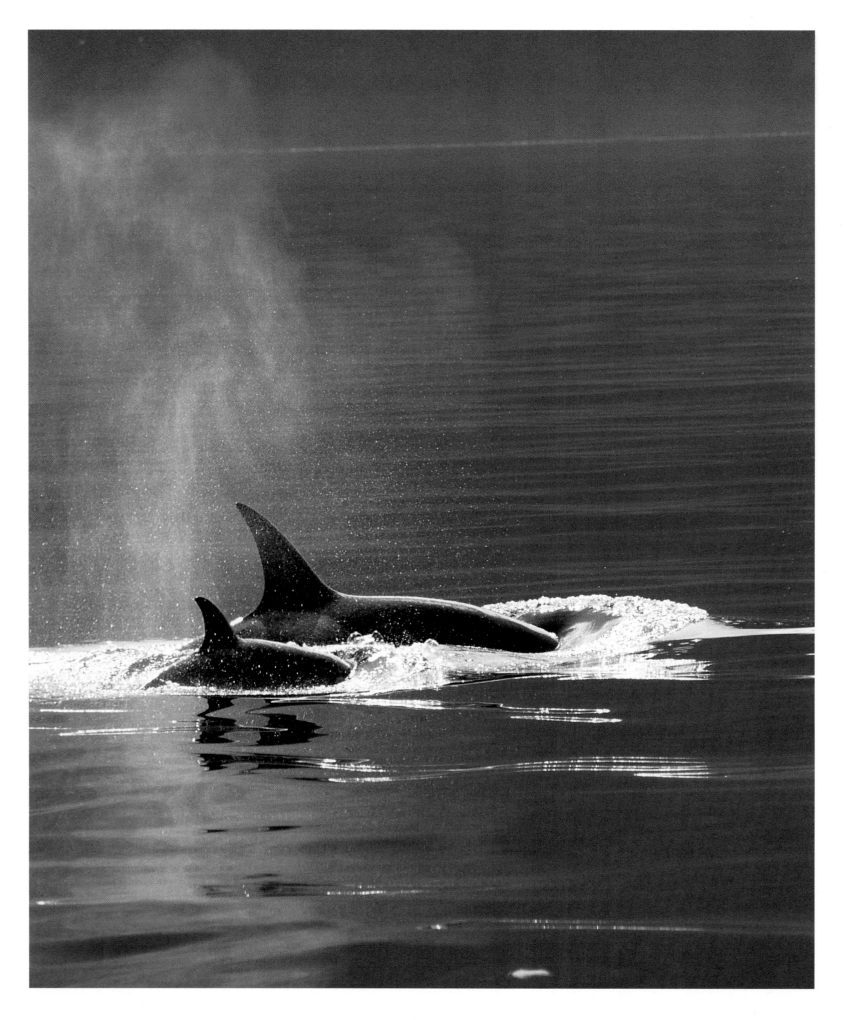

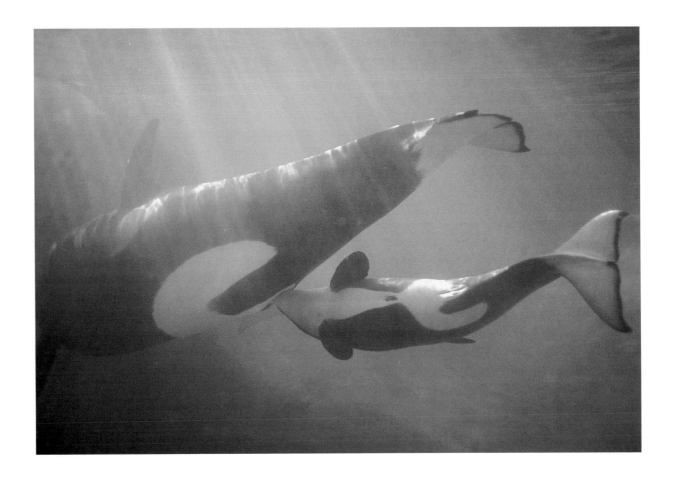

Giants of the deep

The Southern Ocean is home to the largest of the world's mammals, the whales. Ancestors of whales once lived on land, but at some time in their evolution, they took to the water again. Evidence of this can readily be seen in the construction of their skeletons, where the bone structure of the foreflipper closely resembles that of the foreleg of large terrestrial animals. In addition, whales, like all mammals, give birth to live young and suckle the calves with their extraordinarily rich milk.

Whales are divided into the predatory 'toothed whales', feeding mostly on squid and fish, and the predominantly krill-feeding 'baleen whales' which filter huge volumes of water through specialized sieves – baleen plates – designed to trap and engulf krill. Toothed whales have a single blowhole while that of baleen whales is paired. Among the baleen whales,

rorquals have distinct throat grooves, allowing the throat to expand and increase the volume of water filtered. Baleen whales found in the Southern Ocean include the minke, humpback, southern right, fin, sei and blue. Blue whales are the largest creatures ever known to have lived on earth, weighing 150 tonnes (148 tons) and reaching over 30m (100ft) in length. Sadly, their numbers are now extremely low due to the whaling activities of the past. Most commonly seen are the small, agile fin and minke whales which can sometimes be seen leaping, or 'breaching'. Most of the smaller whales are now recovering in numbers under the protection of the International Whaling Commission (IWC), which has imposed a moratorium on commercial whale exploitation, although sadly, not all countries adhere to such restrictions and exploit legal loopholes.

LEFT *Characteristic sickle-shaped dorsal fins identify these as a female killer whale and her calf. Found throughout the world, this species is most numerous in Antarctica with an estimated population of more than 160,000.*
ABOVE *This young killer whale calf is nursing on its mother's milk – a characteristic of all mammals.*

PREVIOUS PAGES *Sixty-five tonnes (64 tons) of humpback whale explode from the sea in a spectacular 'breach'. These whales are strongly migratory from subtropical to polar waters where, in summer, they feed on Antarctic krill.*

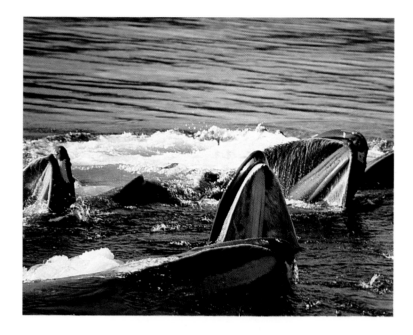

Humpback whales engage in a remarkable behaviour pattern of cooperative feeding. Descending to depths, they form a circle and exhale a stream of bubbles which rise like a circular curtain around swarms of Antarctic krill. Then, rising vertically within the bubble curtain, their mouths agape, the whales engulf both water and krill and strain it through their baleen plates with the help of their large pink tongues in order to capture the nutritious krill. Baleen plates were popularly used in Victorian times as 'stiffeners' for ladies' ballroom gowns.

The best known of the toothed whales are the sperm whale and the unmistakable black-and-white killer whale. Contrary to popular opinion, killer whales are not man-eaters, but feed mostly on penguins and seals. They are primarily denizens of the pack-ice edge and 'pods', as groups are collectively called, can often be seen patrolling and hunting along the edges of open ice leads. Males are easily recognized by their 2m- (6.5ft-) tall, erect dorsal fin while the females have a much smaller and rounded dorsal fin. Sperm whales, originally much sought after for their oil, can dive to depths of up to 3000m (9800ft) into the black, cold interior of the ocean in search of their favourite food, the giant squid. Such prodigious dives may last for well over an hour and raise intriguing questions about diving ability in these marine mammals.

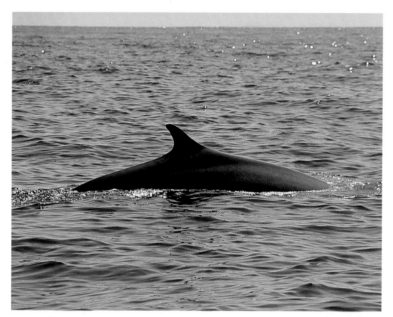

Long, calm, sunny days provide ideal conditions for sighting whales. Sometimes they are spotted lolling lazily at the surface but, if disturbed by an approaching ship, they may dive, or 'sound'. More frequently, whales are sighted by the exhaled 'blow' of spray and exhausted breath which rises unmistakably into the air when they surface to breathe. Particular whale species can be identified by characteristic blow patterns. Many scientists now also make extensive photographic catalogues of fin and fluke patterns to aid in the tracking of whale migration routes across the oceans. Attached satellite transmitters and receivers further add to this information, while pressure sensors can record and transmit the depth and duration of their dives. Estimating the populations of the great whales is extremely difficult and this problem is currently receiving urgent attention. Population estimates in this book were derived from the latest (1995) World Wide Fund for Nature *Species Status Report on Whales*.

Most of the great whales of the Southern Ocean are migratory, moving north into warmer coastal seas during the winter months, when they calve and mate, before moving south again in the austral summer to take advantage of the rich feeding available. Separated by enormous distances, whales have evolved a unique way of communicating which utilizes very low frequency whistles and songs that can travel hundreds of miles through the ocean. Songs of humpback whales in particular have been recorded by scientists and analyzed for patterns of 'speech'. Quite complex songs, and replies, demonstrate that communication is highly structured in this fascinating and mysterious group of animals.

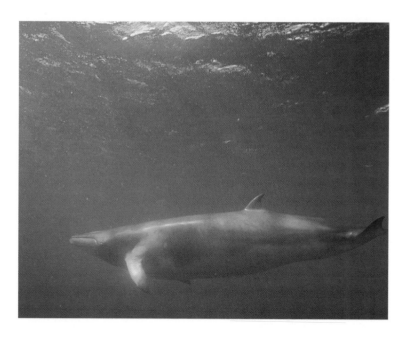

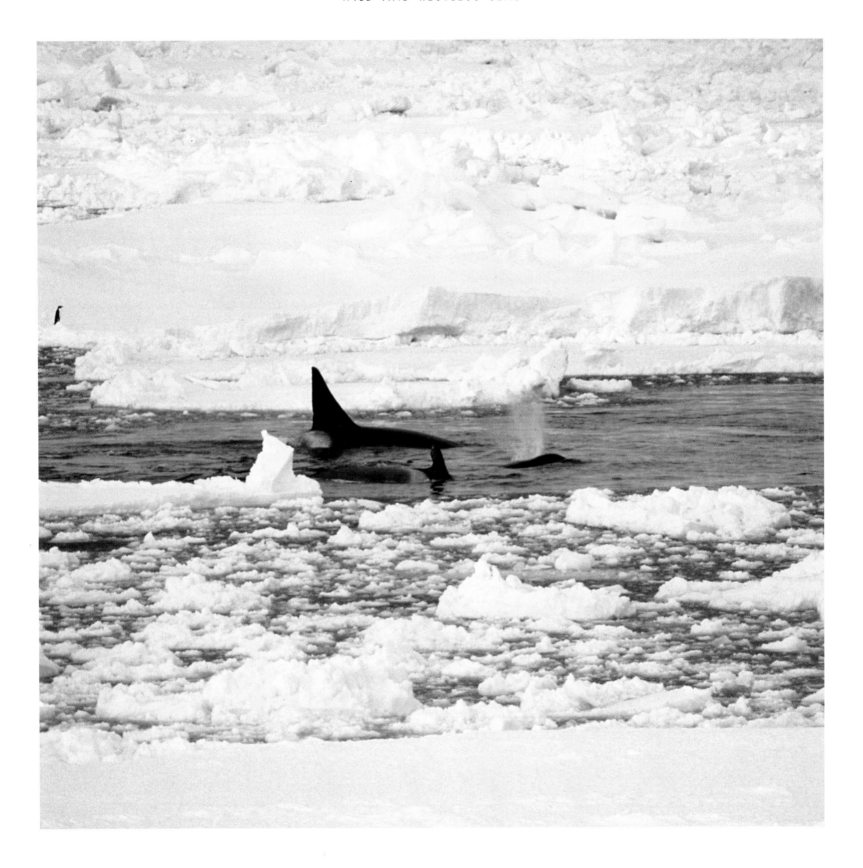

ABOVE *A male killer whale patrols a lead in the ice in pursuit of unwary Adélie penguins or young seals. These highly intelligent hunters have been known to topple penguins off ice floes, while in Patagonia, a group of killer whales has learnt to lunge at and capture seals on the beach.*

OPPOSITE CENTRE *The fin whale weighs about 80 tonnes (79 tons) and reaches 18–25m (59–82ft). The world population is about 120,000.*
OPPOSITE BOTTOM *The small, agile minke whale managed mostly to escape the harpoon while its larger cousins were nearly exterminated.*

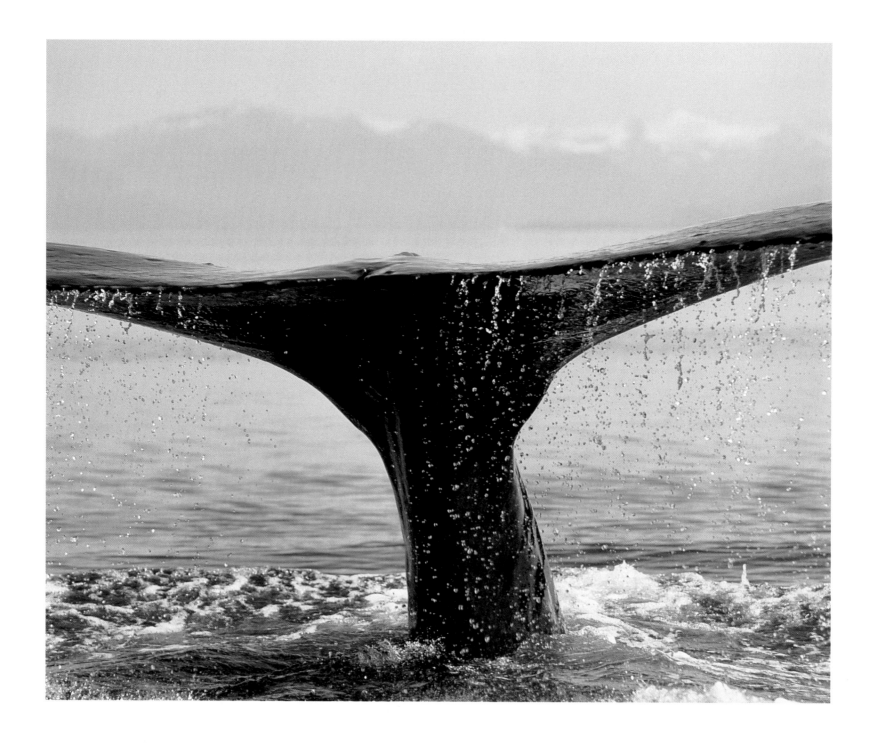

ABOVE *The power and grace of whales is epitomized by the humpback's enormous tail flukes. These will thrust it deep into the cold, dark ocean interior as it 'sounds'. Once a common sight for a whaler's harpooner, it is now tourists and whale-watchers who can experience the thrill of observing these gentle giants dive. During the 1992 season, it was estimated that some four million people worldwide engaged in whale-watching, generating some US$300 million.*

OPPOSITE *Water streams off this humpback's mighty tail flukes. Researchers have successfully established photographic catalogues of fluke patterns and shapes, allowing them to identify individuals and check their migratory patterns. The barnacles on the tail flukes do not harm the whale and filter small food particles from the water as the whale swims slowly along. In total, humpbacks may carry nearly half a tonne of barnacles around on their bodies, however many of them will drop off and perish when the whale migrates from cold to warm waters during the breeding season.*

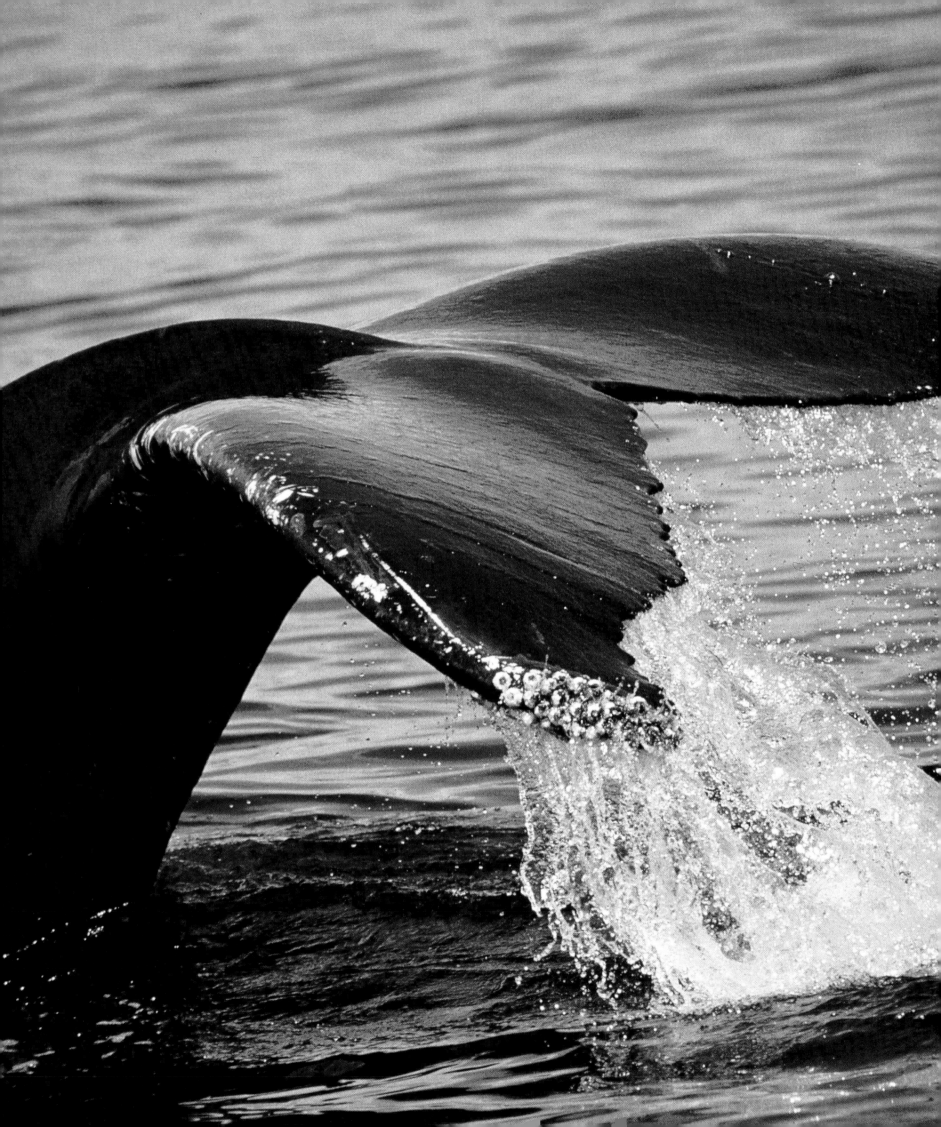

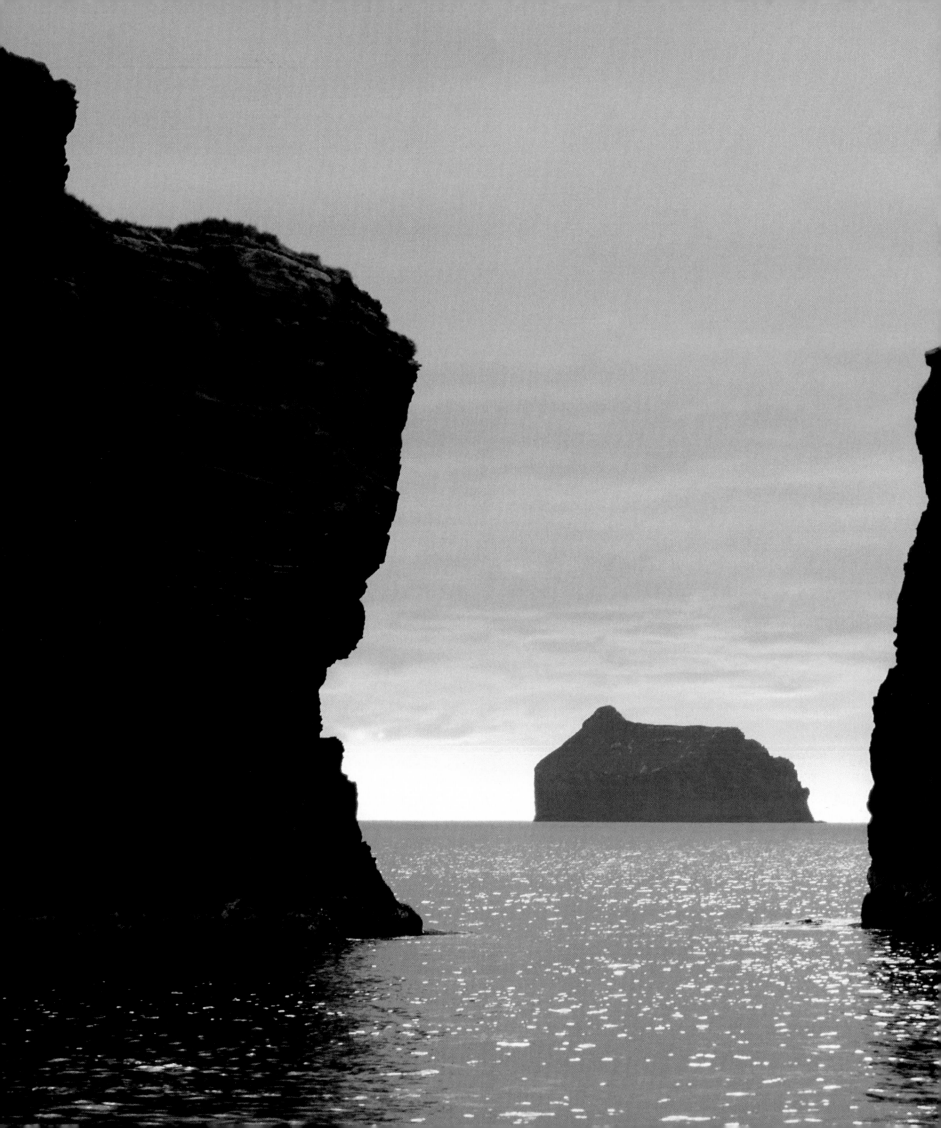

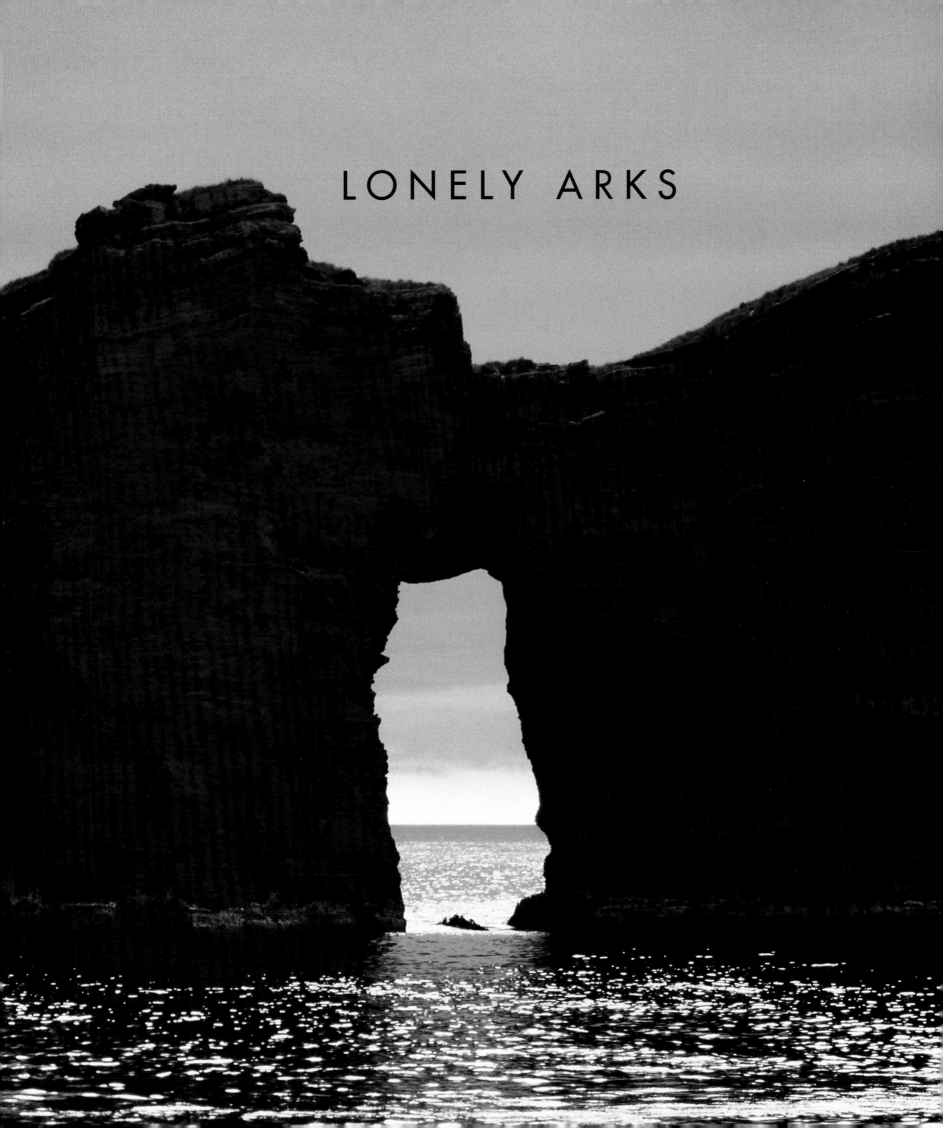

LONELY ARKS

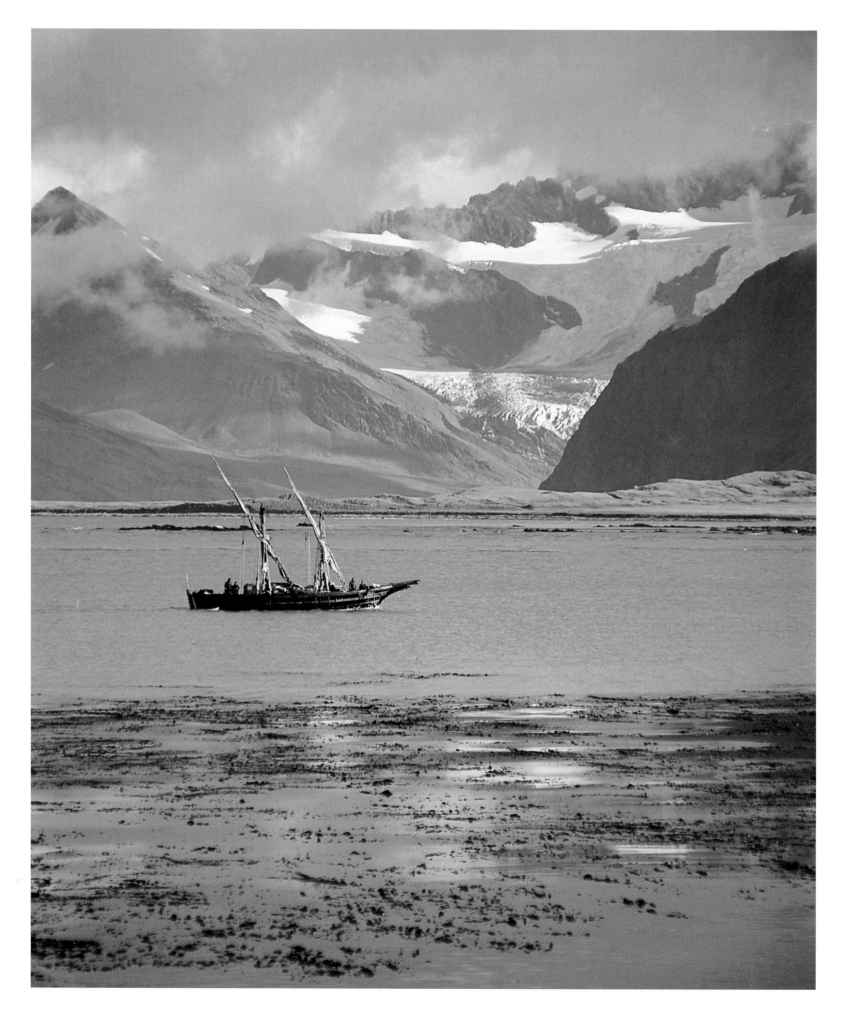

LONELY ARKS

Island oases of the Southern Ocean

Reaching up from the floor of the Southern Ocean, a few isolated and remote mountainous islands ring Antarctica and bear witness to processions of storms which sweep eastwards across the empty ocean. Most islands owe their origins to intense volcanic activity from 100 million years ago to the present, when molten lava spewed through the earth's crust to cool in a steaming cauldron of solidi-

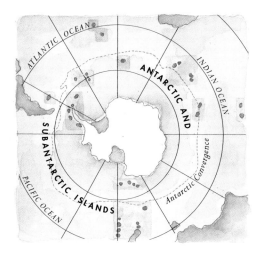

fying rocks and water. On their windward side, huge seas pound and crash against dramatic black volcanic cliffs, hurling wind-swept spray in high arcs across the cliff-top vegetation. Swirling mists and clouds bedeck the craggy, snowy peaks, while lower down, rain-drenched grassy tussock slopes and boggy mires give way to lakes and streams which tumble seawards, returning water to the ocean in a never-ending cycle of evaporation and rainfall.

Further south, on islands where Antarctica's icy breath is felt, frozen glaciers replace running water and grasses give way to reveal bare, unyielding rocks where only hardy lichens cling. Here, in winter, many islands are enveloped and surrounded by advancing pack ice which tames the turbulent seas. If by chance the sun breaks through on the more northerly islands, dazzling rainbows arch across the sky as if pointing to the mythical pot of gold. These islands do, in fact, contain many riches of the natural world. For a few months in summer, colonies of penguins crowd the tussocky slopes and pebble beaches in urban sprawls of noisy, breeding birds. Elephant seals, returned from their distant sojourn

at sea to breed, bask on the beaches or in their favourite muddy wallows. Bulls square up to each other, battling for supremacy and the right to mate. Smaller, more agile fur seals romp around higher up the beaches or on grassy slopes. A myriad oceanic flying birds return from their wanderings to make their nests in burrows, on wind-swept tussock slopes or against dizzying cliff faces. For all, it is a race against time to breed in the short summer months before the winter darkness closes in again. Other dangers lurk too. Predatory skuas and giant petrels often steal unguarded eggs and pick off the young, weak or sick.

Although penguins, flying birds and seals seem to dominate, cushion mosses, lichens, ferns, grasses and flightless insects all have their place in this rich mosaic of island life. And, beneath the waves in shallow sheltered coves, kelp, fish, shellfish, sponges and other sea-floor dwellers linger: a rich larder for birds and seals.

But this natural world has also been witness to the worst of human influences. Sealers and whalers of the 19th century plundered the beaches and surrounding seas, while many of the islands have been subject to introduced animals such as mice, rats, rabbits, cats, domestic animals and even reindeer. These have, without exception, dramatically altered the natural balance of the island ecosystems, something which is only now being redressed.

Depending on their proximity to Antarctica, the subantarctic islands can be roughly divided into different climatic groups, each with its own physical and biological characteristics.

PREVIOUS PAGES *The brooding, rocky sentinels of the Antipodes Islands lie at the northern fringe of the Southern Ocean close to New Zealand. Some have never been exposed to human influences but others, with their treacherous cliffs, have claimed many a ship. Wet and windy, with a near constant temperature due to oceanic influences, such islands are truly arks amongst tempestuous subantarctic seas.*

LEFT *An Italian Antarctic expedition noses quietly into King Edward Cove, South Georgia. This is the most mountainous of the subantarctic islands with 13 peaks exceeding 2000m (6500ft). The highest is towering, snow-clad Mt. Paget at 2934m (9626ft).*

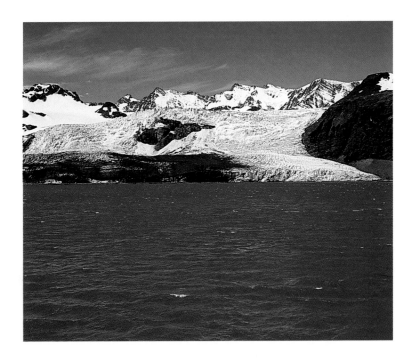
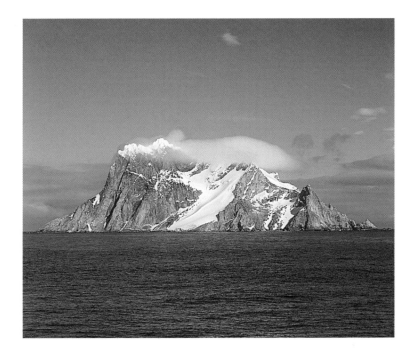

Island diversity

Furthest away from Antarctica, South Georgia, the Falklands, and Marion, Prince Edward, Kerguelen, Crozet, Heard, MacDonald and Macquarie islands lie between latitudes 45 and 55°S and ring the northern edge of the Southern Ocean. Climatically, they are dominated by oceanic influences and the Roaring Forties and Furious Fifties, making them windy and wet, but climatically constant. As many receive more than 2m (6.5ft) of rainfall annually, most are also extremely boggy. There are no trees and the vegetation is dominated by mosses and grasses.

Sea temperatures around these islands to the north of the Antarctic Polar Front average 4–5°C (39.2–41°F), while those to the south fall below 2°C (35.6°F). The ocean therefore has a considerable influence on climate, with subantarctic islands to the north of the Antarctic Polar Front having coastal summer temperatures generally always above freezing (7–8°C; 44.6–46.4°F). In summer, South Georgia can be warm enough for people to brave a brisk dip in the blue-green glacial lakes.

South Georgia is one of the most impressive and larger of the islands. More truly Antarctic than subantarctic, it is today frequently visited by tourist ships leaving from Punta Arenas at the southern tip of Chile and bound for the Antarctic Peninsula. Many of these follow in the wake of the 'Great Explorers' who ventured into uncharted oceans in wooden sailing ships a fraction of the size of the modern, steel, ice-strengthened cruise liners. Icebergs, growlers and the crushing pack ice were real dangers to these early explorers, whose heroic progress is charted in the evocative names of small bays, mountains, glaciers, islands and places throughout the Antarctic and Southern Ocean region.

Further south and more directly influenced by Antarctica and the biting polar winds are South Shetland, South Orkney, South Sandwich, Bouvet, Balleny, Scott and Peter islands. Almost all of these are frozen in by pack ice in winter, while numerous small islands along the coast of the Antarctic Peninsula have practically the same harsh climatic characteristics as the continent itself and are always ice-covered.

Almost all of the subantarctic islands are geologically young and volcanic in origin, except for South Georgia, the Falkland Islands, and some close to the Antarctic Peninsula. Islands such as Bouvet, Heard, the South Sandwich and Peter islands are still active, while Marion, to the southeast of South Africa, and the Crozet group further to the east, have been active until recently. Distinctive red volcanic cones dot these islands, while blackened lava flows, black sandy beaches, lava sea cliffs and flooded valleys provide further evidence of their turbulent geological history. On Marion Island one of the few beaches is covered in black volcanic sand. Against this backdrop, white, black and yellow-coloured king penguins look unquestionably regal.

TOP LEFT *The stark beauty of South Georgia's mountains and glaciers masks a turbulent past. Apart from the island's involvement in whaling, South Georgia also has the dubious distinction of being the only region in Antarctica to have been directly involved in a war, between Britain and Argentina, in 1982.*

TOP RIGHT *Rugged Cornwallis Island is just one of seven volcanically formed islands that together form the Elephant Island group. Elephant Island is best known for its role in Shackleton's heroic voyage to South Georgia in a ship's lifeboat after his vessel,* Endurance, *was crushed by ice in the Weddell Sea.*

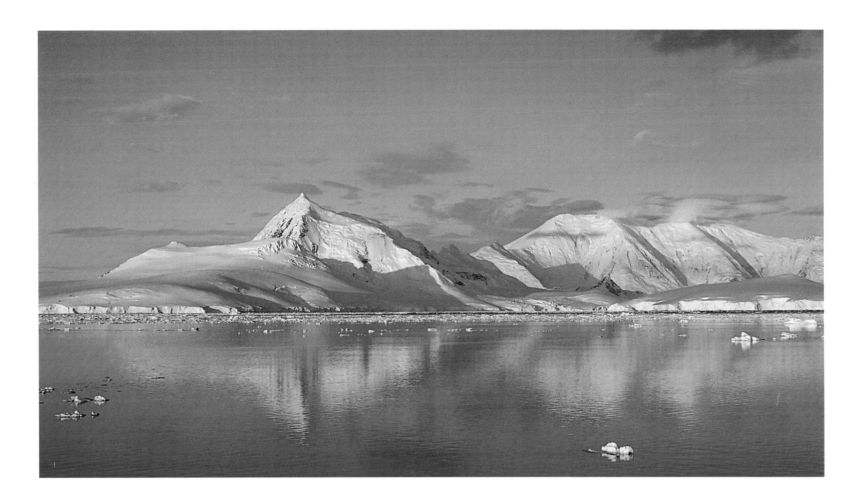

ABOVE *Anvers Island, at nearly 65°S and lying close to the Danco Coast on the western side of the Antarctic Peninsula, is permanently covered by snow and ice, as its climate is strongly governed by Antarctica's dominating influence. The island is home to the United States of America's year-round Palmer Station.*

BELOW *On South Georgia, Lake Gulbrandson has been dammed up by one of the island's glaciers. Apart from being a tourist destination, South Georgia's terrestrial and marine ecosystems are considered to be an area of major research focus and interest for the British Antarctic Survey.*

FOLLOWING PAGES *Volcanic in origin and near pristine, Prince Edward Island is seen only 22km (13.7 miles) across the sea from Marion Island. These remote, rugged islands which lie on the far northern fringe of the Southern Ocean are home to 29 species of breeding seabirds, numbering about 1.6 million pairs.*

BELOW *Coronation Island, part of the South Orkney Island group, has both Southern Ocean and Antarctic continent climatic influences. The island was discovered by a British sealing captain, George Powell, on 7 December 1821, while sailing in the company of American Captain Nathaniel Palmer.*

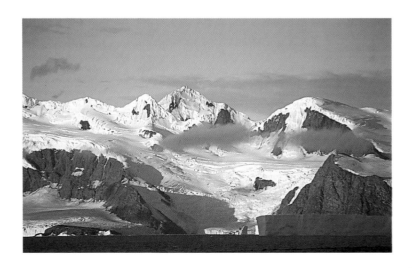

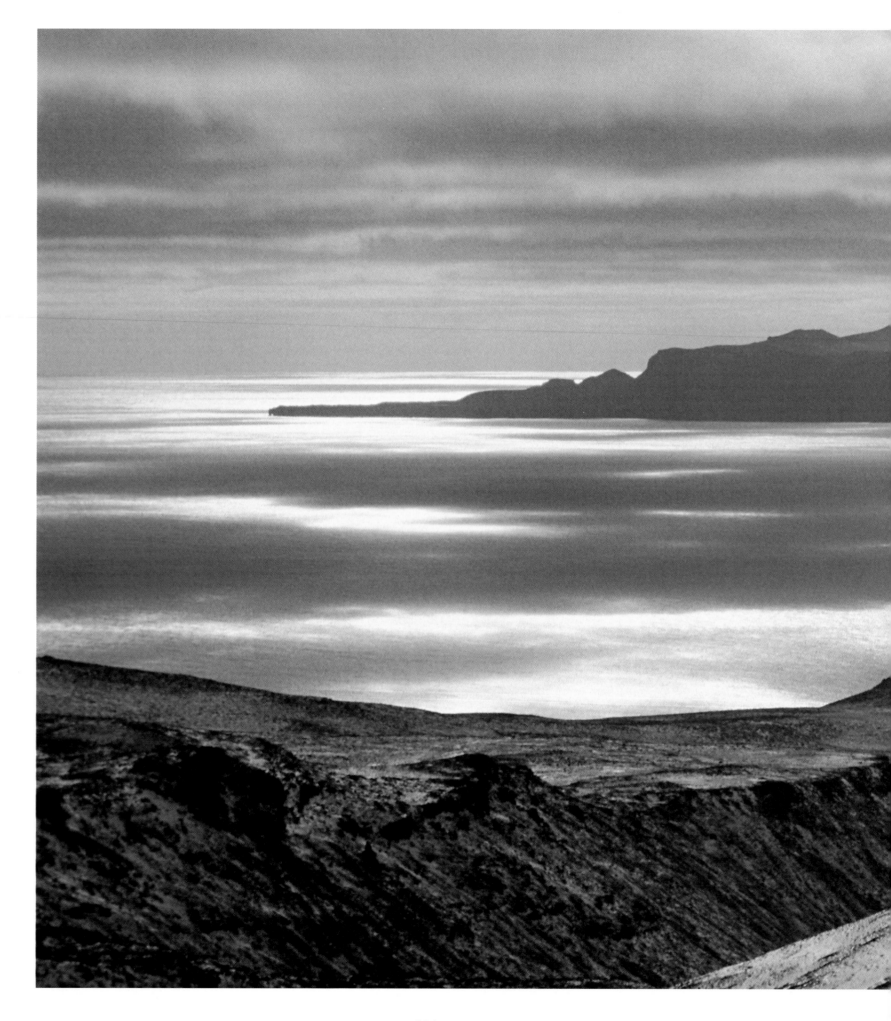

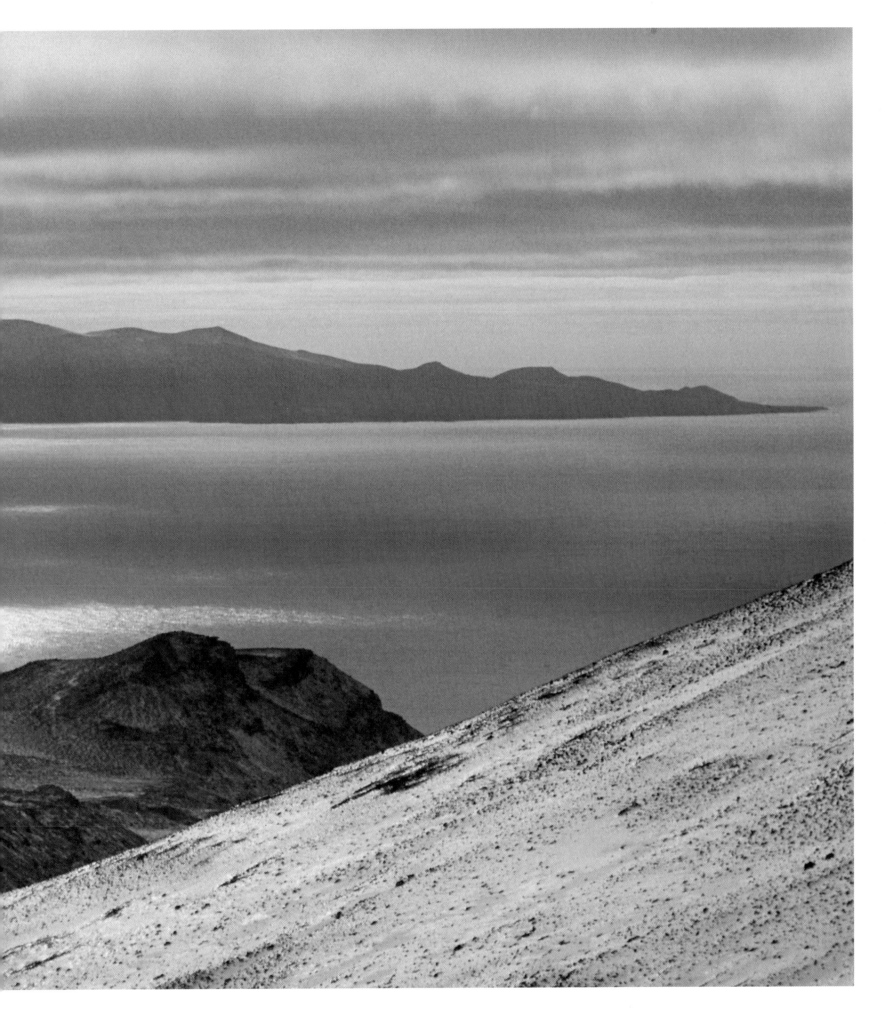

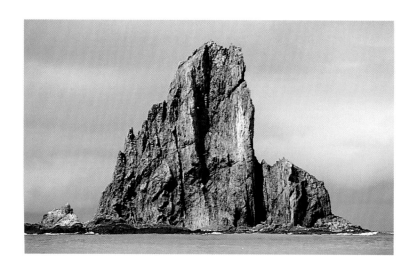

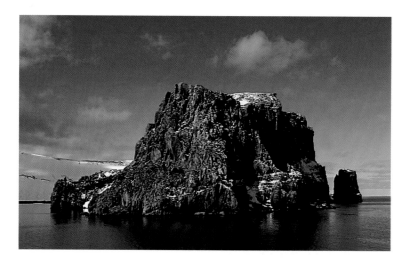

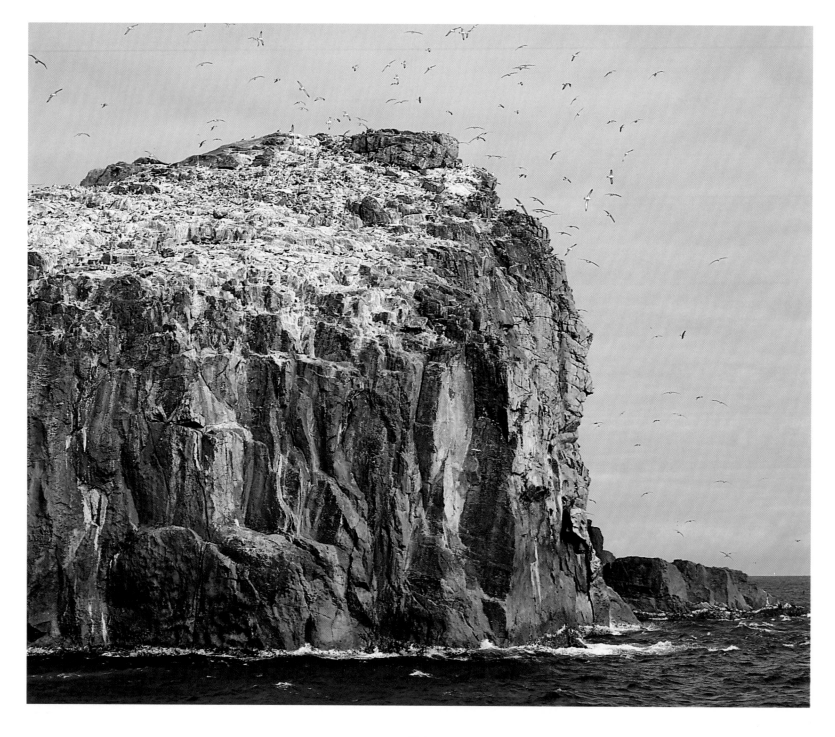

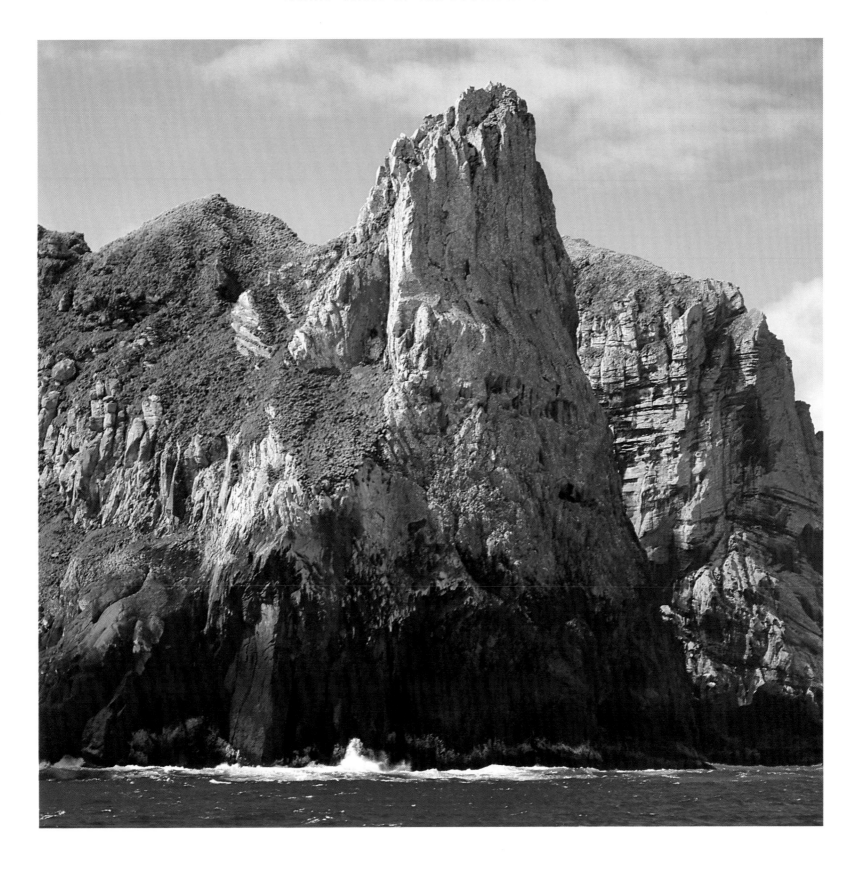

ABOVE *Impressive cliffs of black lava make many of the Antipodes Islands almost inaccessible to people. Subantarctic islands in the vicinity of New Zealand are more northerly and correspondingly much warmer than most. It is this that accounts for their characteristically luxuriant and more diverse vegetation.*

OPPOSITE TOP LEFT *These craggy black volcanic rocks and cliffs form part of the aptly named Point Wild, situated at the northern tip of Elephant Island.*
OPPOSITE TOP RIGHT *The volcanic cliffs of Neptune's Bellows stand guard at the entrance to Deception Island, one of the South Shetland islands.*
OPPOSITE BOTTOM *Salvin's albatrosses wheel above their nesting colony on the guano-splashed rocks of Bounty Island close to New Zealand.*

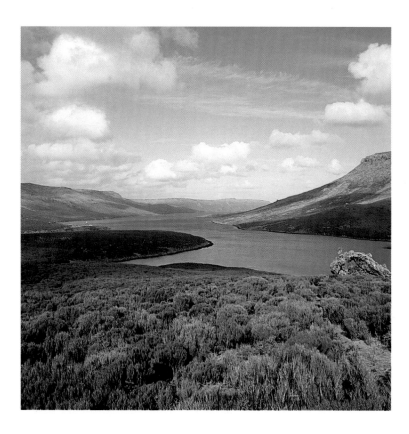

ABOVE *Perseverance Harbour, Campbell Island, lies in the New Zealand subantarctic. James Clark Ross visited here in 1840, and later the Norwegian Henryck Bull focused on the island for his whaling and sealing operations.*

RIGHT *A yellow-nosed albatross stands atop a tussocky knoll on volcanic Inaccessible Island which forms part of the Tristan da Cunha group in the South Atlantic. Tristan, seen in the distance, is the largest of the group.*

BELOW *The abandoned whaling station of Stromness on South Georgia is visible from the head of the valley of the same name. This was just one of five stations established after the one at Grytviken between 1904 and 1917.*

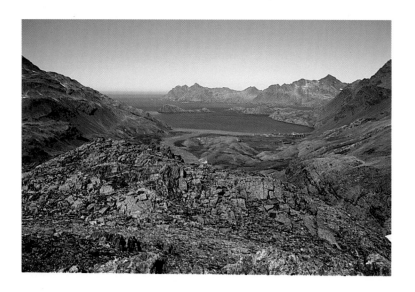

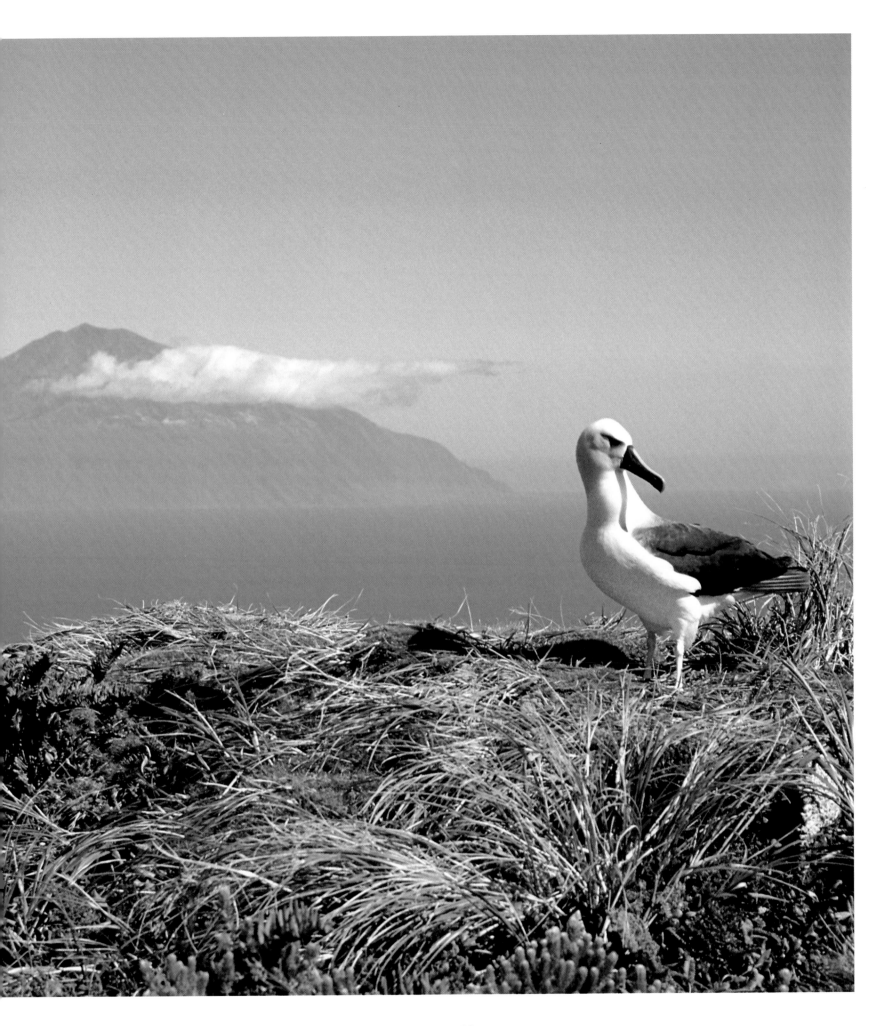

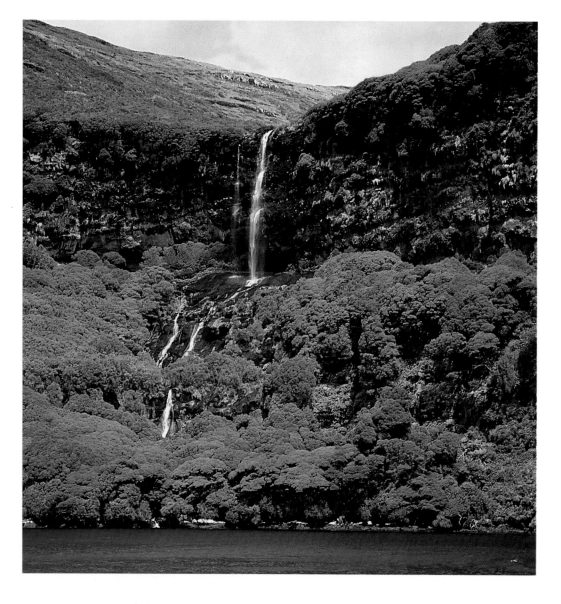

LEFT *A waterfall cascades down the blackened lava cliffs of Harfield Inlet, Auckland Islands, just 400km (250 miles) south of New Zealand. The luxuriant vegetation is the red-flowered rata, Metrosideros robusta, a dense woody bush which is absent on the more southerly of the subantarctic islands.*

BOTTOM LEFT *On the eastern coastal plain of Marion Island, short tussock grasslands of narrow-leaved grasses dominate the tundra-like vegetation. Geologically speaking, the plain is actually a raised lava beach which was once submerged by the sea.*

BOTTOM CENTRE *Verdant green floating rafts of waterweed obscure the many treacherous bogs and mires that cover Marion Island. Underlying layers of peat accumulate over periods of around 10,000 years because the decomposition of dead material takes place so slowly in these oxygen-starved bogs.*

BOTTOM RIGHT *One of the small rivers draining Marion Island's permanent glaciers runs through grassland and volcanic stone-fields, or 'fellfields'.*

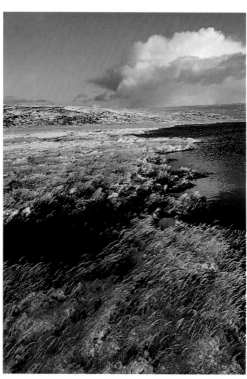
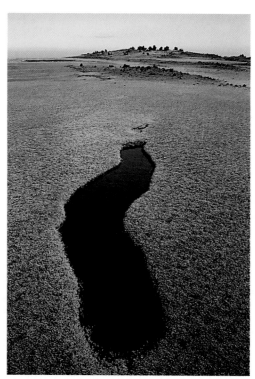
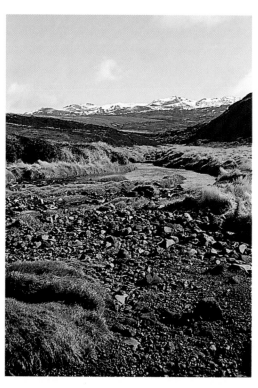

Environments under threat

Vegetation on the northern islands is dominated by grasses, peat bogs, ferns, mosses and lichens, while the southernmost islands lose most of the luxuriant growth and the diversity of plant species. However, it should not be forgotten that a hundred years or more of human influence and intervention have altered these islands in many respects. Most are no longer pristine, while alien plants and animals have invaded many of them, profoundly altering their natural ecological balance and species diversity.

On South Georgia, which has been inhabited since 1904 and occupies an intermediate position between the northern and southern islands, there are over 50 species of alien plants. The introduction of reindeer and sheep by Norwegian whalers as an alternative to whale meat has also had an adverse effect. Today, only the reindeer survive, but their considerable numbers (approximately 2500) cause extensive damage to the natural vegetation. Black rats and striped field mice have also become serious pests on some of the islands, most notably Marion, Crozet, Kerguelen and Macquarie. In addition, rabbits have destroyed much of Macquarie's lush tussock grasses while feral cats, black rats and even a New Zealand bird (the weka) are important predators of eggs, chicks and burrowing petrels. Recent control measures have, however, eliminated 95 per cent of the rabbits and also reduced the feral cat population, while the weka is apparently gone.

RIGHT, TOP TO BOTTOM *'First Red Hill'*
on Marion Island is a volcanic cone of red iron-rich
scoria rock; mosses of King George Island — these are
extremely slow-growing and indiscriminate trampling
causes severe damage; of all plants, the lichen Usnea
antarctica *has adapted the best to the cold; small*
encrusting lichens grow into bare rock — of the 150
species of lichen that occur here, most are grey or
black; tufts of Antarctic 'hair grass', which is
mainland Antarctica's only grass species.

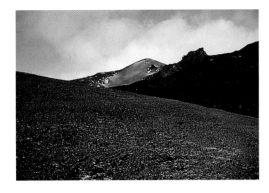

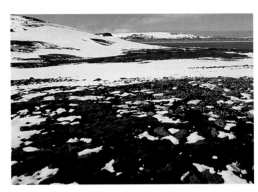

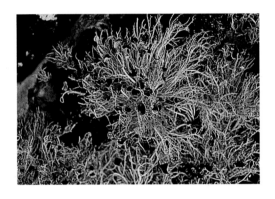

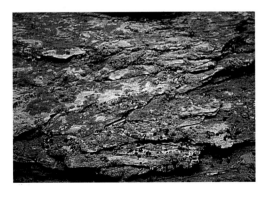

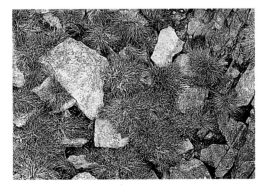

THE CATS OF MARION ISLAND

The story of the feral cat problem on Marion Island graphically illustrates the dangers of introducing alien creatures to environments where they do not naturally belong.

In an attempt to control the mouse problem (caused by 19th century sealers) prevalent at the main base on Marion Island, five pet cats were introduced in 1949. By 1975 the cat population, now feral and ranging across the 290km² (112 sq mile) island, had grown to an estimated 2139 individuals and was rapidly increasing by 13 per cent annually. About 450,000 small burrowing petrels were being killed each year, while the common diving petrel was wiped out as early as 1965.

In 1977, as a first control measure, the feline flu virus, feline panleucopaenia, was introduced to the population, then estimated to be around 4500 cats. The resulting epidemic reduced numbers to about 615 cats by 1982. However, even this vastly smaller cat population posed a serious threat, especially since the surviving cats had developed immunity to the virus. A full-scale hunting effort across the whole island was then initiated in the spring of 1986. Eight two-man teams armed with 12-bore shotguns and battery-operated searchlights for night-time hunting were deployed. From 1986–89 a total of 807 cats were accounted for. The use of baited traps reduced cat numbers even further and since 1993, no cats have been sighted. Since then, the breeding success of burrowing petrels has substantially recovered.

Introduced alien species often severely disturb the natural ecological balance of the environment. Typically, the introduced animal or plant does not have a predator in its new environment and, in the absence of such natural control, the alien species can run riot causing widespread devastation.

RIGHT *A southern giant petrel at its nest with its young chick. The eggs are laid in mid-September and hatch in late November; the chicks are reared by early April. Like all petrels, the giant petrel freely drinks seawater. The excess salt is excreted from a gland in its head and through the prominent nasal tubes on top of its green-tipped bill. The northern giant petrel's bill is red-tipped.*

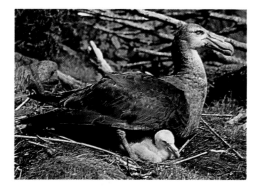

BOTTOM *Giant petrels are voracious predators of young or small birds and scavenge on penguin and seal carcasses. The smaller females usually feed at sea as the much larger males use their robust size to prevent the females from feeding at carcasses.*

OPPOSITE *A nesting colony of southern fulmars on their characteristic nesting site of rocky cliffs.*

Havens of the Southern Ocean

Despite the threat of introduced fauna and flora, many of these islands are still welcoming oases lying just out of reach of the paralyzing coldness of the Antarctic winter. Millions of Southern Ocean birds and seals return each year to their place of birth, to renew the struggle to find a mate, breed and feed their young during the short austral summer.

Sooty, yellow-nosed and blackbrowed albatrosses return to breed each spring, while the magnificent wandering albatross makes landfall only on the more remote subantarctic islands. Held aloft on the prevailing westerlies, it is possible for this bird with its 3m- (10ft-) wingspan to soar effortlessly right around the Southern Ocean. During periods of calm when there is no wind to assist their flight, albatrosses will sit on the ocean in desultory groups, rising and falling in the gentle swell, until stirring winds give them enough lift to take wing once again.

Living for 50 years or more, the wandering albatross only becomes sexually mature after eight years, when it will return home to find a mate. Together with the grey-headed albatross, they breed only every two years because of the length of time it takes to rear the large demanding chicks. The mating 'dance' of the wanderer is one of the most elegant and beautifully intimate courtships to observe. With outstretched wings, heads extended skywards and accompanied by a sharp clapping of bills, the partners dance around each other, cementing the bonds that will keep them together for life. Nesting sites are established singly rather than in groups, on windy tussock meadows across the island. After mating in the late spring, one egg is laid which hatches after two months. All through the following winter, the downy white chick remains on the nest, fed alternately by the male and female. Wandering albatrosses feed mainly on squid and larger zooplankton and forage thousands of kilometres from their nest, returning to feed their young at intervals of up to 10 days. Squid, krill and other delicacies retained in the crop are regurgitated into the bill of the juveniles, which waste no time in swallowing them!

Both light-mantled and sooty albatrosses prefer to nest on grassy cliffs above the sea from which they effortlessly soar using the updrafts along the cliff edge. Pairs of these birds can often be seen flying a breathtaking pas de deux along the crests of the cliffs in perfectly timed harmony.

Spring sees the arrival of the Arctic tern. Migrating from the Arctic in the autumn, this tern makes one of the longest migrations in the world (an almost 4000km [2500 mile] round trip), taking advantage of the plentiful food in the summer months of both regions. Similarly, white-chinned and pintado petrels, subantarctic skuas, shearwaters, prions and the diminutive Wilson's storm petrel, which flits across the wave crests, flock to the islands in huge numbers. The smaller petrels nest in rock crevices or in deep burrows beneath the tussock grasses; they are thus confined to the northern islands as the grassless southern islands would be unsuitable for breeding purposes. Together with the prions, these birds emerge from their cover only at night when they feed collectively on small crustaceans found at the sea's surface. This behaviour protects these delicate species from the voracious predatory skuas and giant petrels which will knock them out of the sky if they are caught unawares.

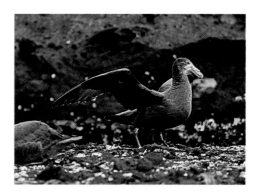

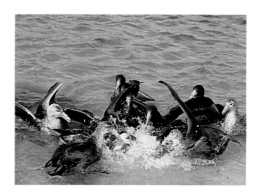

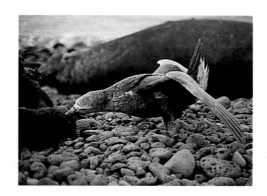

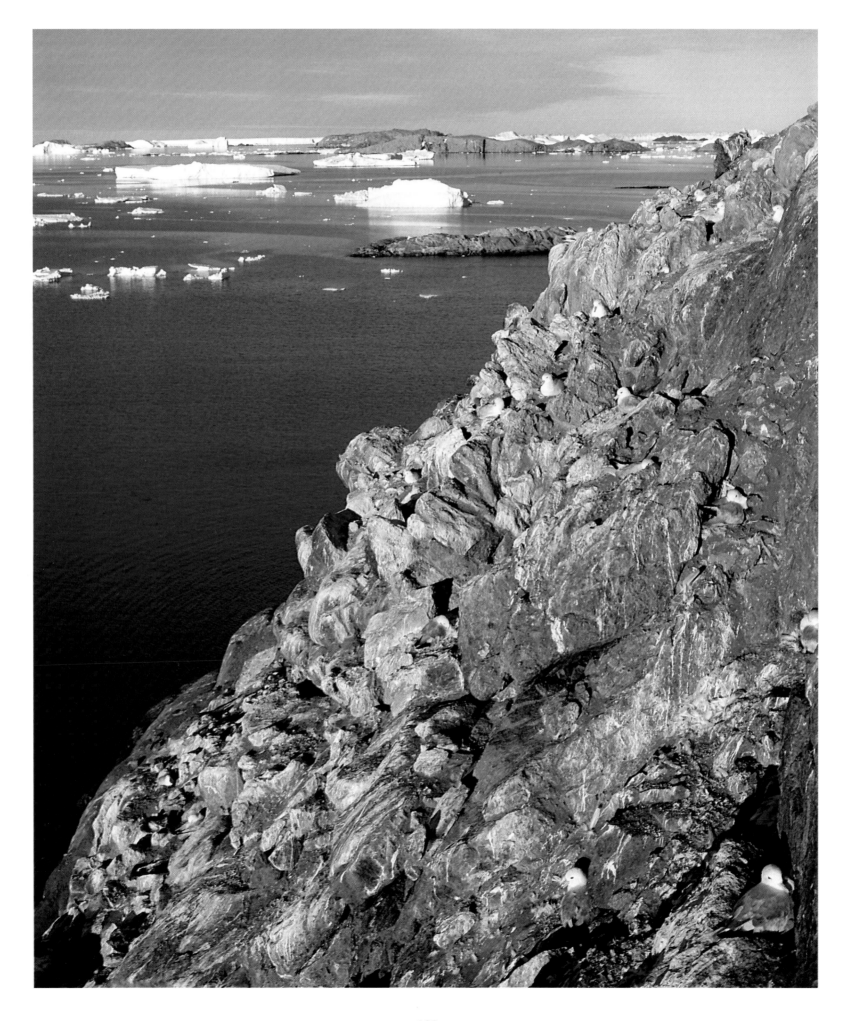

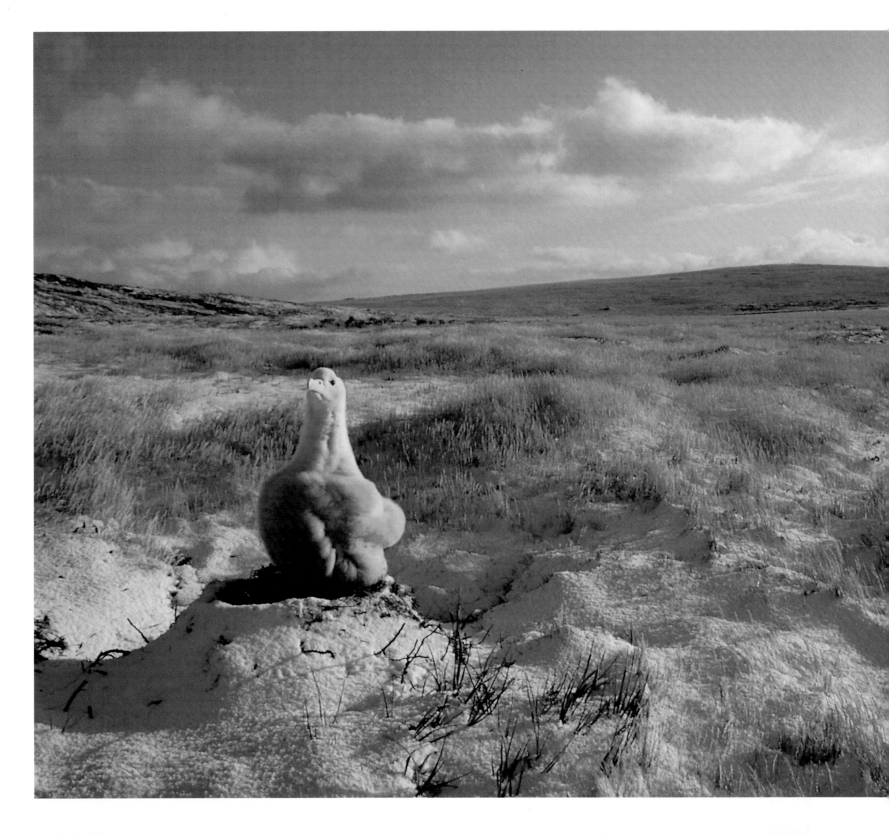

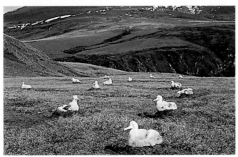

ABOVE *A wandering albatross chick waits for the arrival of a parent bearing a meal of mashed-up squid and fish in its crop. The chick will remain on the nest throughout the coming winter.*

LEFT *Albatross Valley on Marion Island boasts the highest density of breeding wanderers in the world.*

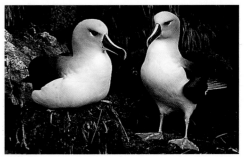

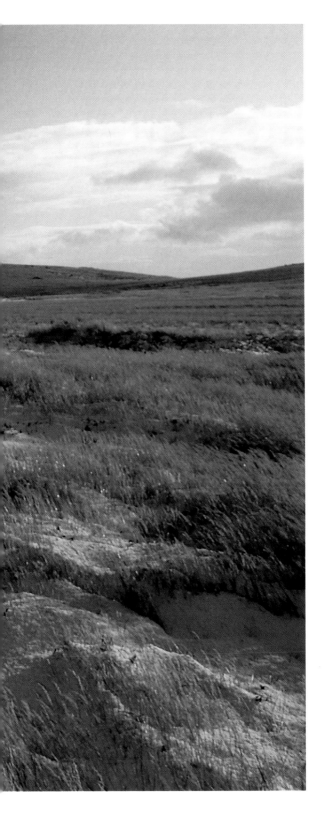

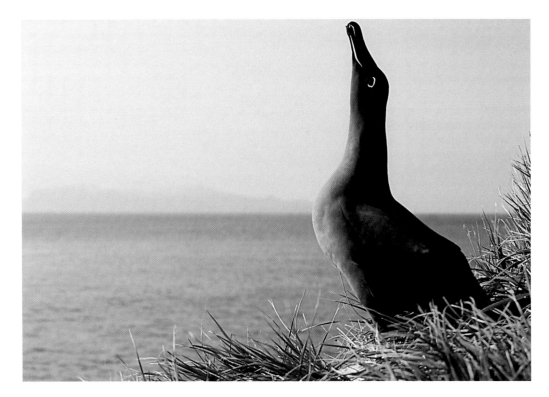

ABOVE *A sooty albatross engaged in 'skycalling' on Marion Island. Pairs of these beautiful birds can frequently be seen flying high along the crests of cliffs in perfect harmony. Prince Edward Island lies in the background.*

BELOW *Wandering albatrosses have the largest wingspan of any living bird and nest on windy, tussocky slopes where they can run downhill into the wind. Ungainly on land, they are exceptionally graceful once airborne.*

BELOW LEFT *A light-mantled sooty albatross sits at its nest with her young chick. At this age, the chicks are extremely vulnerable to skuas and giant petrels and the parents must maintain a constant vigil.*

OPPOSITE BOTTOM RIGHT *A pair of grey-headed albatrosses tend to their nest site on Prince Edward Island.*

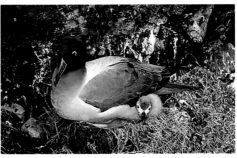

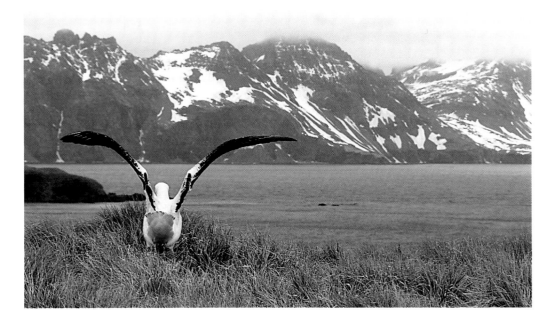

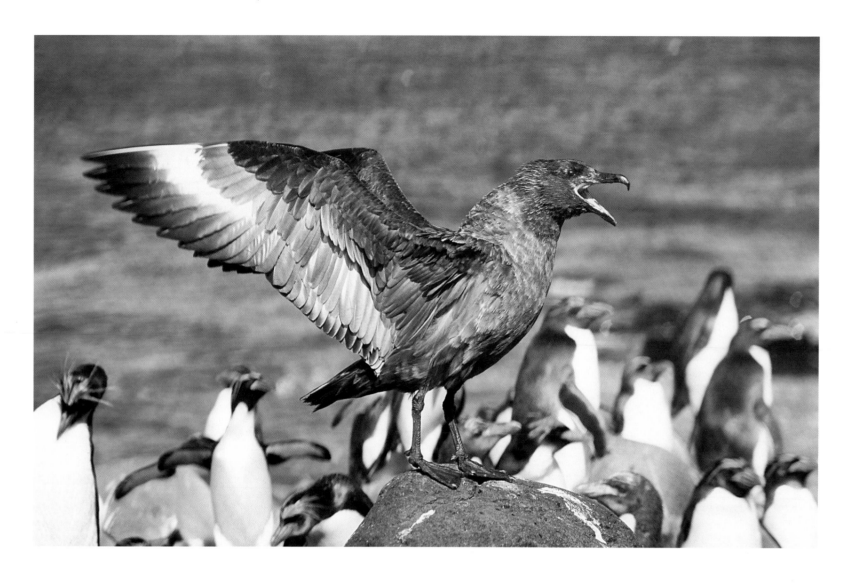

ABOVE *A large, aggressive subantarctic skua shrieks menacingly in a macaroni penguin colony. Few Antarctic birds can escape the unwelcome attentions of these avian highwaymen who rob nests of eggs and young chicks as well as harassing adults in flight, forcing them to jettison food destined for their young.*

BELOW LEFT *By frequently preening themselves, imperial cormorants maintain their water-resistant feathers in good condition after dives of up to 100m (330ft).*
BELOW RIGHT *A whitecapped albatross, or 'shy', sits on its cliff-side nesting ledge. These birds breed only in the Australia and New Zealand regions.*

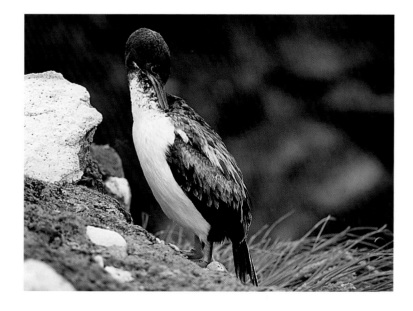

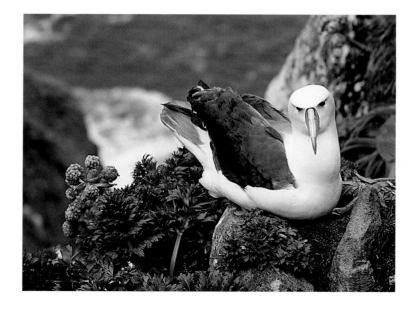

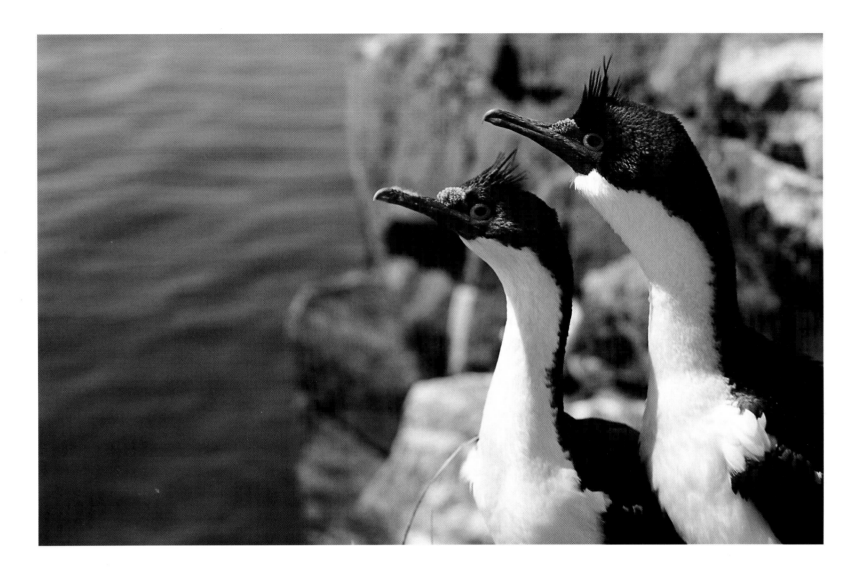

ABOVE *A pair of imperial, or blue-eyed, cormorants at their nest. The prominent orange nasal caruncles vary in colour seasonally, but are brightest during the breeding season. These cormorants occupy scattered locations along the western Antarctic Peninsula, Scotia Arc islands and most of the subantarctic islands.*

BELOW LEFT *A flightless teal of Enderby Island. Originating from the flighted teals of New Zealand, these birds became flightless in the absence of predators.*
BELOW RIGHT *Antarctic terns breed throughout the subantarctic and maritime Antarctic, migrating to temperate southern latitudes during the austral winter.*

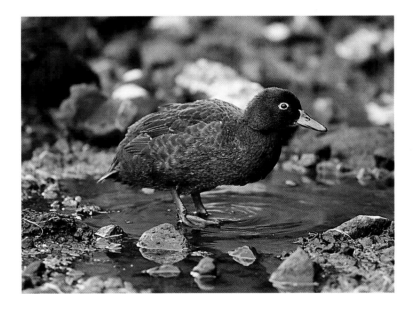

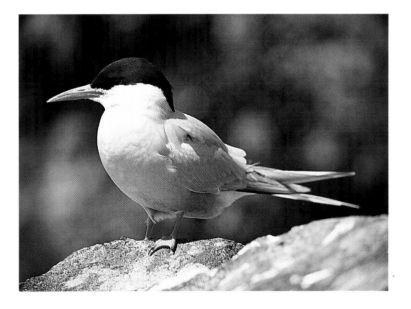

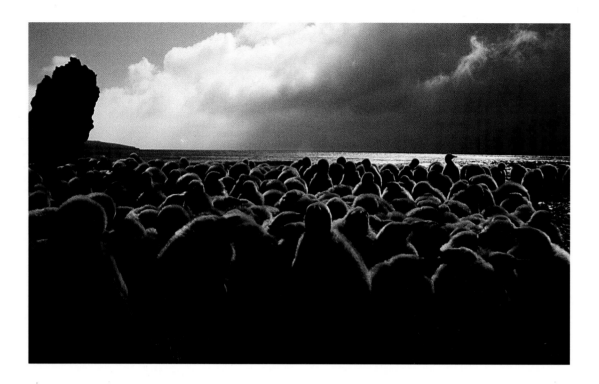

Colonies and crèches

Early summer sees advance parties of king, macaroni, gentoo, chinstrap, and rockhopper penguins jostling and bobbing in the more sheltered bays, coves and inlets, before allowing themselves to be hurled up the beach or onto the rocks by the surf. Amazingly, there are few injuries. Although supremely adapted to 'fly' through the water with their stubby flippers, penguins are not particularly agile on land. Nevertheless, now fat and sleek from months of feeding at sea, the penguins begin to establish vast, noisy rookeries of calling and squabbling birds, each pair trying to establish their own small territory. The mating ritual begins.

Quarrelsome macaronis have extravagant orange feather-plumes sweeping back from their eyebrows, and form vast, densely packed rookeries on low rocky slopes. After the breeding season, empty macaroni rookeries stand silent, devoid of grass, trampled and scoured out by thousands of restless feet. Only the feathers, skeletons and bones of those that did not survive the struggle are left as testimony to the metropolitan, sprawling and noisy colony that once existed.

Elsewhere, small and comical rockhopper penguins choose rocky outcrops and tussocky nooks and crannies on which to build their nests. Similar in appearance to the macaronis, they have a distinctive yellow feather head crest. Brilliant red eyes reflect the rockhoppers' cocky, self-assured personality – except during moulting when they sit around in forlorn groups waiting patiently for their new suits of clothes! They breed in loose colonies consisting of hundreds to thousands of pairs of birds and, being inquisitive and confident, it is common to find them nesting

beneath the huts and walkways of many of the island bases and weather stations. Nests are rudimentary or nonexistent. Usually two eggs are laid and incubated in a brood pouch by both males and females who take it in turns to go to sea and feed. Amazingly, when the mates return, they find their partners amongst the seemingly identical birds. Songs and calls amidst the cacophony of sound seem somehow to bring the right couples together again. A short ritual 'dance' and greeting confirms the choice.

Regal and curious, king penguins look like smaller cousins of the Antarctic continent's emperor penguins. Being less agile, they are not inclined towards long treks from the sea over rough ground, and form huge colonies close to sheltered beaches. They, like emperor penguins, have a complex breeding cycle forced on them as a result of their large size. A single egg is laid in November and then incubated on the feet of the adults for about eight weeks until the chick hatches in early April.

After hatching into chocolate-coloured fluffy chicks in mid-January, they grow rapidly in protected crèches and are safe from predators such as skuas and giant petrels by mid-April. After breeding, the adults moult so that by the time autumn comes they are ready to return to the sea. All through the winter, the chicks remain huddled together on land, while their parents return to feed them every two to three weeks. With the arrival of spring the adults return permanently to the rookery and by the end of the second summer the chicks are ready to fledge. Of course, this lengthy breeding cycle extending over two seasons means that adults only breed once every two to three years instead of annually.

OPPOSITE *The woolly, chocolate-brown king penguin chicks in this crèche are nearing the end of their second summer at the rookery. Soon they will moult into their exotic adult plumage.*

TOP RIGHT *The urban sprawl of this king penguin breeding colony reaches its peak from late October to late March. The braying penguins drown out the sound of the crashing surf, and thousands of feet trample any remaining vegetation to death.*

CENTRE *Rockhopper penguins conceal their chicks on rudimentary nests in the breeding colony.*

BOTTOM RIGHT *Interspersed with crèches of fluffy chicks, a king penguin colony surrounds a subantarctic island lake. The greatest number of king penguins are to be found on Marion Island, home to an estimated 215,000 individuals. The world population stands at about two million and is still recovering from 19th-century exploitation, when king penguins were killed for their oil.*

BELOW *Aggressive and agile, chinstrap penguins have located this breeding colony on the volcanic slopes of Deception Island. Nests may sometimes be commandeered from Adélie penguins, such is the competition for ice-free ground in the maritime region where this species normally breeds.*

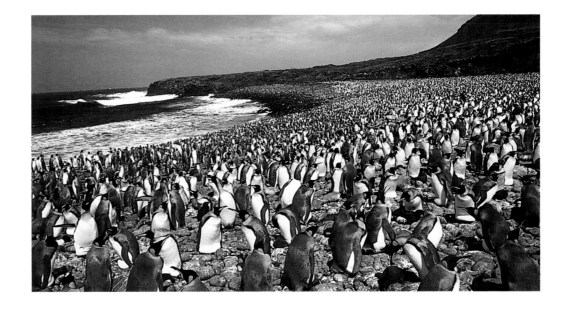

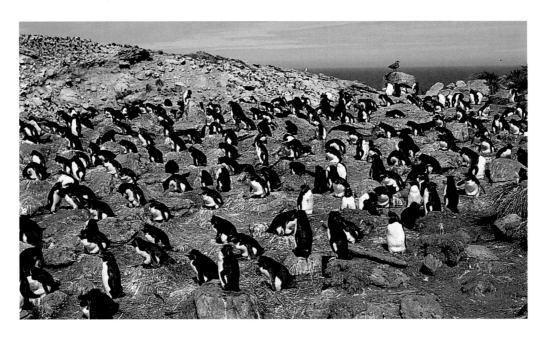

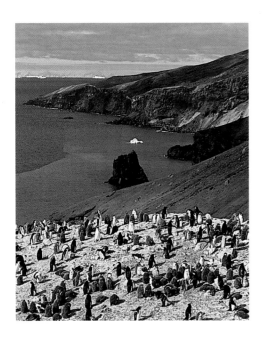

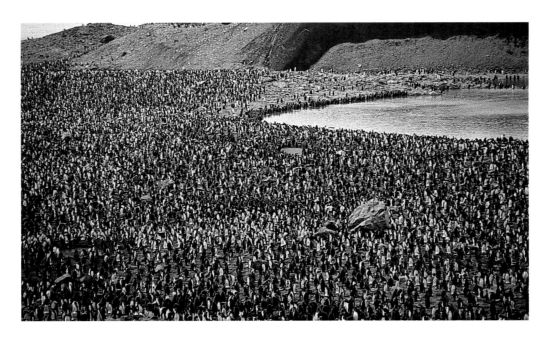

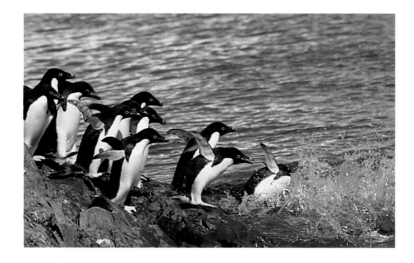

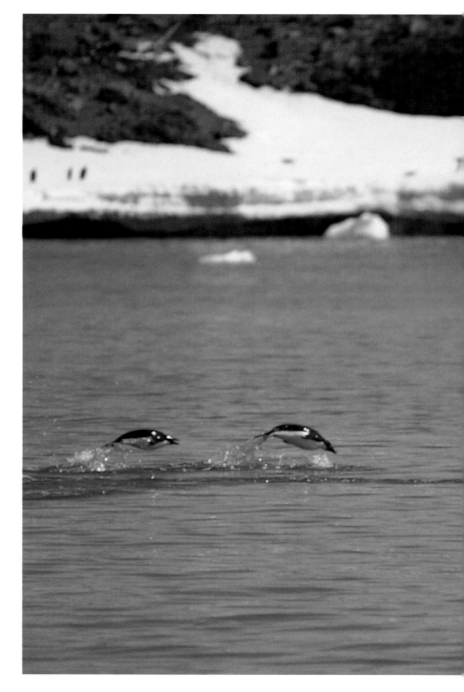

ABOVE *Adélie penguins play follow-the-leader and dive into the sea on a foraging expedition for zooplankton and larval fish – their preferred food.*

RIGHT *Rather clumsy on land, penguins are transformed in the water and swim with consummate ease and agility. These Adélies are 'porpoising', a swimming technique that allows them to snatch a breath without any loss of speed.*

BELOW LEFT *King penguins approach the 4°C (39.2°F) sea without fear of the cold as they are covered in a 2cm (0.8in) layer of fat and have oily waterproof feathers so that they can maintain their constant 38–40°C (100–104°F) body temperature. Apart from insulation, penguins also depend on their fat for energy while they are at the rookery incubating their eggs, and later, moulting.*

BELOW RIGHT *'Porpoising' Adélie's can travel at 20kph (12.5mph) over long distances. In short bursts, they reach speeds of 30kph (19mph).*

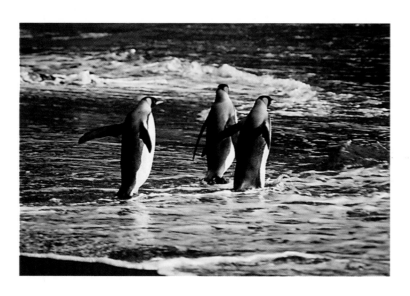

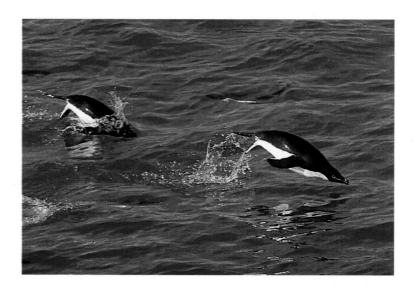

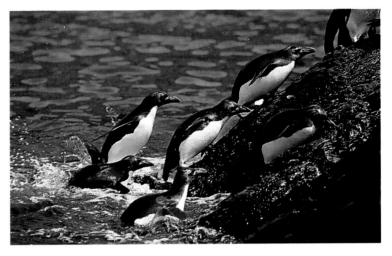

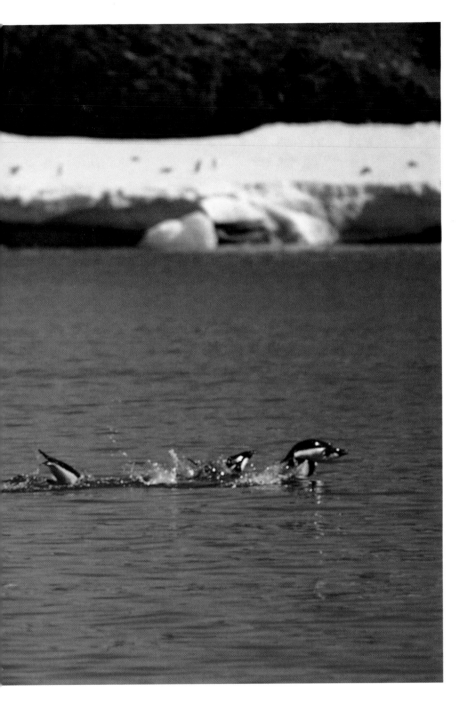

ABOVE *Plump macaroni penguins struggle ashore at Hercules Bay, South Georgia. One of them is using its beak to lever itself up the slippery rocks.*

BELOW LEFT *Macaroni penguins form a small flotilla in the choppy surf before going off to feed. They feed as far as 200km (125 miles) offshore at Marion Island and can often dive to depths of up to 100m (330ft). Macaronis feed mostly on subantarctic euphausiid species and other small zooplankton species.*

BELOW *A king penguin surfs ashore after foraging as far as 300km (190 miles) offshore. These penguins have been recorded to dive to depths of 250m (820ft) in search of lanternfish species – their favourite food. Lanternfish, most less than 160mm (6.5in) in length, belong to the myctophid family and possess light-organs along their sides. By day, they live at depths of around 1000m (3300ft), but migrate closer to the surface at night. These fish form 86 per cent of the diet of the around 220,000 king penguins on Marion Island. About 12,000 tonnes (11,800 tons) are consumed annually by these birds during the breeding season.*

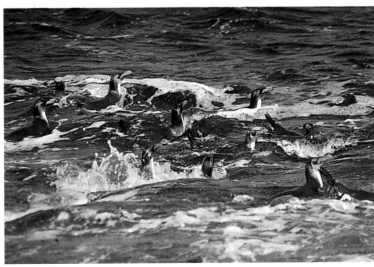

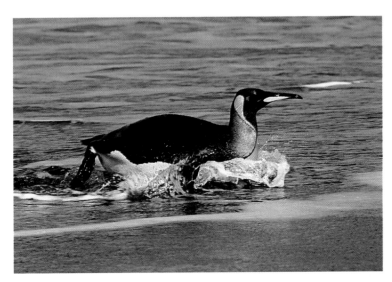

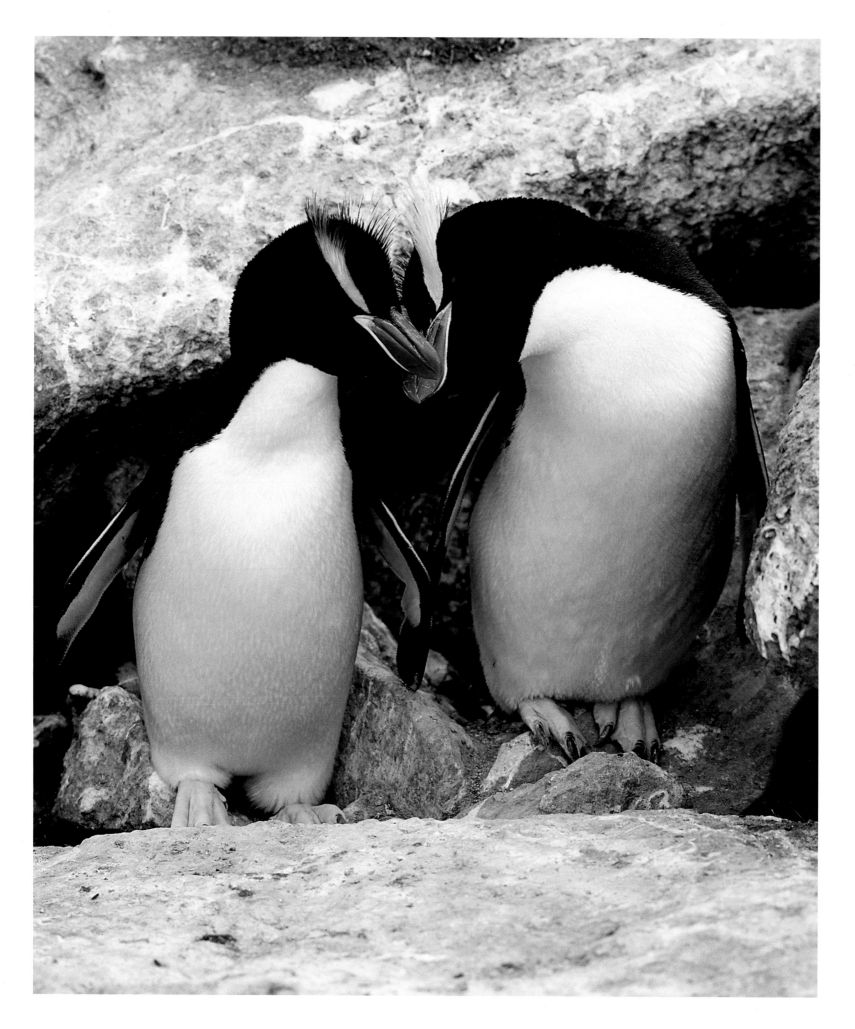

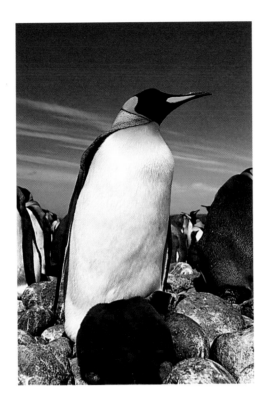

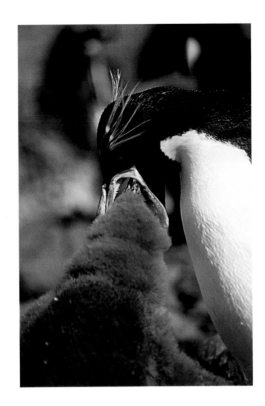

OPPOSITE *Many of the penguin species, including this pair of erect-crested penguins, carry out elaborate 'nest-relief' ceremonies of recognition and greeting when one partner relieves the other at the nest.*

ABOVE LEFT *Neither king nor emperor penguins have a nest; instead they incubate the egg on their feet.*
ABOVE RIGHT *A macaroni penguin disgorges a crop full of large zooplankton species to its chick. Note the backward pointing barbs on the adult's bill which are used to prevent items of prey from escaping.*

BELOW LEFT AND CENTRE *These penguins belong to the genus Eudyptes, characterized by yellow and orange head crests which they flourish during courtship. Crested penguins lay two eggs, one much larger than the other.*
BELOW RIGHT *The unusual and attractive yellow-eyed penguin is the most threatened of all penguin species.*

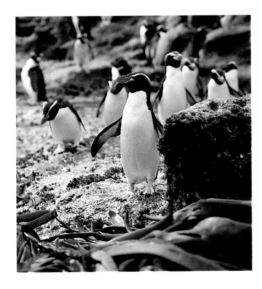

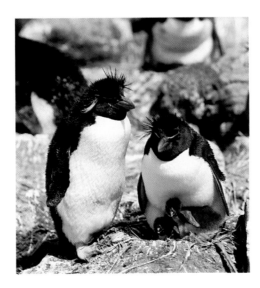

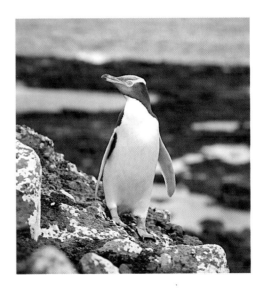

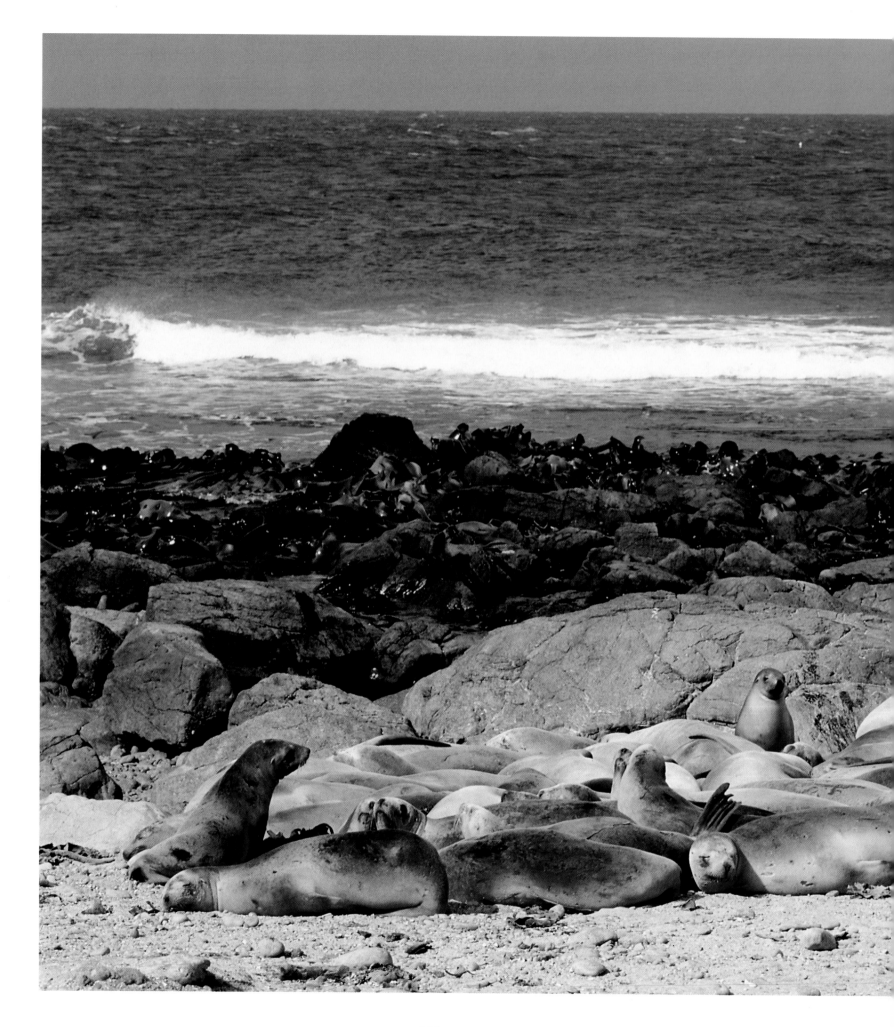

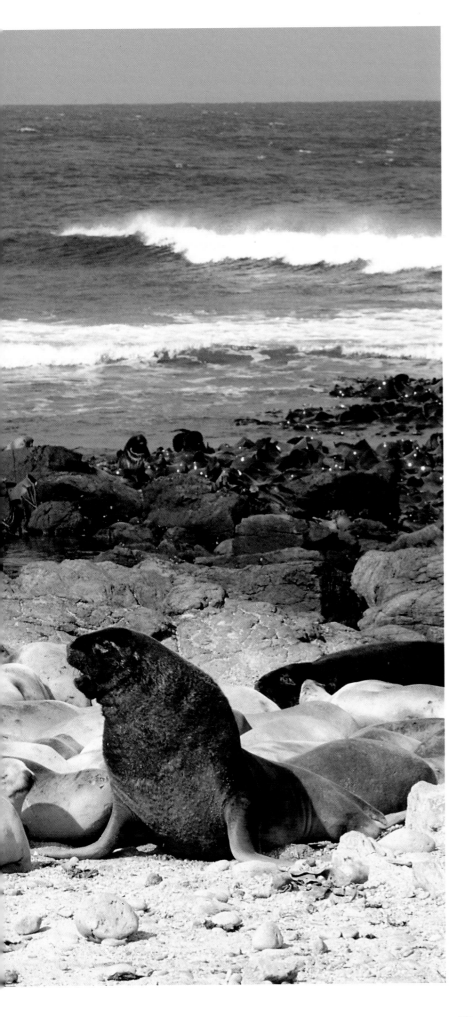

Seals of the islands

On islands all over the subantarctic, a similar script is being followed. Elephant seals are just one of the seal populations that make use of these islands to breed. There are three major breeding stocks on South Georgia, the Kerguelen and Crozet Islands and a fourth on Macquarie. Although elephant seals are found on the other subantarctic islands and on parts of the Antarctic mainland, these are usually the nonbreeding subadults.

Elephant seals are prodigious divers and have been recorded to dive to depths of 1000m (3300ft), lasting as long as 45 minutes, in search of squid and fish. Using tags and satellite tracking of transmitters implanted under the seals' skin, researchers have established that they migrate huge distances from the edge of the pack ice to their island breeding grounds.

Male bulls, characterized by their remarkable trunk, can reach vast proportions of up to 4000kg (8820 lb), making them one of the largest animals other than whales and elephants. Females are smaller, and gather in large breeding herds on beaches which are controlled by the dominant male. The bulls are the first to haul out onto the beaches and it is these 'beachmasters' who will defend their territories and try to protect their harem of females from being poached by young but more inexperienced males. It is tough work and the 24-hour day, seven-day week takes its toll. Most males become heavily scarred from fights and lose up to 25 per cent of their body weight – there is simply no time to go to sea to feed. Pups are born from September to November.

LEFT *On Enderby Island in the New Zealand subantarctic, a Hooker's sea lion bull watches over his harem of females. Unlike true seals, sea lions are able to stand on their foreflippers and turn their hindflippers forward, making them quite agile on land and enabling them to gallop along the beach if required.*

BELOW *Young bull elephant seals doze peacefully in front of the old whaling station at Husvik, South Georgia. In the early part of the 19th century, southern elephant seals had virtually disappeared from all but the most remote islands.*

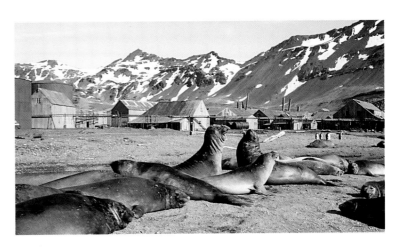

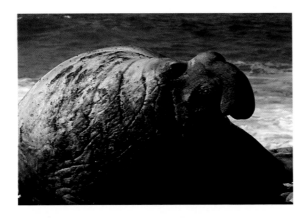
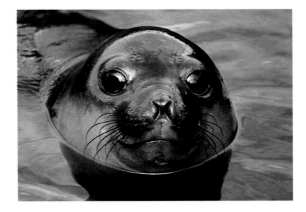
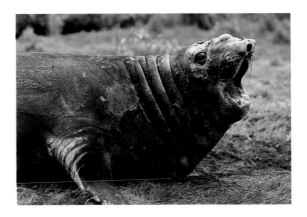
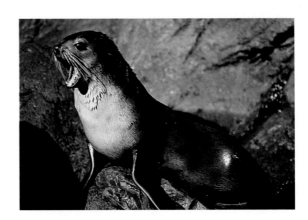

TOP LEFT *A mature southern elephant seal bull. The inflatable trunk, or proboscis, is used primarily for display purposes.*
TOP RIGHT *The southern elephant seal's large eyes may be an adaptation which allows them to see in the dark depths.*

ABOVE LEFT *This elephant seal is moulting but depends on its blubber, a third of its weight, for insulation against the cold.*
ABOVE RIGHT *A subantarctic fur seal stands on a rock on Marion Island — true seals cannot stand on their foreflippers.*

OPPOSITE *A southern fur seal hugs her pup. Fur seals depend on their valuable fur coat, instead of blubber, for insulation.*

The world population of southern elephant seals stands at about 600,000. Inexplicably, however, the numbers of elephant seals in the South Pacific and South Indian oceans have been declining in recent years, despite their protection from the sealers, while elephant seal populations in the South Atlantic have returned to their pre-exploitation numbers. Nevertheless, numbers still exceed the population of the early 1960s when elephant seals were exploited extensively for their blubber. Perhaps this is all part of a long-term change in the delicate natural balance of the Southern Ocean ecosystem, caused by human interference. It will still be some time before all the answers to such questions are unravelled.

Also present on the islands are the southern fur seals. Although not considered to be true seals because of ancestral differences, Antarctic fur seals nevertheless form an important group. They were hunted extensively for their pelts in the late 1700s and early 1800s until their numbers were driven close to extinction, making hunting unprofitable. Since the Convention for the Conservation of Antarctic Seals came into force in 1978, the populations of fur seals have continued to recover rapidly.

Fur seals are quite agile and surprisingly fast on land. Unlike the more placid Weddell and elephant seals, they can be aggressive and temperamental, particularly the larger bulls. These weigh close to 100kg (220lb) and have an impressive mane of fur around their neck when fully grown. The mature males haul out onto traditional beaches from September onwards in order to establish territories and harems which they will then defend ferociously against intruders.

Black woolly pups are born in November and December and are weaned for an extended period by the mothers. When these go to sea to feed in order to maintain their supply of milk, the pups are left behind in crèches. Attractive fur seals are now increasing in number everywhere.

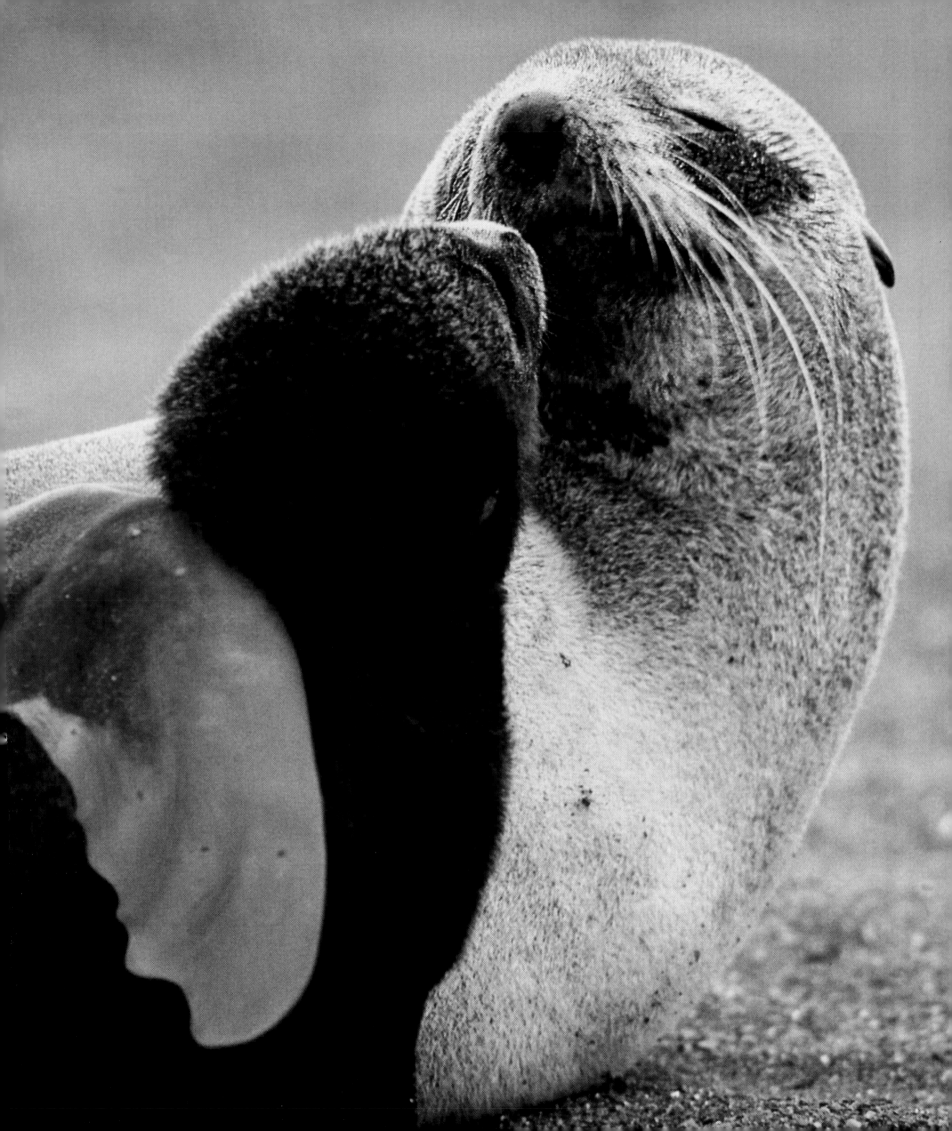

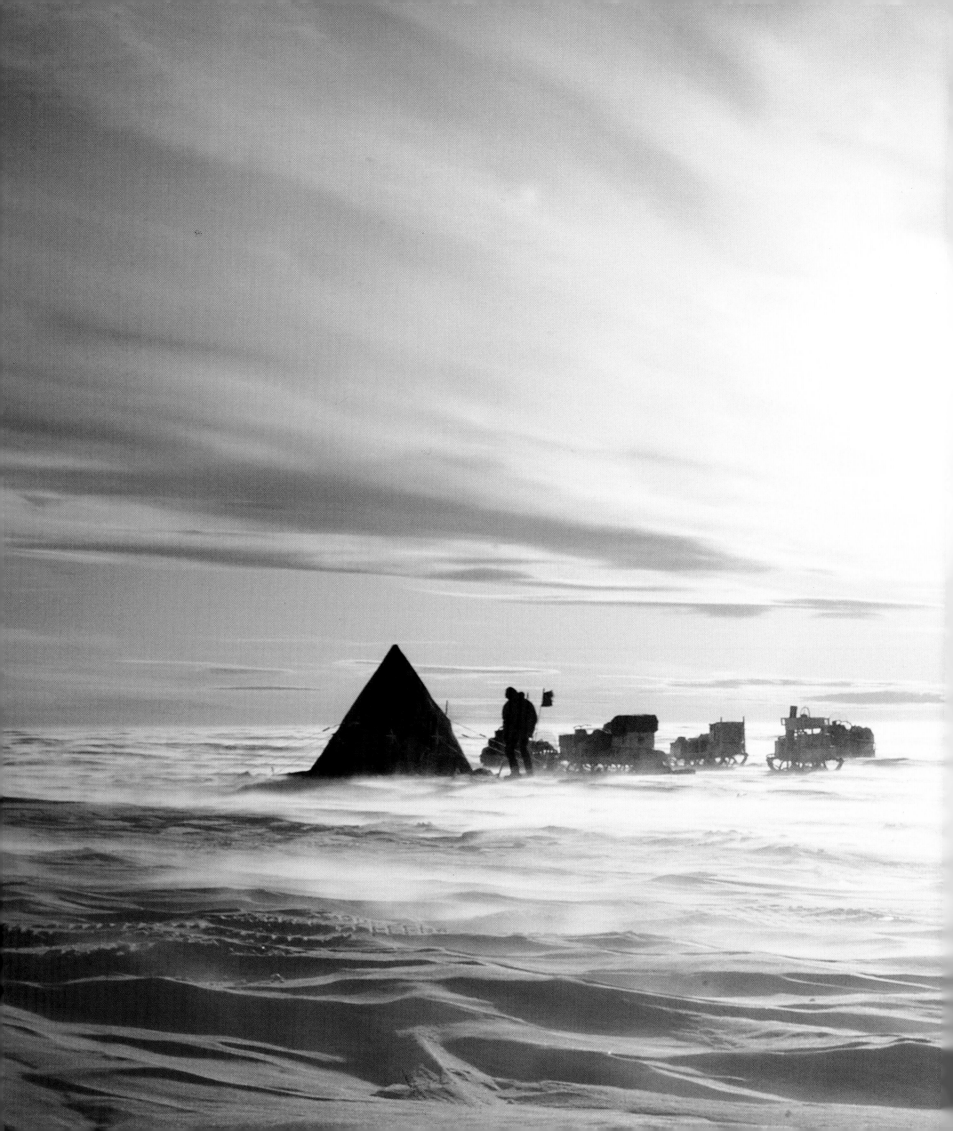

HUMAN INFLUENCES
IN ANTARCTICA

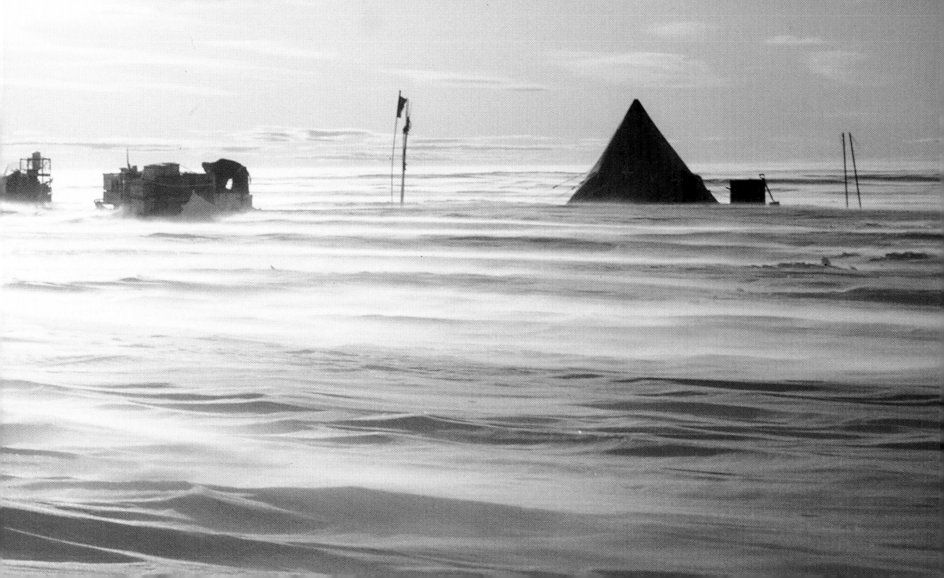

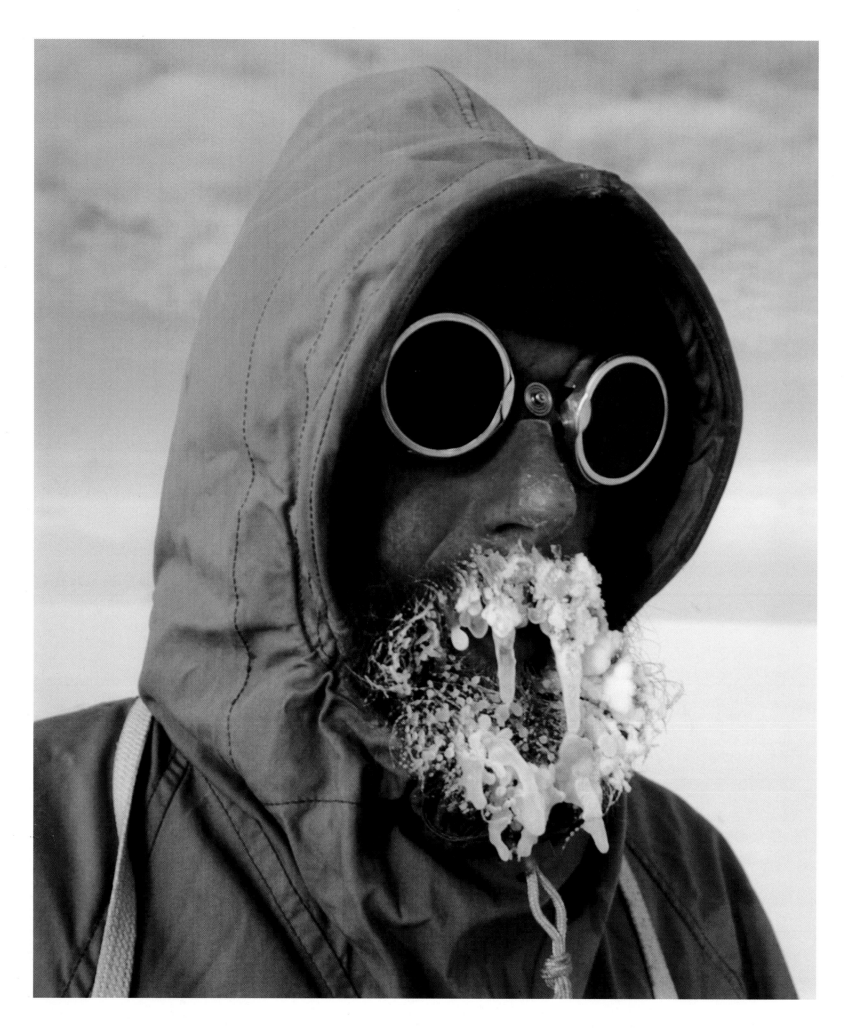

HUMAN INFLUENCES IN ANTARCTICA

From exploitation to conservation

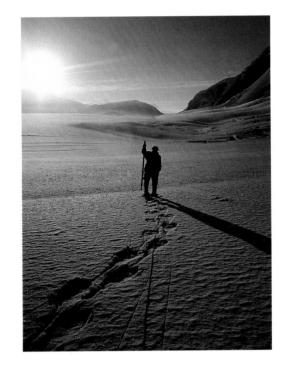

It was less than 200 years ago that exploration of Antarctica first took place. Yet in the intervening years the Antarctic region has been subjected to a series of intrusions by humankind. Initially, some of its natural living resources were severely exploited, followed gradually by the establishment of numerous scientific research bases. And recently, Antarctica has been gaining in popularity as a tourist destination, a development that risks further damaging this already threatened region. In addition, the effects of past as well as present activities have yet to be fully established.

The island of South Georgia witnessed some of the most active whaling and sealing activities in the Antarctic region. Early explorers, seeking *Terra Australis Incognita*, discovered seals and whales in abundance, and whalers and sealers soon established a thriving and profitable trade in oils, blubber, meat and furs to satisfy the demands of Europe and the rest of the world.

In 1904, the Norwegian whaling pioneer, Captain C.A. Larsen, founded the first Antarctic whaling station at Grytviken, in King Edward Cove, South Georgia. Over the next 60 years, more than 54,000 whales were processed there, producing oil to the value of about £25 million (US$40 million). Finally, in 1965, whaling operations ceased almost overnight in response to dramatically declining whale stocks which rendered the whaling industry unprofitable. The whaling station was abandoned but remains there to this day. A museum is located in the old wooden Manager's House, while the chains used to haul the whale carcasses onto the wooden flensing platform, and trypots which sealers used to boil down seal blubber can still be seen on the beaches. In the large rust-streaked sheds, discarded harpoon heads, packed in boxes, are ready to fire from the harpoon guns. Huge boilers, silent forges and the rusting hulks of whalers which lie partially sunken in the harbour at Grytviken all bear mute testimony to the area's sad history of exploitation.

At the height of activities, the station at Grytviken had accommodation for 300 men and even included a cinema, a wooden ski-jump slope and a beautiful wooden church. The station produced whale and sperm whale oil, whale meat, whale bone meal, meat extract and, when freezer ships became available, frozen meat. The factory facilities were capable of processing 25 20m (65ft) whales daily. Initially, only the blubber from the whales was used, boiled down to make edible fats and cooking oils. The carcasses were then simply discarded. Such profligate waste prompted the South Georgia British Administration to introduce legislation compelling the whalers to utilize all of their catch. This resulted in the production of bone meal for fertilizer and the processing of whale meat for human consumption.

ABOVE *Wearing snow shoes and securely roped to his colleague, a scientist probes cautiously ahead for crevasses with a long thin pole.*

LEFT *Icicles, formed as breath condenses in the freezing air, drape the beard of this scientist. In this harsh environment, it is impossible to overestimate the importance of having the right equipment — snow-goggles are essential to prevent snow-blindness from the glare.*

PREVIOUS PAGES *Alone in a wind-blown snowy wilderness, a remote field camp at 79°S emerges from a clearing blizzard beneath the midnight sun. Weather patterns are notoriously unpredictable in Antarctica, as many explorers and scientists have found to their cost.*

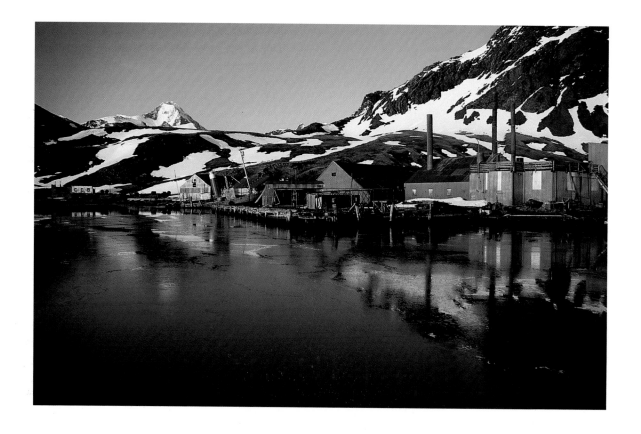

ABOVE *The abandoned whaling station at Grytviken, South Georgia, lies in silent testimony to a once-thriving industry.*

With hindsight and a better appreciation of the reproductive biology and distribution of whales, it is clear that such heavy exploitation of whales was not sustainable. However attitudes then were different and the seriousness of the whalers' impact on whale stocks was not sufficiently well appreciated. Although the South Georgia British Administration attempted to control whaling by restricting the numbers of whale-catcher vessels and shore-based stations, as well as protecting females and their calves, this was not enough. The nail in the coffin came in 1925 with the invention of stern-slip factory ships which allowed whales to be pursued, caught and processed on the high seas without the constraints of international law or national sovereignty.

Recognizing this problem, the League of Nations instituted the International Convention for the Regulation of Whaling in 1935, in a first attempt to control the industry. It provided protection for some species and also set aside a sanctuary, but it did not go so far as to regulate the number of whales that could be caught. Furthermore, five major whaling nations refused to accede to their regulations. Later, in 1946 the International Whaling Commission (IWC) was established to protect whale stocks. However, the IWC proved to be just as ineffective as the previous Convention, for similar reasons. In 1960, the year in which the

Antarctic Treaty became effective, whaling nations killed the largest number of whales ever: 66,000 worldwide. Whale stocks around South Georgia had ceased to exist. Killed by its own hand, the industry collapsed overnight and the station at Grytviken was abandoned in 1965. In the last season of worldwide commercial whaling (1985–86), fewer than 8000 whales were caught, mostly the smaller species that had previously been overlooked. Many of the larger species had been pushed to the brink of extinction, including the blue whale.

To halt this decline the IWC, in 1982, introduced a moratorium on all whaling operations, effective from 1986. Now, under the protection of the IWC and with the cooperation of the Commission for the Conservation of Antarctic Marine Living Resources (CCAMLR), signed in May 1980, whales enjoy much better protection than in the past. Some whale stocks have shown a pronounced recovery, including that of the southern right whale which migrates to South African, South American and Australian waters from the subantarctic to calve and mate, before returning to its feeding grounds. Their increased numbers form the basis of an expanding whale-watching tourist industry along these coasts. Another success story is the population growth of southern minke whales which now stand in the range of 514,000 to 1,138,000 individuals. But, for the blue whale, the largest animal ever known to have lived on earth, it may be too late: of the estimated 25,000 which once roamed the Antarctic seas, only about 460 now survive. Researchers are still unsure whether the blue whales will ever recover to anything approximating their former numbers, despite having been protected since the late 1960s.

There is hope for the future, however. The Indian Ocean was declared a sanctuary for whales, dolphins and porpoises in 1979. The establishment of a Southern Ocean Whale Sanctuary was approved at the IWC's meeting in Puerto Vallarta, Mexico, in 1994 by an overwhelming majority, with only Japan voting against it. The sanctuary encompasses an area of some 50 million km^2 (19 million sq miles). Environmentalists claim that this vast whale haven will protect at least three-quarters of the world's remaining baleen whale population, which has been diminished by years of commercial whaling to about 1.6 million individuals in 1995.

Although the economic value of whales as a harvestable resource is substantial, the economic returns from whaling are now rivalled in many instances by those generated from benign activities, such as whale-watching, which generated a staggering US$300 million worldwide in 1992. Undeniably there are stocks of minke whales that could be harvested on a sustainable basis, but a worldwide shift in attitudes and ethics means that today, whales have a greater value alive than dead.

BELOW *Grytviken whaling station provided the whale oil that lit London's street lights in the early 1900s. The clearly visible white wooden house, the old Station Manager's house, has now become a whaling museum along with the rest of the station. It was established in 1992 by the Commissioner for South Georgia and was then placed under the guidance of the South Georgia Museum Trust.*

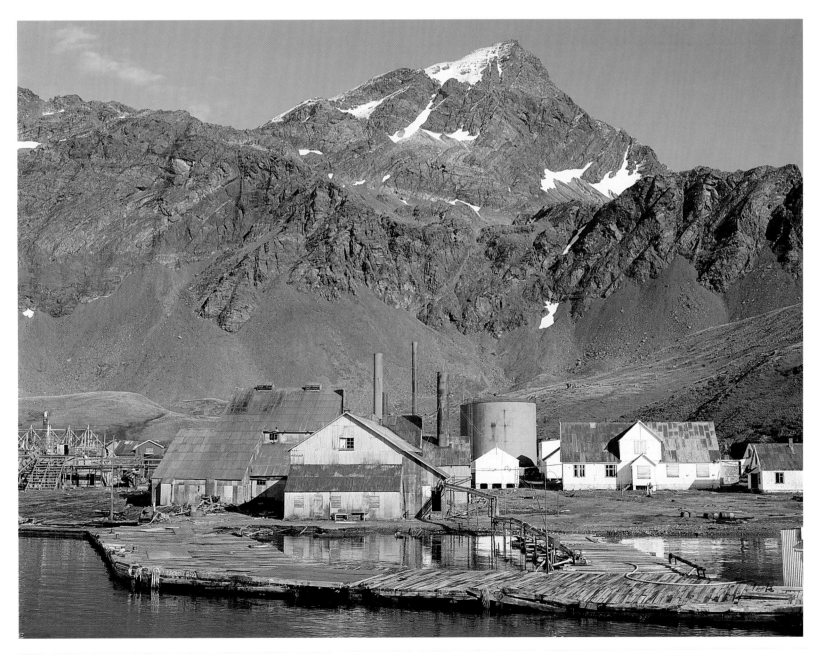

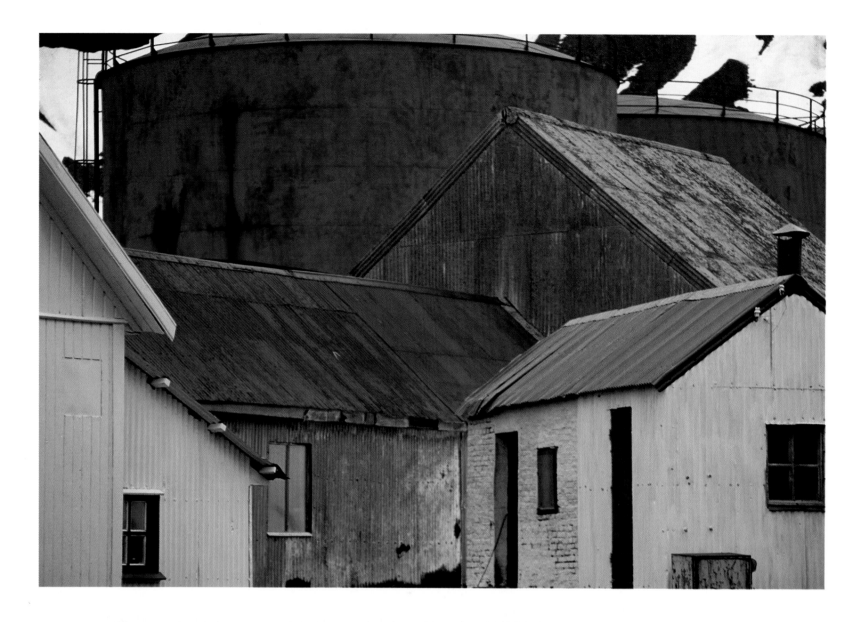

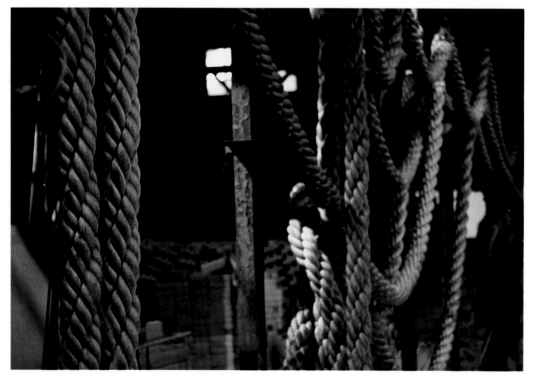

ABOVE *Wooden buildings, rust-streaked corrugated iron roofs and huge whale-oil storage drums at Grytviken are all reminders of its tragic history.*

LEFT *Braided mooring ropes, which were used to secure the floating whale carcasses to the boats, still hang neatly coiled in Grytviken's sheds.*

OPPOSITE *The Grytviken museum complex includes three whale-catcher vessels. Petrel, shown here, is the best preserved and the only vessel still floating. Built in 1929 in Oslo, she was converted from whaling to seal-catching in 1957 when whale stocks were scarce. Partly restored, the boat is now permanently moored alongside the whaling station; the harpoon and gun platform are visible on the prow, while the 'crow's nest', or lookout point, is high up on the mast.*

Elephant seals and fur seals were also harvested – for their blubber and pelts respectively – particularly, in the case of elephant seals, once whale stocks had been depleted. Exploitation began in the late 1700s and, along with fur seal hunting, continued widely until 1822 when the reduction in numbers made hunting uneconomical. The sealing industry lingered on until the early 1900s at Macquarie and until 1964 at South Georgia. Antarctic seals are now fully protected by the Convention for the Conservation of Antarctic Seals (CCAS) which came into force in 1978 and, since then, there has been no more commercial sealing of any of the Antarctic species.

Seals in temperate waters around the world enjoy much less protection. Furious debate, and antagonism, exists between fishermen who view seals as competition, those conservationists who would support sustainable exploitation, and the public who generally abhor seal culling.

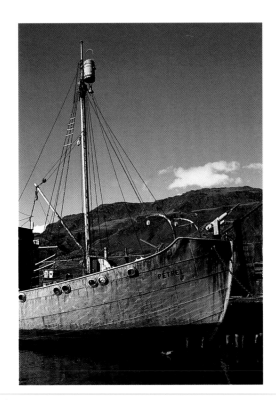

Commercial fishing

Before 1960, commercial fishing in Antarctica was not a serious proposition since fish stocks worldwide had been sufficiently abundant closer to home. But, with diminishing stocks and political changes which extended national sovereignty to 200 nautical miles from the coast for many nations, access to the world's richest coastal fishing grounds was now denied to many. Fishing fleets looked to Antarctica, and commercial fishing was soon established. During 1970, 400,000 tonnes (393,600 tons) of fish were taken, mainly near South Georgia. However, this rate of exploitation was not sustainable and the catch fell to only 50,000 tonnes (49,200 tons) in 1971. Since then, stocks have recovered somewhat and fishing is regulated with an annual quota of about 100,000 tonnes (98,400 tons).

Before whale stocks were severely depleted due to whaling activities, it was estimated that baleen whales consumed some 800 million tonnes (790 million tons) of Antarctic krill annually. By 1965, however, whale stocks were so low in number that only about 190 million tonnes (187 million tons) were consumed. A huge surplus seemed there for the taking. Tales of a vast and lucrative industry abounded, but it was not that simple. In the absence of whales, it is believed that other consumers of Antarctic krill such as birds, seals and fish took advantage of the surplus, while estimates of Antarctic krill abundance were fraught with difficulty and inaccuracy. Nevertheless, by 1977 a commercial Antarctic krill fishery was in existence which, by 1982, was harvesting about 500,000 tonnes (492,000 tons) annually. The annual take has moderated to about 250,000–300,000 tonnes (246,000–295,200 tons), making it the largest crustacean fishery in the world and accounting for 10 per cent of crustaceans taken worldwide.

THE SOUTHERN OCEAN WHALE SANCTUARY

THE SOUTHERN OCEAN WHALE SANCTUARY

Antarctic Convergence

WWF IN ANTARCTICA

Founded in 1961 by, among others, Sir Peter Scott, only child of Captain Robert Falcon Scott, the World Wide Fund for Nature (WWF) is one of the world's largest independent, international conservation organizations with 29 affiliate and associate national organizations around the world. With its headquarters in Gland, Switzerland, and with almost six million regular supporters, its aim is to raise money to support conservation projects worldwide.

In Antarctica, WWF was instrumental in the establishment of the International Whaling Commission's (IWC) Southern Ocean Whale Sanctuary, an area of approximately 50 million km² (19 million sq miles) which was set aside in 1994 for whale protection (see map, left). It has been demarcated as an area that would exclude hunting should the IWC decide at some future date to allow sustainable whale harvesting, but is concerned only with the whales themselves and not with their food supply or habitat requirements. Nevertheless, it is an important victory for the WWF conservation lobby and in keeping with the principles of the Madrid Protocol and CCAMLR.

One of the other Antarctic conservation projects supported by WWF–Australia is a 1995/96 population census of albatrosses and other threatened seabirds on subantarctic islands such as the Antipodes, Disappointment and Auckland. It is estimated that as many as 44,000 of these birds die annually when they swoop after the bait on tuna long-lines paid out from commercial boats. In New Zealand, it is thought that between one and five birds die each time a single bluefin tuna long-line is set. Such profligate slaughter cannot be allowed to continue, and it is the aim of the WWF to prevent this. Supported by WWF, Japanese, Australian and New Zealand fishermen are seeking ways to reduce the albatross bycatch.

Global dangers

It is not just marine life which needs to be protected. The Antarctic region is being increasingly affected by human activites elsewhere in the world. Due largely to industrial activity since the 18th century, 'greenhouse gas' concentrations are increasing, notably that of carbon dioxide originating primarily from fossil fuel combustion. Atmospheric carbon dioxide concentrations are expected to double from 1950s' levels by the year 2050. Models of resulting global warming anticipate temperature increases of about 0.5°C (0.9°F) per decade, perhaps more over Antarctica. A question frequently asked is whether or not this will cause the ice sheet to melt. This depends on the relative rates of ice accumulation and ice melt. Recent studies predict that polar latitudes will warm faster and more than equatorial regions, but that this will result in increased precipitation over the ice sheets and in an accumulation of ice.

Since 1960, there has indeed been an increase in the East Antarctic ice sheet accumulation rate, but by contrast, the Wordie Ice Shelf on the western side of the Antarctic Peninsula has shrunk considerably from 2000km² (772 sq miles) in 1966 to approximately 700km² (270 sq miles) in 1989. In August 1995, Norwegian scientists reported that sea ice in Antarctica is decreasing in extent by about 1.4 per cent per decade. This coincides with an increase in average southern hemisphere temperature of 2.5°C (4.5°F) in the last 50 years, emphasising the link between ice cover and climate.

Could this be evidence for global warming or simply natural changes in the earth's climatic cycle? It is still too early to say, but by probing deep into the ice sheet, glaciologists are uncovering a treasure chest of scientific information about the world. Air, dust and elements trapped in the ice allow scientists to look back in time and unravel the climate history of the earth, possibly providing a window into the future. Results from the 2083m- (6834ft-) long Vostok ice core retrieved in 1961 show that the earth's climate has undergone considerable natural variability with a strong link between 'greenhouse gases' in the atmosphere and global warming or cooling. Today, we are participating in a global experiment of our own making in which only future generations will know the results.

In the mid-1970s, two British scientists, Farman and Molina, made the startling discovery that stratospheric ozone concentrations in the atmosphere over Antarctica had been decreasing steadily over the last 20 years, leading to the description of the 'ozone hole' which occurs each spring. Indeed, in each successive year since, the size and extent of the ozone hole has worsened so that countries such as Argentina, Chile, South Africa, Australia and New Zealand in particular, are adversely affected. Ozone is of immense global importance as it protects the earth from the harmful rays of the sun, notably excessive and damaging UV-B radiation which has hazardous health implications for humans, plants and animals.

The culprits identified in the destruction of the ozone layer are chlorofluorocarbons (CFCs), a group of extremely stable, long-lived, low-toxicity, man-made industrial gases. When released into the atmosphere, they slowly accumulate above the stratospheric ozone layer. Here, a photochemical reaction involving chlorine and ozone takes place in the presence of sunlight and UV-B radiation, resulting in the breakdown of ozone.

The extent of the seasonal ozone hole is determined mainly by the strong circumpolar winds occurring during the extreme cold of winter, known as the Polar Vortex, which isolate the air over Antarctica from the rest of the global atmosphere. When these winds relax in summer, ozone from beyond the reaches of the Polar Vortex floods into the ozone hole so that by December, ozone concentrations in the hole have risen again. Recently, ozone depletion over the Arctic region has also been observed.

THE GREENHOUSE EFFECT

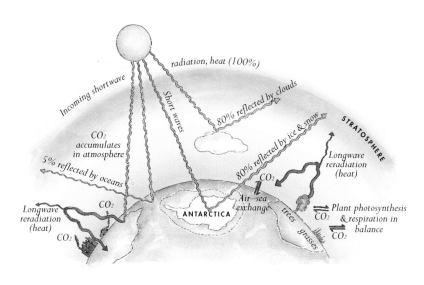

LEFT The so-called 'greenhouse' gases, notably carbon dioxide (CO_2), methane, CFCs, nitrous oxides and water vapour act like a blanket for the earth, keeping it about 33°C (91°F) warmer than if they were absent from the atmosphere. The gases act by being transparent to incoming shortwave radiation, but are mostly opaque to outgoing longwave radiation. However, due largely to industrial fossil fuel combustion, atmospheric CO_2 concentrations are expected to double to about 560 parts per million by the year 2050, with an expected increase in global temperatures of about 0.5°C (0.9°F) per decade. The most important of the greenhouse gases, CO_2, is produced mostly in the industrial northern hemisphere and atmospheric circulation distributes the CO_2 right around the globe. Importantly, clouds, snow and ice reradiate about 80 per cent of the incoming heat. The oceans and plants (through photosynthesis and respiration) normally control the concentration of atmospheric CO_2, but now it is not really known when, or even if, these natural processes will be able to slow down or stop global warming.

OZONE SHIELD AND FORMATION

OZONE DESTRUCTION

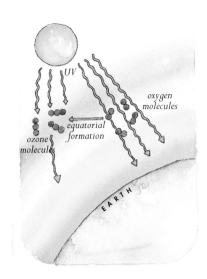

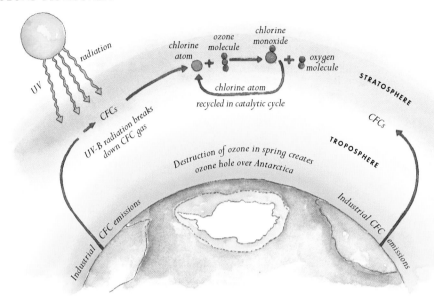

ABOVE *This illustration explains how ozone shields the earth from UV-B radiation and also how ozone is formed from oxygen in equatorial latitudes where UV-B radiation is strong. UV-B splits up two oxygen molecules into four oxygen atoms which then regroup into ozone and a single oxygen atom. This seeks more single oxygen atoms with which to combine, thus producing O_2 or O_3 in a continuing process.*

ABOVE *The illustration explains how UV-B radiation from the sun destroys Antarctica's protective stratospheric ozone layer in the austral spring (October) when the sun once more illuminates the region. When the CFCs are released into the earth's atmosphere, UV-B breaks this gas down into its components of chlorine, fluorine, bromine and carbon (see text). Chlorine gas then catalytically combines with an ozone molecule (O_3), splitting it to form chlorine monoxide and oxygen. However, in a catalytic cycle that is not yet completely understood, the chlorine monoxide molecules combine with other chemicals which in turn decompose to liberate free chlorine again. Thus, each chlorine atom released by the decomposition of a CFC molecule can go on to destroy many tens of thousands of ozone molecules before the chlorine atom finally returns to the earth's surface.*

However, satellite imagery shows that this is considerably less marked because the stratospheric temperatures here are warmer than over the Antarctic. Consequently, the circumpolar wind vortex is much weaker than in Antarctica, resulting in a better mixing of air in the atmosphere.

In 1987 most of the major industrial nations became signatories to the Montreal Protocol (later revised in 1990). This called for a 50 per cent reduction in substances that deplete the ozone layer by 1995, an 85 per cent reduction by 1997 and a complete phase-out by the year 2000. Between 1986 and 1991, worldwide consumption of CFCs decreased by 40 per cent, particularly in the developed world. However, the picture is less rosy for developing countries where the economics of phasing out CFCs are likely to be costly and rather protracted.

The marine environment is also at risk from global pollution. The oceans are not static and currents originating in the northern hemisphere ultimately arrive in Antarctica. These atmospheric circulation patterns can also introduce foreign material into the Antarctic marine system. In this way, radioactive material produced in above-ground nuclear tests during the 1960s later reached Antarctica's waters. Toxins such as DDT and other chemical insecticides have been found in Adélie penguins, while traces of mercury have been discovered in Adélie and emperor penguin eggs. Higher concentrations may be found in petrels and skuas which migrate annually to the northern hemisphere.

The danger to marine birds posed by plastics, particularly polyethylene beads, is also significant. Again, those species which migrate into equatorial or northern hemisphere latitudes are the ones most affected. Blue petrels and great shearwaters in particular ingest these floating beads, mistaking them for small crustaceans, and present them to their chicks.

LEFT *This satellite image reveals the average monthly ozone concentration over Antarctica for October 1992. The image was recorded by the Total Ozone Mapping Spectrometer (TOMS) instrument on the NIMBUS-7 satellite. Images such as these now allow for daily ozone measurements and warming forecasts. Since 1970, total ozone over Antarctica in spring has fallen by 50 per cent.*

The human factor

It is vital that Antarctica be spared further damage but, at the same time, it is unrealistic to expect human involvement to cease altogether. If the region is to become a World Heritage Site, as some have argued for, then parts of the continent must still be made accessible to people wishing to experience this wilderness. Outmoded concepts of conservation in which an environment could only be preserved if humans were removed from the scene are giving way cautiously to more pragmatic approaches.

In the 1992–93 Antarctic summer season about 6500 tourists (twice that of previous seasons) on 21 tour ships visited the continent, primarily exploring the ice-free and beautiful Antarctic Peninsula. This rapid increase in Antarctic tourism has resulted in a conflict of interests between scientists and tourists who are inevitably drawn to research bases where they run the risk of disrupting scientific programmes and disturbing the penguin and seal colonies being studied. Trampling of slow-growing mosses and other vegetation can also be serious, particularly on some of the subantarctic islands. Proper management measures need to be adopted and, to this end, the tourist industry finally introduced internal regulations in 1991, forming the International Association of Antarctic Tour Operators (IAATO).

RIGHT *A tour ship pushes slowly south from Paradise Bay through the dramatic Lemaire Channel. This is a narrow waterway lying in a geological fault line flanked by the towering cliffs of the Antarctic Peninsula and Booth Island.*

BELOW *In the tranquil beauty of Paradise Bay on the Danco Coast, along the Antarctic Peninsula, inflatable boats give tourists an unparalleled opportunity to leave the ship and get closer to nature: to feel the spray, to touch the ice floes and to see penguins and seals twisting and turning in the clear blue water.*

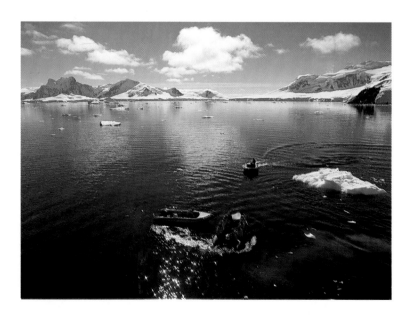

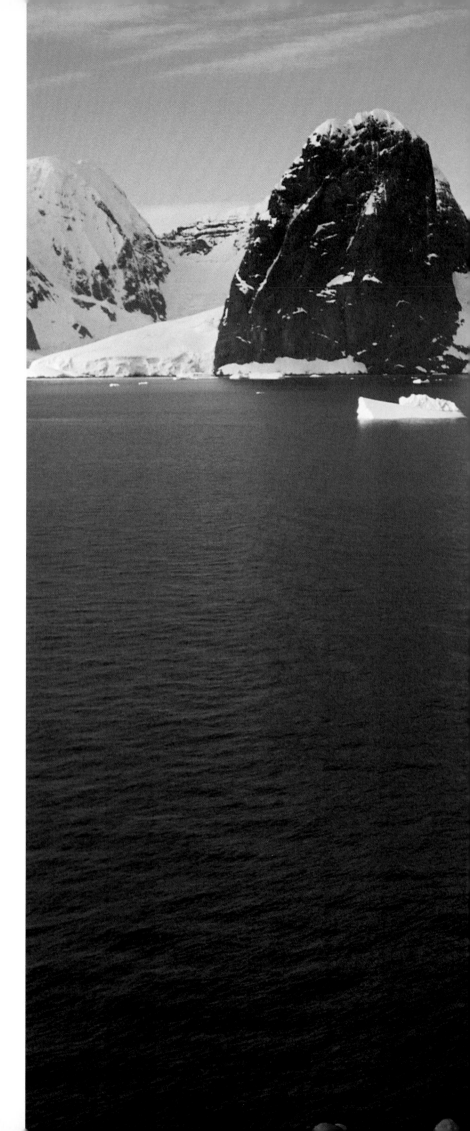

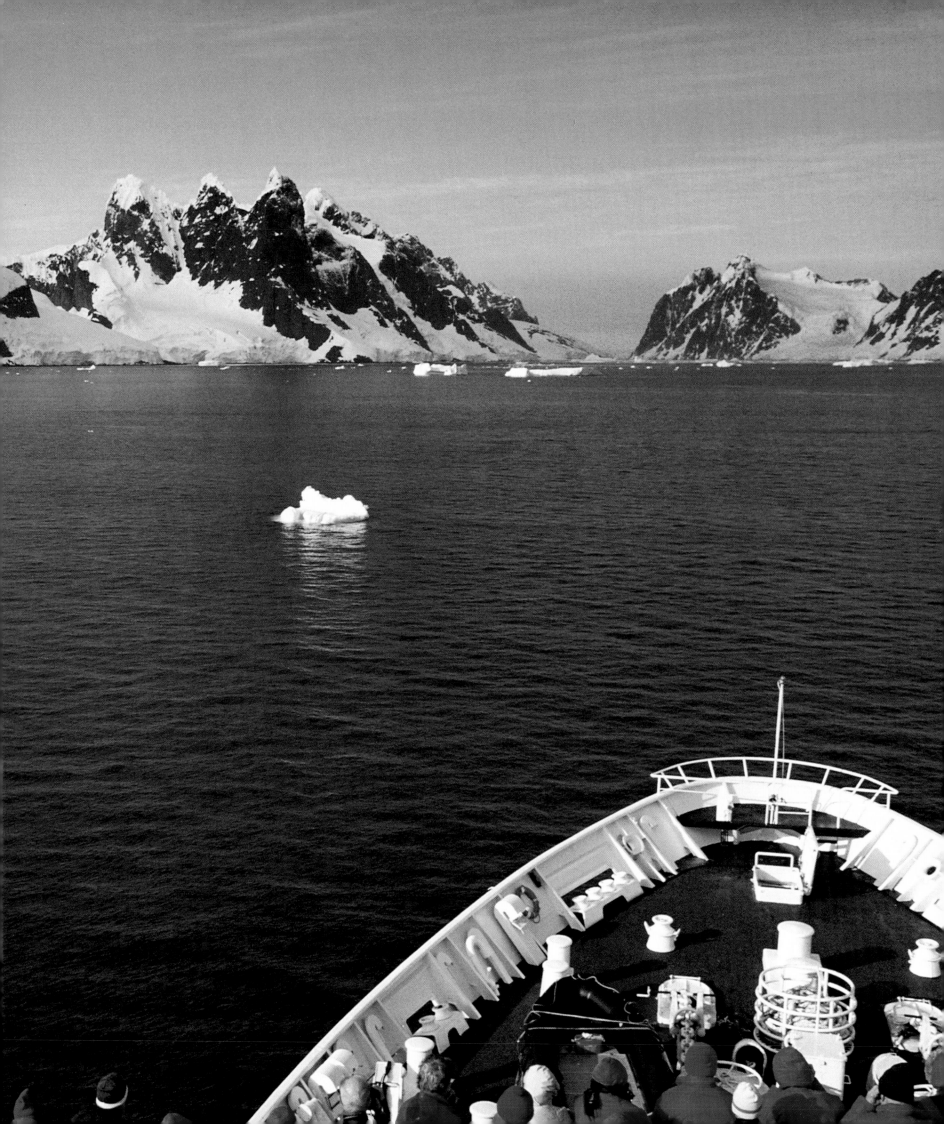

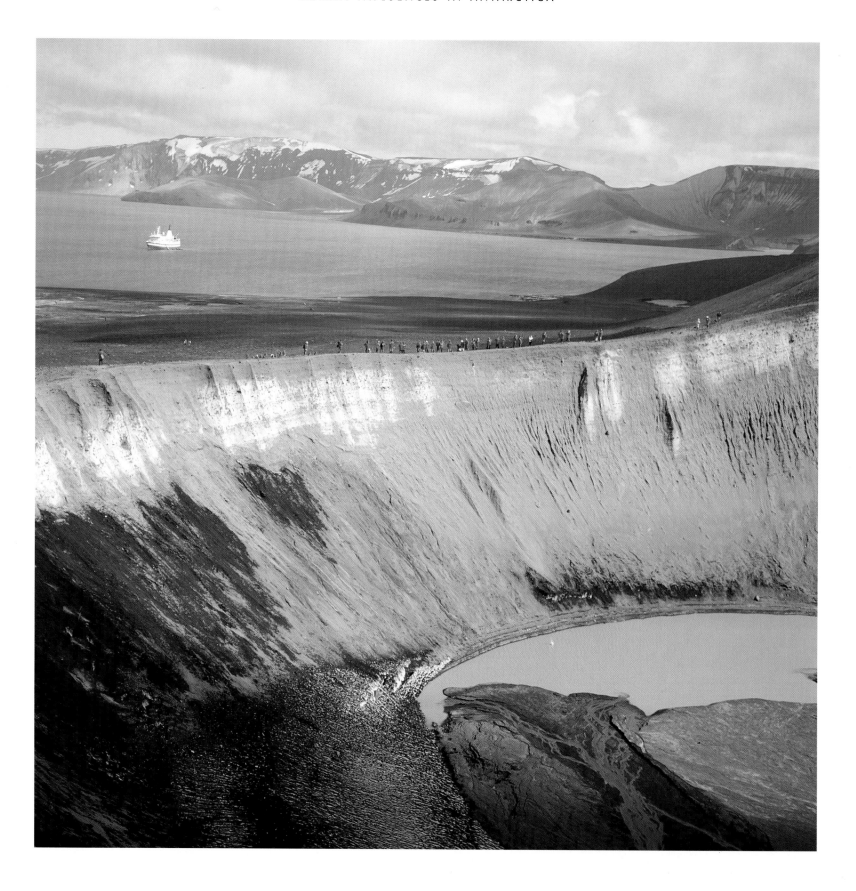

ABOVE *Brought ashore by inflatable boats from the Society Explorer, tourists explore the ash-covered rim of a volcanic caldera on Deception Island, part of the South Shetlands group. In 1968, volcanic activity destroyed the deserted whaling station.*

OPPOSITE TOP *A wandering albatross has its space invaded by no less than 40 curious enthusiasts. While the albatross may seem unconcerned, by monitoring the bird's heartbeat for signs of stress, scientific tests have shown that this is actually far from true.*

OPPOSITE BOTTOM LEFT *Tourists watch the bows of their ship slowly force a way through the pack ice.*
OPPOSITE BOTTOM RIGHT *A group of tourists on board an inflatable boat stares in fascination at the cathedral-like beauty of an ancient blue iceberg.*

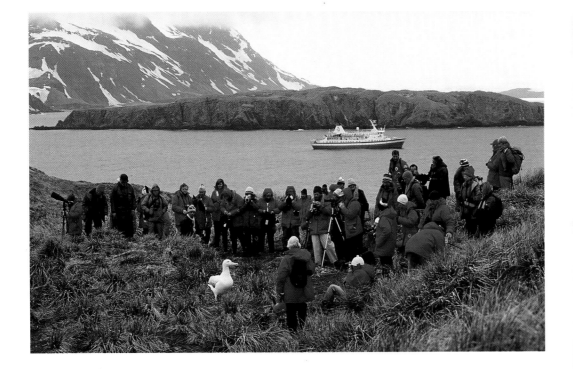

- Regular scheduled visits for the general public began in the 1950s; most ships sailed from South America to the Antarctic Peninsula.
- Chartered flights to the Antarctic Peninsula ice strips and scenic flights to the Ross Ice Shelf, the Transantarctic Mountains and Mt. Erebus were common from 1977 to 1980. However, these were discontinued after an Air New Zealand DC-10 crashed on the slopes of Mt. Erebus in November 1979, killing all 257 people on board.
- Seaborne tourism took off in 1984 with the regular sailing of two luxury purpose-built cruise ships, *Lindblad Explorer* and the *World Discoverer*, from New Zealand and Australian ports to the Ross Sea region, and from South America to the Antarctic Peninsula.
- During the 1987/88 season, about 3000 tourists visited Antarctica; by 1992/93, this figure had doubled.
- Since the collapse of the Soviet Union, a number of their logistical polar resupply and research vessels have been bought by tour operators. Powerful ice-breakers, these ships can penetrate into the pack ice of the Ross and Weddell seas, making new areas accessible.
- Facilities on board these ice-breakers include *en-suite* cabins, gymnasia, an auditorium where experts provide lectures, libraries, bars, excellent cuisine, an experienced captain (often Russian), and a tour manager. Some ships even boast an indoor heated swimming pool and a sauna. There is also always a ship's doctor and onboard hospital. Helicopter flights and inflatable boat landings are a regular feature.
- By far the majority of tourist ships follow the western Antarctic Peninsula route to about 66°S. But, during the 1996/97 season, the first Antarctic circumnavigation will take place aboard the *Kapitan Khlebnikov*. The voyage is scheduled to take 66 days.

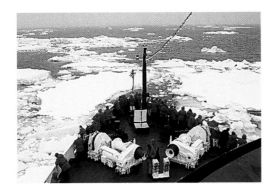

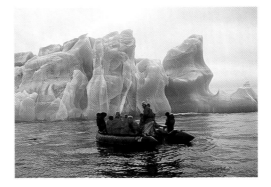

However, it is not just tourists who are visiting Antarctica in increasing numbers; there are now over 60 scientific research bases on Antarctica and the subantarctic islands. All require logistical support by air or sea and the infrastructure is considerable. In the early years there was little concern for environmental conservation. Seals and penguins were used for food and oil, and some king and emperor penguin colonies were severely affected. Older bases at the turn of the century accumulated an impressive amount of rubbish which was usually dumped into a convenient gully or the sea. Oil spills have occurred and human waste disposal was also rather haphazard initially. Today many of the older bases need replacing, but some are now 20m (65ft) or more beneath floating ice shelves.

Current legislation, in the form of the 1991 Protocol on Environmental Protection, states that they and all pollutants be removed, and where new bases are proposed, exhaustive Environmental Impact Assessment procedures are mandatory before permission can be granted for any building to take place.

Fortunately, most scientific bases are now models of responsibility and their impact on the environment is negligible. Furthermore, the sad history of environmental degradation elsewhere in the world has provided a salutary lesson. With the Antarctic community largely freed from political pressures and bound by Antarctic Treaty regulations and the Madrid Protocol, the conservation of Antarctica and the management of science has every likelihood of success.

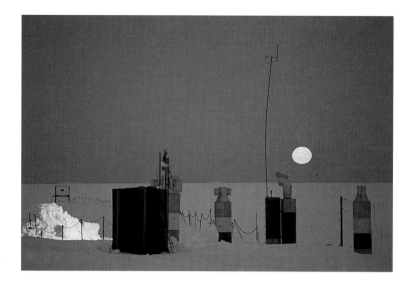

ABOVE *The moon rises dramatically over the South African SANAE III base. Light floods out onto a snow pile from the base's entrance, a trap door which leads to the buckled scientific and living quarters 25m (80ft) beneath the ice. Inexorably crushed by the weight of the ice, the base was declared unfit for occupation in January 1995 and the scientists were evacuated as a result.*

RIGHT *Tending to his instruments, a meteorologist appears silhouetted against a blood-red sky as he strains to see the spring sun appear over the horizon after the long dark winter months. The base is SANAE III, now unoccupied. In the interests of environmental conservation, it will have to be painstakingly removed piece by piece and returned to South Africa. A new base is being built on the nunatak of Vesleskarvet, 150km (90 miles) inland. By building the base on rocks, it is hoped that its lifespan will exceed that of bases built on the ice. Weather conditions permitting, completion and occupation have been planned for 1995/96.*

BELOW *A remote scientific field party, in pyramid tents on the Ronne Ice Shelf, experience the ultimate in solitude under a hazy midnight sun.*

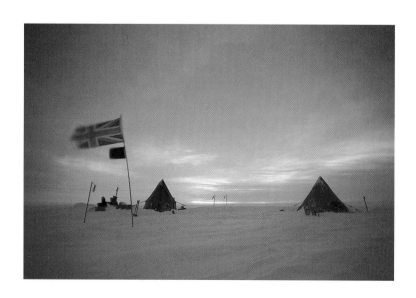

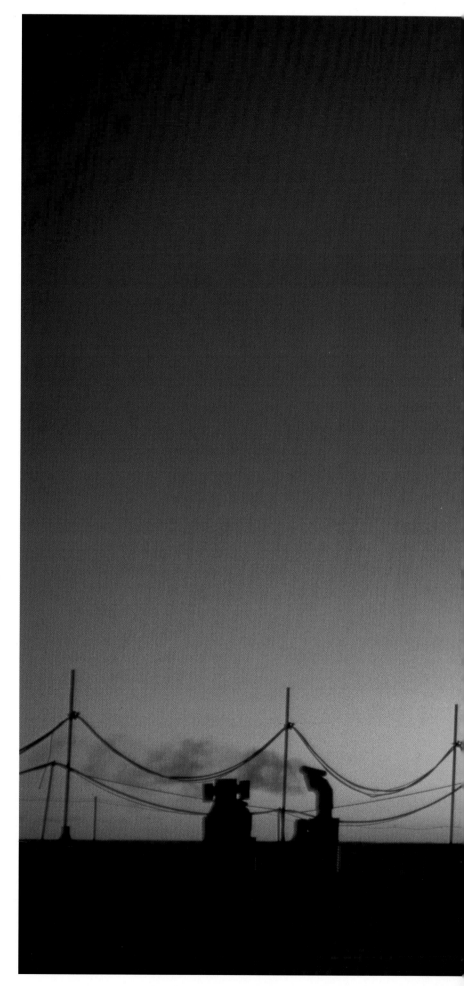

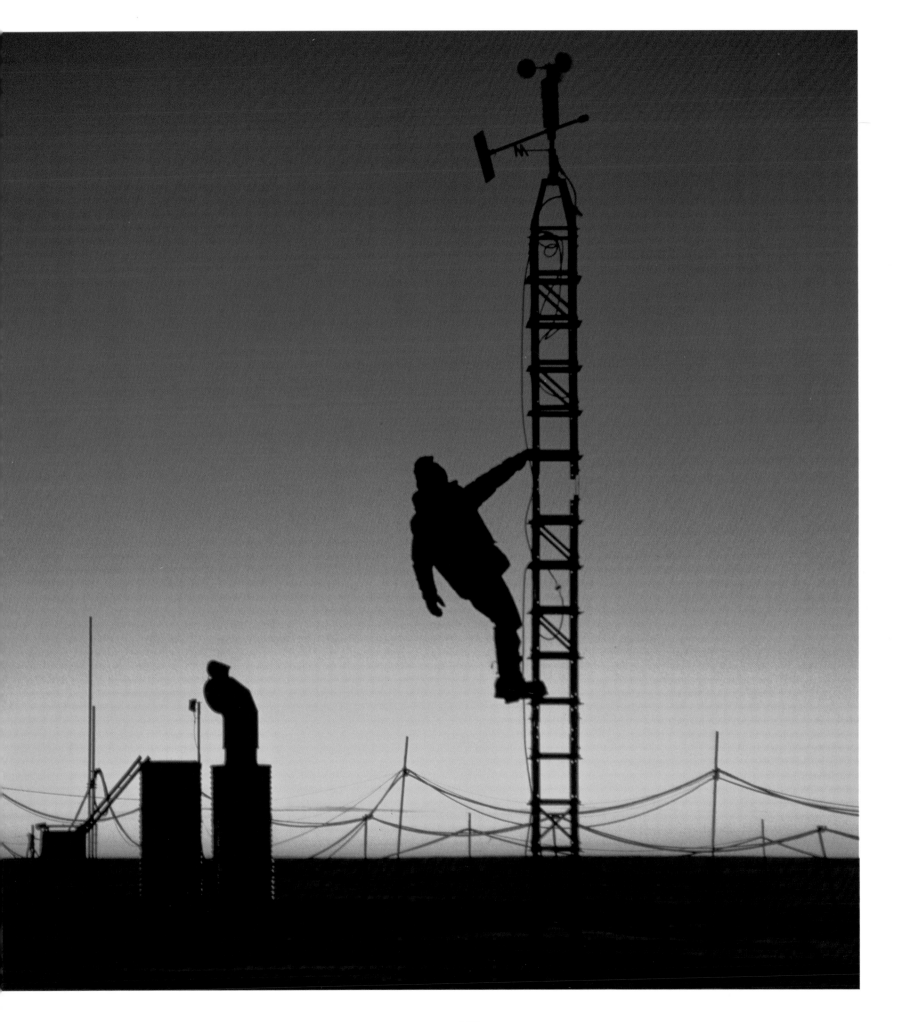

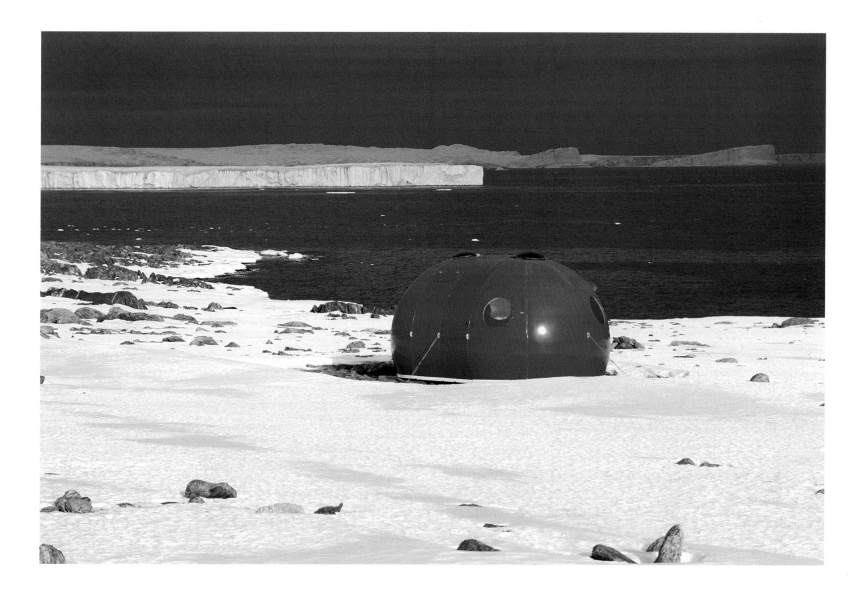

ABOVE *At Terra Nova Bay, a modern plastic and fibreglass summer field hut at Germany's Gondwana Station offers cost-effective transportable modules with minimal environmental impact. Improved environmental awareness, supported by new legislation, is reversing the effects of many Antarctic activities of the past.*

BELOW LEFT *A fish hut on the sea ice in McMurdo Sound. Protectively covering a hole in the ice, huts similar to this allow divers safe access to the silent world beneath the ice where observation and filming of Weddell seals becomes possible.*
BELOW *One of the British Antarctic Survey's bases, Rothera Point Station.*

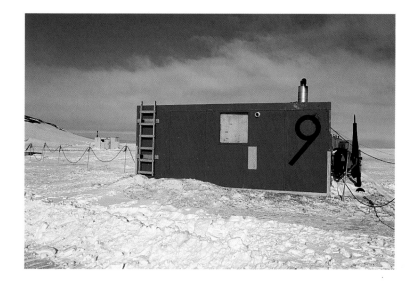

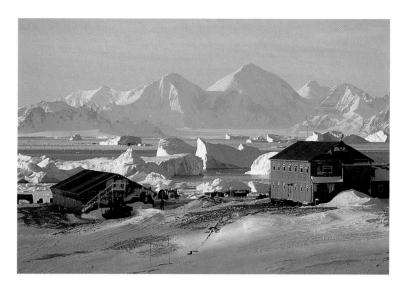

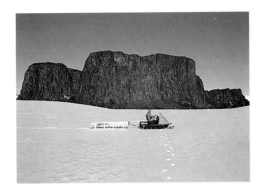

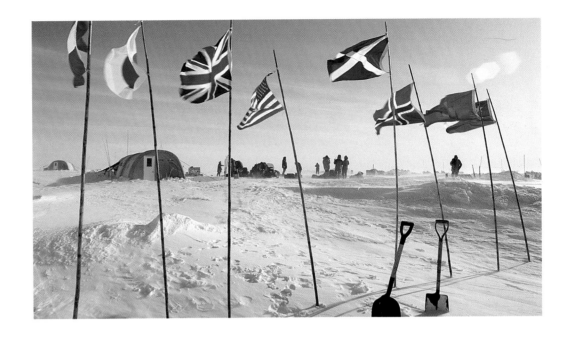

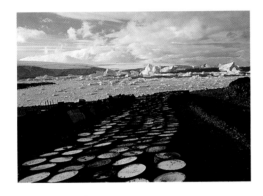

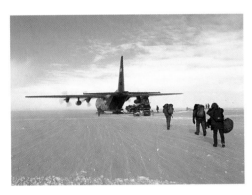

ABOVE *National flags flutter at Patriot Hills base camp. The blue-ice runway and landing strip has been the starting point for many modern expeditions such as the 1992–93 crossing of Antarctica by Fiennes and Stroud.*

LEFT, TOP TO BOTTOM AND BELOW *In the 85 years since the South Pole was conquered, modern equipment and transportation have opened up every realm of Antarctica. Skidoos are noisy but fast, replacing dog teams; Hercules aircraft fly almost daily to the South Pole while polar resupply vessels carrying helicopters navigate the seas and master the air. Dry suits have also allowed divers to explore the world of seals and penguins.*

FOLLOWING PAGES *Humankind, the most destructive animal on earth, holds the key to the future of this last remaining wilderness. As we ponder the future of this vast and fascinating Antarctic continent, we all have a responsibility to ensure that tomorrow's dawn over Antarctica will not be destroyed by our own heavy hand.*

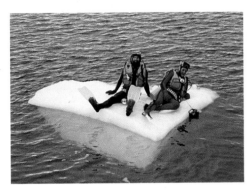

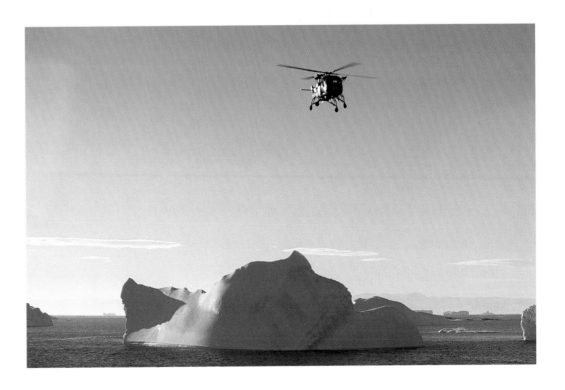

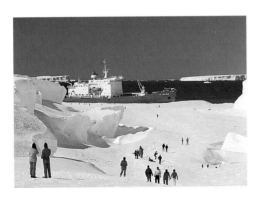

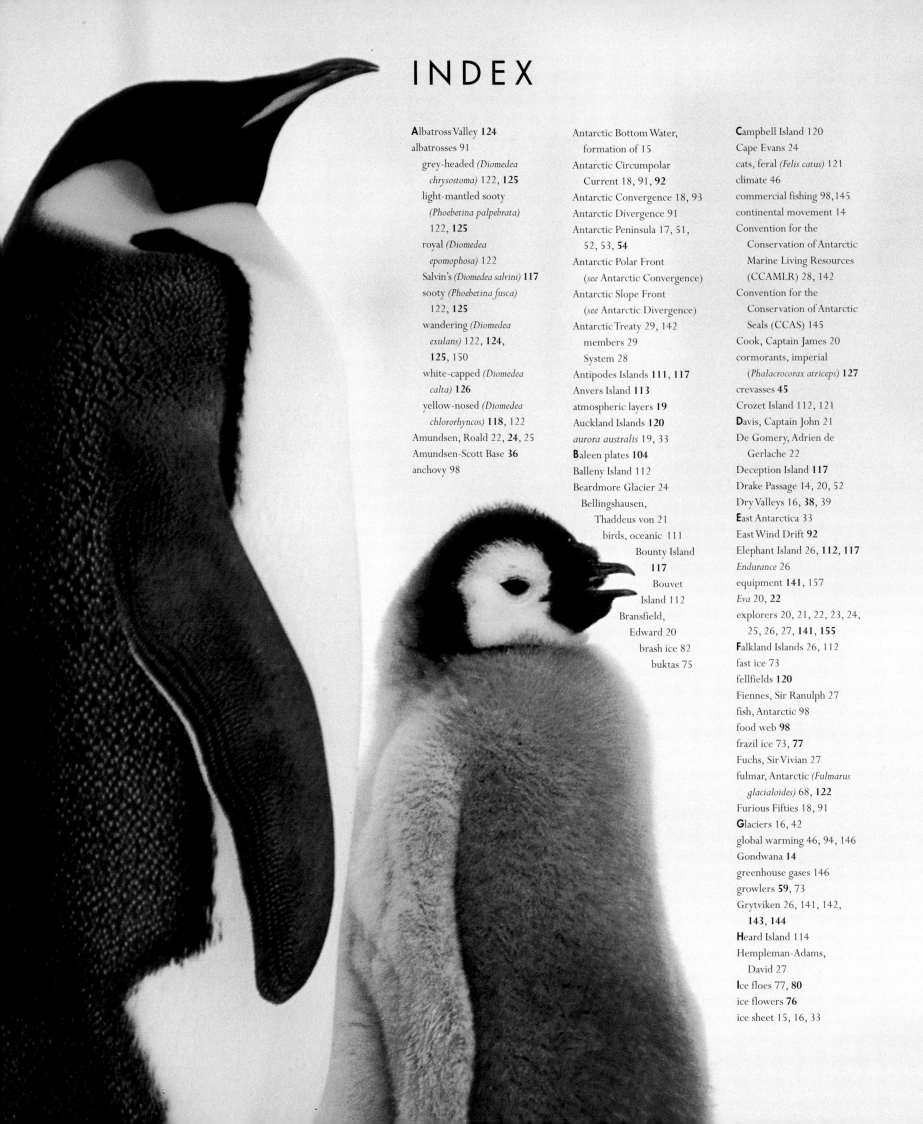

INDEX

BIBLIOGRAPHY

Bonner, W.N. (1989). **The Natural History of Seals**. Helm, London.

Evans, P.G.H. (1987). **The Natural History of Whales and Dolphins**. Helm, London.

Fiennes, R. (1993). **Mind over Matter: The Epic Crossing of the Antarctic Continent**. Sinclair-Stevenson, London, Auckland, Melbourne, Singapore and Toronto.

Harrison, P. (1995). **Seabirds: An Identification Guide**. Croom-Helm, London.

Hempel, G. (Ed) (1994). **Antarctic Science: Global Concerns**. Springer-Verlag, Berlin, Heidelberg, New York, London, Paris, Tokyo, Hong Kong, Barcelona, Budapest.

Kerry, K.R. & Hempel, G. (Eds) (1988). **Antarctic Ecosystems: Ecological Change and Conservation**. Springer-Verlag, Berlin, Heidelberg, New York, London, Paris, Tokyo.

Knox, G. (1984). **The Biology of the Southern Ocean**. Cambridge University Press, Cambridge.

Reader's Digest. (1985). **Antarctica: Great Stories from the Frozen Continent**. Sydney, London, New York, Montreal, Cape Town.

Walton, D.W.H. (Ed) (1987). **Antarctic Science**. Cambridge University Press, Cambridge, New York, Port Chester, Melbourne, Sydney.

Watson, L. (1991). **Whales of the World**. Hutchinson, London, Sydney, Auckland, New York.

ACKNOWLEDGEMENTS

Although this book bears the name of just one author, the ideas and information contained within the text stem not only from my own passion and curiosity but also from the extracted wisdom of colleagues and students at the University of Cape Town (UCT) and at other overseas institutions of Polar Research. To all of these people, I am indebted for their willingness to share many of the ideas and insights outlined in these pages. However, any errors of fact or interpretation are my sole responsibility. The research that forms the basis of this book would not have been possible without the funding provided by my sponsors, the South African Department of Environmental Affairs and Tourism, and UCT.

Originally, I had thought that writing a 'popular science' book about Antarctica would be relatively easy but instead, I received an education from my editors Mariëlle Renssen and Anouska Good who simplified the text into orderly but colourful life. For their patience and cajoling I owe them some roses! But text alone is not enough. Layout and design bring creative excellence and I feel fortunate that we were able to achieve this through the work of the designer, Trinity Fry, who took the project to heart and moulded pictures, diagrams and text into a pleasing tapestry. The artist, Annette Busse, deserves recognition for bringing a delicate brush to the illustrations, while I would similarly like to thank Scarla Weeks of the Oceanography Department, UCT, for generating the satellite imagery she obtained numerically from America.

Lastly, the support and encouragement of friends and colleagues is greatly appreciated, especially that of Ingeborg Ewen. My parents have a special place, since it was they who first gave me the opportunity to follow a wondrous path into the world of natural history.

Publisher's acknowledgements The publishers would like to thank Darrel Schoeling of Quark Expeditions, USA, for the information on tourism in Antarctica, and Éva Plagányi and Peter Ryan, both of the University of Cape Town, for their invaluable scientific advice.

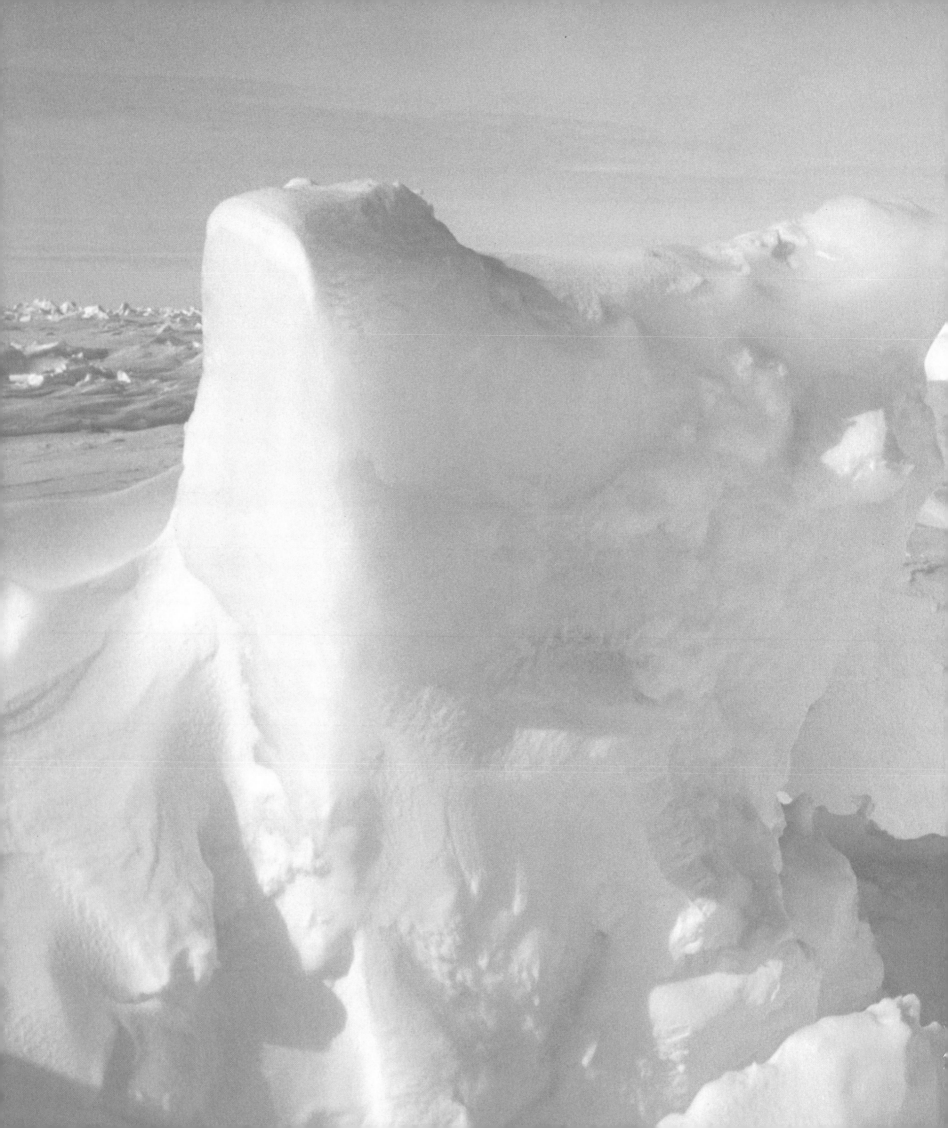